338.76887221092
G362
OCLC Record

DATE

Barbie and RUTH

ALSO BY ROBIN GERBER

Fiction
Eleanor vs. Ike

Nonfiction
*Leadership the Eleanor Roosevelt Way: Timeless
Strategies from the First Lady of Courage*

*Katharine Graham: The Leadership Journey
of an American Icon*

Barbie and RUTH

The Story of the World's Most Famous Doll
and the Woman Who Created Her

ROBIN GERBER

COLLINS BUSINESS

An Imprint of HarperCollins *Publishers*

For Ariel, Julia, and Tasha

HarperCollins books may be purchased for educational, business, or sales promotional use. For information, please write: Special Markets Department, HarperCollins Publishers, 10 East 53rd Street, New York, NY 10022.

FIRST EDITION

Designed by Renato Stanisic

Frontispiece: Photo courtesy of UCLA Charles E. Young Research Library, Department of Special Collections, *Los Angeles Times* Photographic Archives, © Regents of the University of California, UCLA Library

Library of Congress Cataloging-in-Publication Data

Gerber, Robin.
    Barbie and Ruth : the story of the world's most famous doll and the woman who created her / Robin Gerber.—1st ed.
        p. cm.
    Includes bibliographical references and index.
    ISBN 978-0-06-134131-1
    1. Handler, Ruth. 2. Dollmakers—United States—Biography. 3. Barbie dolls. 4. Mattel, Inc. I. Title.
    NK4894.2.H324G47 2009
    338.7'6887221092—dc22
    [B]
                                                                    2008029838

09 10 11 12 13 OV/RRD 10 9 8 7 6 5 4 3 2 1

Contents

Introduction

On the afternoon of December 11, 1978, a woman in her sixties with well-coiffed snow-white hair climbed the steps of the federal courthouse in downtown Los Angeles, her husband at her side. Looming over the couple was the seventeen-story building's slab-like tower of polished granite veneered in pale pink, glazed terra-cotta, with lower portions massed in front. As the workplace for government and law, the complex boasted an ordered geometry. Stylized eagles soared fifty feet over the double bronze doors of each of five entryways as Ruth and Elliot Handler entered.

Following Ruth's lawyers, the couple entered Judge Robert Takasugi's cavernous courtroom on the second floor. Elliot sat in the audience as Ruth took her place at the defense table. The handsome young assistant U.S. attorney John Vandevelde, from the Special Prosecutions section, had settled himself at the prosecution table when the bailiff called the courtroom to order. Ruth's sentencing hearing was about to begin.

Ruth was not the first celebrity defendant to carry a worried frown into this Los Angeles courthouse. Clark Gable and Charlie Chaplin had both argued paternity cases there in the 1940s. Bette Davis had forced Warner Brothers to defend itself in a breach-of-contract suit in the second-floor courtrooms. Only a few years earlier, the federal government had prosecuted Daniel Ellsberg, a military analyst for the RAND Corporation, for leaking the Pentagon Papers. But there had never been a felon like Ruth.

She had founded Mattel, the biggest toy company in the world; created Barbie, the world-famous iconic doll; and helped build the modern toy industry. At a time when few women had any corporate power, she was in the top echelon. She got there not by rising through the ranks or by heredity, but by creating a company that she controlled. She had also allowed padding and other falsifying of the company books, and her protestations of innocence, her refusal to take responsibility, made the prosecution determined to push for a severe sentence.

Ruth had been well represented, but she still sat in anxious silence. Herbert "Jack" Miller, a powerhouse lawyer from Washington, D.C., headed her defense team. He had served four years as assistant attorney general in the Criminal Division of the U.S. Department of Justice under Attorney General Robert Kennedy. There he helped convict Teamsters Union boss Jimmy Hoffa, and later he represented President Richard Nixon in the Watergate tapes case. That day, Miller, as always, wore the PT 109 tie clasp given to him by President John Kennedy.

Two months earlier, after various legal skirmishes had failed to defeat the charges, Ruth had pleaded nolo contendere, or no contest, to federal fraud charges involving Mattel, Inc. She knew the charges could land her in jail, a fate she hoped to forestall with her plea. The Justice Department, however, had other ideas. To them she was a criminal, a woman who had lied and defrauded people. It did not matter that she was beloved by fiercely loyal employees and the woman who had given children countless hours of fun, or that she had eased the pain and embarrassment of hundreds of breast cancer survivors with the prosthetics she had manufactured after her own mastectomy. For prosecutors, she had committed a federal crime. That crime was all the prosecution and the shareholders who had lost millions of dollars cared about.

Ruth anxiously watched Judge Takasugi, hoping the unreadable jurist would be lenient. Before him sat a wife and grandmother beset by illness, beaten down by years of litigation, and terrified she would be incarcerated.

How had it come to this moment? Ruth and Elliot had celebrated their fortieth wedding anniversary that summer. How had she gone from that time of hope and promise so many years before to this moment of fear and despair? She had conquered so many challenges. She had controlled her destiny, fought for it, gambled with it, but always she had won—until now. Try as she might, she could not find anything in her vast arsenal of talent or charm or brains or guts that could help her.

The courtroom fell into a cold, expectant silence. Judge Takasugi was ready to announce Ruth's fate.

Chapter 1

The Doll Nobody Wanted

Little girls just want to be bigger girls.
—Ruth Handler

Ruth Handler could sell anything. In 1959 she arrived in New York for the nation's Toy Fair, confident that she could sell a new doll she had created. She had been fighting naysayers, however, for seven years. The doll was a terrible idea, they had told her.

As the forty-three-year-old executive vice president of Mattel, Inc., Ruth had created an industry upstart in 1944 that was now the third biggest toy company in America. Mattel, based in Hawthorne, California, just outside Los Angeles, was a $14 million business. Ruth, a petite 5-foot–2 ½-inch hard charger with a quick smile and quicker temper, had tripled the size of the business since the start of the decade. With her husband, Elliot, as chief toy designer, she had outmarketed and outmanaged her chief rivals, Louis Marx and Company, and Kenner Products. Her revenues would soon exceed theirs.

Ruth headed straight for the New Yorker Hotel, where a room had been converted into display space. So many companies came to Toy Fair with so many toys to display that they overflowed into hotels neighboring the main hall. Beds, chairs, and desks were all carted out to make room for elaborate displays like the one for Ruth's doll.

Ruth dressed that morning to look sharp and show off her slender waist and full bust. Moving restlessly around the room, she adjusted and scrutinized each twelve-inch scaled scene, no doubt thinking about what was at stake. She had ordered a huge amount of inventory from her Japanese manufacturers. Twenty thousand of her petite-size fashion dolls were on weekly order, along with forty thousand pieces of the various outfits that had been designed to fit the doll's tiny, voluptuous figure. But the cost of moving that inventory onto and off store shelves was not all that was on Ruth's mind.

Ruth was also worried about her credibility. She had founded the company, and the men in her mostly male industry gave her credit for brilliance as an entrepreneur. But she had never invented or designed a toy. She also possessed the sometimes irrational optimism that fuels leaders and allows little tolerance for failure. Even though her designers told Ruth many times that making this doll profitable would be impossible, she pushed it through anyway.

Ruth lit one cigarette off the last. She barked orders laced with four-letter words and swiped at specks of dust. Her bravado hid another more personal reason that made this toy important to her. For her, this doll was more than a plaything. She was determined to make the buyers understand that this small plastic toy had a giant place to fill in the lives of little girls.

Toy Fair shimmered with all the hype and hoopla of a three-ring circus and a Broadway show rolled into one. The extravaganza was about innovation, design, a touch of genius, and companies betting on hitting the cultural zeitgeist. Toy manufacturers, intent on mesmerizing retail store buyers, spilled out of the main convention venue, the Toy Center at 200 Fifth Avenue, a legendary address in the history of toy making. Built just after the turn of the twentieth century, the building saw tenants move in as World War I ended and the center of toy manufacturing moved from Germany to the United States.

Large, gaudy banners draped the entrance to the fair. Adults promenaded in character costumes, and toys blinked, whirled, and stared from elaborate displays. Child's play cloaked the serious business of making toy sales. Nearly seven thousand retail buyers milled around 200 Fifth Avenue on an unseasonably warm day. New items at the 1959 fair included a working child-size soda fountain, a walking hobbyhorse, a gas-operated car that could go as fast as 22 miles per hour, and a Dr. Seuss zoo.

Starting in 1903, toy companies had arrived at Toy Fair to unveil their inventions and try to grab the attention, and shelf space, of store buyers. The first fair had been held near the docks to accommodate toys imported from Europe. That year, the American toys included the Humpty Dumpty Circus, Crayola crayons, Lionel trains, and teddy bears, supposedly named for the president who had refused to kill an orphaned bear cub.

Before Toy Fair started, the media had ignored Ruth's doll. With the space age dominating Americans' imaginations, the *New York Times* focused on Mattel's two-stage, three-foot-long plastic rocket, which could shoot two hundred feet into the air. Jack Ryan, a former project engineer on the U.S. Navy's Sparrow missile project, was lured from a job at Raytheon Company to design the miniature missile. Mattel had the trappings of a major aircraft company, with its own research and development department and twenty graduate engineers with a large budget to dream up the next hot toy. Picked for their unique creativity and fierce competitiveness, they were called the blue-sky group, and they were expected to think two to four years into the future.

A toy like the plastic rocket would be sent to a team of ten industrial engineers, who planned the production. "On a new item," Ruth explained to a reporter, "we will run as many as a hundred cost sheets before we fix on a design." She had boundless faith in the management and productions systems she had designed. Mattel's factories were more mechanized and its costs more refined than any of its competitors. With typical grandiosity, Ruth told the *New York Times*, "With our system we might just as well be turning out real airplanes or missiles." Instead, fueled by Elliot's genius for invention, Ruth sold toys to a postwar marketplace starved for them.

Ruth and Elliot had built a reputation for clever, well-priced toys that capitalized on popular culture. To avoid having their ideas stolen, Ruth never unveiled her products until Toy Fair. She also used designs difficult for others to copy and easy for Mattel to copyright. By 1959 Mattel's showrooms spilled over into the hotel where Ruth waited for buyers to arrive. Hundreds of smaller companies would be corralling buyers in lobbies and hallways, trying to coax them to see a new toy, but Mattel gave out appointments for their scripted, dramatic presentations. Buyers for the biggest companies might turn their badges upside down to try to avoid aggressive salespeople from the smaller companies, but they sought out Mattel representatives. As she smoothed her thick brown hair, which she had swept into a roll off her broad forehead, Ruth kept a sharp eye out for the man who could make all the difference.

Of the thousands of registered buyers at Toy Fair, none was more powerful than Lou Kieso from Sears, Roebuck. He could make or break a toy in the marketplace. An order from him meant shelf space across the country and page space in Sears's coveted Christmas catalog. Kieso had done well by Mattel in the past, and Ruth was determined to convince him that her pet toy that year belonged in his company's stores.

The nation's store by 1959, Sears had been building large stores in the suburbs for more than a decade. Americans relied on Sears's credit cards for everything from clothes to toys to appliances and the service contracts that went with them. Some people even lived in Sears houses assembled from mail-order kits that were sold until 1940.

In the room where Ruth waited, the heavy hotel curtains were closed so that the lighting could be adjusted to highlight each of the displays. The most dramatic setting featured a doll-size curving white staircase that seemed to come out of nowhere. A lone doll, just eleven and a half inches tall, stood two steps from the top. She wore a white wedding gown, her broad skirt sweeping the stairs. A tiny, realistic veil hung over her blond hair and smooth face. Her arms, moveable at the shoulder, carried a proportionately large bouquet of flowers, and she seemed balanced on her toes, although an invisible rod through each tiny foot anchored the doll to a stand. Around the room, twenty-one other outfits, including a Plantation Belle striped sundress and matching hat, and a simple zebra-striped strapless bathing suit with tiny sunglasses, gold hoop earrings, and open-toed shoes, were displayed in thematic settings on dolls that varied only by hair color. Blonds outnumbered brunettes two to one.

Ruth had spent years convincing her designers, including Elliot, that there was a market for a mass-produced adult doll. Watching her daughter, Barbara, playing with friends in the early 1950s first brought the idea to mind. Ruth listened many times at her home in the Beverlywood section of Los Angeles as the girls played make-believe with paper dolls.

There were many manufactured paper dolls on the market in the early 1950s. Animals, babies, toddlers, families, and folk characters were popular. Of all the choices, though, Ruth noticed that the girls focused their attention on one type of doll: grown-up women.

Barbara and her friends did not play with the popular Betsy McCall paper doll, found in *McCall's* magazine, or others like it. Betsy, a girl about their age, was shown each month playing the piano, gardening, baking a cake, or doing other wholesome activities. But Barbara and her friends were drawn to the kind of dolls that were often pushed in the pages of comic books. To attract girls as readers after World War II, comic book publishers included paper dolls in their pages. They even invited readers to send in fashion designs. The reader with the best ideas had her name published along with her design. Many of these paper dolls were portrayed as models, a career that gave girls good reason to change the dolls' clothes.

The way the girls held the thin cardboard women up like puppets and carried on conversations about adult life as they imagined it fascinated Ruth. She saw that they were seeing themselves in the role that they imagined for the doll. They were also mimicking adult conversation.

The cardboard cutout dolls had the advantage of a changeable paper wardrobe, but the clothes attached with frustratingly ineffective tabs and never looked right. The dolls themselves were one-dimensional placards, the barest tools for imagination.

How much richer would the girls' play be, Ruth wondered, if instead of flimsy paper dolls they had a real grown-up doll? "I knew that if only we could take this play pattern and three-dimensionalize it," she told interviewers years later, "we would have something very special." She imagined a miniature woman made from molded plastic with realistic clothes, perhaps some makeup, and manicured nails.

There were fashion or glamour dolls at the time: Dollikin, Little Miss Ginger, Sindy, Miss Revlon, and others, and although some were labeled "teenaged," they looked like baby dolls with makeup and styled hair. Although they had changeable adult outfits, their bodies were childlike or pubescent and varied in size. "They were so ugly and clumsy and had child bodies for grown-up play situations, it just did not go," Ruth recalled. Ruth envisioned a more sophisticated version of these dolls, more obviously a woman and more lifelike than any then available. She wanted a doll like the King Features Syndicate cartoon character of the time, Tillie the Toiler, and her adolescent male counterpart from the Chicago Tribune Syndicate, Harold Teen. Tillie worked at a fashionable women's wear company run by clothing mogul J. Simpkins. She worked in the office, did a little modeling, and even joined the army during World War II. All the while, Tillie was impeccably dressed.

Manufacturers of fashion dolls were not sensitive to the subtleties required to give the doll the kind of imaginative value Ruth envisioned. Their dolls had baby faces, cramped necks, rounded stomachs, flat chests, and straight legs, and looked comical in bridal or prom costumes. Ruth believed that teenagers could not engage in teenage play with these babyish dolls.

Fashion dolls were a 1950s innovation on the ubiquitous baby doll. Newly developed plastics, and later vinyl, made it possible to manufacture smaller, detailed dolls. Retail store buyers saw potential for selling them as collectibles as well as toys. But the buyers clung to the conventional wisdom of the 1950s. In that postwar era, little girls were encouraged to hold marriage and motherhood as their highest aspiration. As a result, baby dolls still dominated the market. Toy companies, their designers also predominantly male, followed suit.

Ruth and Elliot had been considering getting into the doll business, but they wanted to find a unique point of entry. "We never entered any business the same way other people entered. We never copied people, ever," Ruth recalled. But when Ruth suggested her idea for an adult doll to Elliot, he balked. "Ruth, no mother is going to buy her daughter a doll with breasts," he told her, despite his usual support for his wife's ideas. "She was devastated by his reaction," Ruth's friend Fern Field said. The rest of the all-male team agreed with Elliot. They were comfortable with toy guns and rockets, musical instruments and pop-up toys, but the doll Ruth described defied their imagination. They told her that mothers would be horrified by a sexual-looking doll. What she was proposing was much too curvaceous. Parents would object. Boys and girls did not just play with different toys; they grew up to be men and women who created different toys.

Further, a small plastic doll with the detail Ruth wanted could not be made, they told her. Besides, even if it could be made, it would be too expensive to sell. Ruth wanted realistic clothing, with zippers, darts, and hemlines. She wanted eyeliner and rouge on the tiny face and colored polish on the fingers. The costs for engineering the molds and machinery, not to mention postwar wages, made Ruth's vision a very expensive experiment. "Why doesn't she stick to management and marketing," the designers muttered.

But nothing fueled Ruth's drive like being told something could not be done. She pushed back, and the impasse dragged on as Barbara entered her teen years still playing with paper dolls. Then, in 1956, on a Handler family vacation in Europe, Ruth found exactly what she needed to change the minds of her designers.

The Handlers had arranged for a six-week grand tour of Europe from mid-July to early September. With their two children, they sailed on the *Queen Mary* from New York to England, where they stayed a week in London, and then went on to Paris. From there, a private car drove them into the Alps to the Grand Hotel National, overlooking the lake in Lucerne, Switzerland. The first day they rode the railway to the top of Mount Pilatus and later did a grand alpine tour, seeing the spot where the Rhine and Rhône rivers rushed from glaciers. Before they left for Venice, they had a free day in Lucerne to shop and tour the picture-perfect Swiss town. As they wandered the cobbled streets, they found a toy shop, likely the Franz Carl Weber shop, named for the famous toymaker. Ruth's son, Ken, who was twelve years old, wanted to go right in, but Ruth and fifteen-year-old Barbara stood outside, transfixed by a display in the window. Wooden dolls hung next to a hard plastic doll. That doll was named Lilli.

The Lilli dolls looked elongated and cartoonish and were dressed in gorgeous costumes. One was in a ski outfit; another had a distinctly European costume. Ruth and Barbara had never seen dolls like these before, and Ruth offered to buy one for Barbara to put on display in her room since she had passed the age for playing with dolls. Barbara was delighted, but she had a hard time choosing among the dolls with their distinct outfits. Ruth wanted to buy the clothes separately but was told that they were not sold that way. If a customer wanted a different costume, she had to buy the doll that went with it.

Later in the trip, in Vienna, Ruth and Barbara saw more Lilli dolls in a local store, packaged in clear round plastic cases, with different outfits that Barbara loved. Ruth was certain the Lilli doll manufacturers had made a mistake by not offering separate costumes. Ruth bought several dolls to bring back to Mattel, as well as another for Barbara.

The plastic Lilli dolls were just under a foot tall, all with the same face of an adult woman, narrow eyebrows sloping up in a sharp inverted V, eyes glancing to the side, and red lips provocatively puckered. They had long, shapely legs; well-endowed breasts; and tiny waists.

"Bild-Lilli," as the doll was called, was not primarily a child's toy in Europe. She started life as a sex toy. She originated in a comic strip in a tawdry gossip-sheet newspaper called *Bild-Zeitung*. Lilli pursued rich men by striking provocative poses in revealing clothes and spouting comic-strip bubbles of suggestive dialogue. In one cartoon, as she holds a newspaper over her naked body, Lilli tells a friend, "We had a fight and he took back all the presents he gave me." She was naive and clever at the same time, with her hair pulled back in a tight ponytail and one large curl coming down over her forehead.

Lilli had been born as a doll only four years before Ruth's trip to Europe when Reinhard Beuthien, her cartoonist, teamed up with designer Max Weissbrodt. The two saw the potential in taking Lilli off the page and making her a lascivious three-dimensional toy. Weissbrodt worked for the Hamburg-based company O & M Hausser, famous since 1904 for its molded figures made of Elastolin and by the 1950s for its innovative work with molded plastic. Lilli, her long legs ending in a molded black shoe, was a high heel away from being a prostitute, which in Hamburg was a job licensed and allowed by the government.

Lilli dolls could be bought in tobacco shops, bars, and adult-themed toy stores. Men got Lilli dolls as gag gifts at bachelor parties, put them on their car dashboard, dangled them from the rearview mirror, or gave them to girlfriends as a suggestive keepsake. Lilli was also a marketing tool for the *Bild* newspaper. Over time, the unusual doll with her wardrobe and accessories became a children's toy as well. But Ruth knew nothing of Lilli's past and did not care. She finally had the model for a doll she was certain would be a hit. Back in California, dolls in hand, she went to work.

Jack Ryan, head of Mattel's research and design team, was about to fly to Japan on a project. Ruth stuck a Lilli doll in his suitcase. "While you're over there," she said, "see if you can find someone who could make a doll of this size. We'll sculpt our own face and body and design a line of clothes, but see if you can find a manufacturer."

In a rare admission of her own vulnerability, Ruth later said that the doll could have been made in the United States "if someone had had the will and the motivation, but we did not have anyone that had that strong motivation during that period, and even I was not that secure." She wanted to soften the brittle hard plastic of the German doll, but softer plastics were a recent innovation and suppliers were scarce. Then there was the problem of casting the new material to get the detail Ruth envisioned in the doll's face and body. And finding workers to mass-produce the doll and its tiny, realistic clothes at wages that would keep the toy affordable was daunting. Ruth believed Ryan would find a manufacturer in Japan, known for its workers' skill with detailed design. But Ryan would find problems in Japan, too. The Mattel designers had been right about the difficulty of producing the doll Ruth wanted.

When Jack Ryan and Frank Nakamura, a young product designer Ryan took with him to Japan, showed Lilli to Japanese manufacturers, they reacted with distaste. "They thought she looked kind of mean—sharp eyebrows and eye shadow," Nakamura, who spoke Japanese, explained. Finally, Ryan found Kokusai Boeki, a small company that distributed toys and other items in Japan. Their rotocasting equipment, used to make low-cost dolls, was very crude, and they were accustomed to working with hard plastic. They melted hard granular polymer material that formed the plastic into a liquid and squeezed it into a mold, filling its cavities. The plastic was then chilled to its original hard state, shrinking during the process, and thus easily removed from the mold. But softer vinyl did not always fill the tiny indentations during this injection molding process. If Mattel wanted Kokusai Boeki to make the odd-looking doll, the Japanese told Ryan and Nakamura, a better material and molding method would have to be found.

Back in the States, Ruth started the plastics search and soon learned about a malleable form of polyvinyl chloride, or PVC. In 1926, Waldo Semon, an organic chemist for B. F. Goodrich, was attempting to bind rubber to metal. As he experimented with the polymer vinyl chloride, he discovered that he could turn it into the jellylike plastic we now know as vinyl. He tried his new material out, making golf balls and shoe heels. Semon later found that vinyl was inexpensive, durable, fire resistant, and easily molded, but it was not until the late 1930s that this plasticized PVC was commercialized for tubing and gaskets. World War II boosted the industry through military-funded PVC plants for the vinyl-coated wire used aboard U.S. military ships. By war's end, B. F. Goodrich dominated the market, producing more than ten million pounds of PVC a year. Polyvinyl chloride was used for everything from pipes to beach balls, squeezable toys, syringe bulbs, soft-sided bottles, air-filled cushions, and upholstered couches.

For all its advantages, however, the new vinyl still required a special casting method called "rotational molding" in order to get the fine detail of the doll Ruth wanted. This technique required near constant turning of the hollow metal mold over an open flame, and the process was slow and inconsistent. But early in the 1950s, Goodrich discovered a form of powdered PVC that worked particularly well in rotation molding, and the process itself was revolutionized by a new type of hot air oven. With more control over the heating, the special grade of plastic powder could be coaxed into the tiny channels of the mold as it was rotated during the heating and cooling process.

While the process was faster and produced more predictable results, the advances were so new that neither the doll makers in Japan, nor Seymour Adler, head of production and engineering, whom Mattel sent from the United States to help, had ever tried the new method. "They had to basically figure it out," explained a Mattel designer. "They had to create the manufacturing process and to work perfectly with the Japanese to do that. They had trouble working out the molding. When they took the hand out the fingers would break off . . . there were bubbles on the nose." Adler landed in Japan clutching the latest plastics industry journals, but he and his Japanese colleagues had to make up the process as they went along.

As the Japanese team worked on perfecting the mold process, simple castings from the electroplated molds were sent back to Mattel for approval. The doll looked too much like a prostitute for the company's taste, so she was being put through a makeover. Mattel hired Bud Westmore, who had been a makeup artist since the 1930s and worked on dozens of movies as well as the television show *Alfred Hitchcock Presents*, to do the doll's face. Lilli's widow's peak curved like the top half of a heart, accenting a high forehead. Her hairline was altered to make it more conventional. Designers relaxed Lilli's exaggerated puckered lips, although they were still bright red. Her arched eyebrows sank into a straighter line, and her face became less pointy, while her hair was rooted so it could be brushed and styled. The changes were subtle, but Ruth wanted them anyway. In the end, Lilli and her new sister were barely distinguishable except to the new doll's creator.

Each change in the mold required at least six sample castings. Language and cultural barriers led to mistakes. The Japanese did not understand American taste or quality standards, and their factory was fairly crude. Mattel felt that the first shipment of dolls had eyes that were too slanted. Then the doll's breasts were made with nipples, despite Jack Ryan's repeated requests that they be smooth. Finally, he abandoned words and picked up a doll. "I took my little fine Swiss file," Ryan said, "and very daintily filed the nipples off."

Ruth treated her creation like a child, naming it early in the design process for the doll's inspiration—her daughter, Barbara. She wanted to use her daughter's nickname of Babs, but that name was copyrighted, as was the name "Barbara." But "Barbie" was available, so she took it. Consumed with the doll's manufacturing, Ruth sometimes called her daughter by the doll's name, a mistake the teenage Barbara did not appreciate.

As Barbie's manufacturing moved ahead, Elliot made a trip to Japan to check on the doll's progress and to start the production of dollhouse furniture he had designed. Ruth loved the new doll furniture, which was modern and made from wood. She saw the possibility of using Elliot's idea as an accessory for her new doll, but Elliot would have to make his furniture Barbie-size. As Ruth explained later, however, when she tried to talk to him about it, Elliot's bias against the doll came out. He insisted that his furniture was "something totally different," although he could not explain why. Ruth felt that they were not communicating, and she was certain he was making a mistake. She sensed that he was going along with Barbie but did not really believe in the doll. Faced with the many production and marketing problems that Barbie created, Ruth gave up trying to convince him.

Ruth did succeed in getting her doll a couture wardrobe. She had started gathering ideas by contacting Obletter Spielwaren, the German toy retailer, in November and ordered more Lilli dolls. Although the Lilli doll clothing could not be bought separately at toy stores, Ruth convinced the company to send her individual outfits. She ordered six dolls in different costumes, including a light blue dress and a carnival costume. She also picked out nine other outfits, including a blue evening dress, a woman's blouse, and a dirndl dress with a short yolk and belt. The next month she ordered twelve more Lilli dolls from the Franz Carl Weber stores.

Armed with her trove of Lilli doll models and clothing, Ruth searched for a dress designer. Elliot suggested calling Los Angeles's Chouinard School of Art. There they found Charlotte Buettenback Johnson, an American fashion designer who had worked in the New York City garment industry from the time she was seventeen. Divorced with no children, Johnson had moved to California, where she had a business designing and sewing children's clothes. She was also teaching a fashion design class at Chouinard. Ruth asked her to become the personal clothing designer for a new doll, telling her, "I want American clothes, and I want play situations which teenage girls would go through. I want things like prom dresses, wedding dresses, and career-office dresses. I want her to be able to dress up, and I want slacks." Interchangeable outfits, Ruth decided, would be the key to enhancing the doll's play value. Clothes also had the potential to be the most profitable part of the new project.

Johnson influenced every part of the design process, and some people said the final doll had the same shape head and hair as the statuesque designer. At first, Ruth brought dolls to Johnson's apartment once or twice a week at night, and together they decided on the outfits. Johnson found a Japanese woman in her neighborhood to sew the tiny samples. But as the line developed, Ruth's production staff told her that all the zippers, snaps, buttons, darts, and hemlines made the clothes far too detailed to be manufactured cost effectively in the United States.

Johnson quit her jobs and spent the next two years in Japan working with local suppliers to design a wardrobe appropriate for an adult woman or a teenager, in accord with Ruth's sense of little girls' desires. She searched for fabrics that had the right weight and small enough designs for the proportions of the clothes she planned, all fashioned with tiny snaps, buttons measuring less than an eighth of an inch in diameter, and miniature zippers.

Born a year after Ruth and raised in Omaha, Johnson was tenacious. She also held strong opinions about fashion and design, which served her well in her new job. In Tokyo, living at the Frank Lloyd Wright–designed Imperial Hotel, she made unrelenting demands on the Japanese designer and two seamstresses she met with six days a week. She convinced textile merchants to make cloth to her specifications in small, and therefore costly, batches. She insisted on pastel-colored tricot for the undergarments. Her early designs included two strapless brassieres, one half-slip, one floral petticoat, and a girdle. No detail escaped her attention.

Ruth emphasized that detail was the key for making this doll unique and marketable. She believed mothers and their daughters would appreciate the care that went into the clothes. In later years, Ruth said that her competitors never successfully copied Barbie because they did not create the quality product that she insisted on.

Barbie's assembly was done by Japanese workers who worked either in factories or their homes. Part of what made the doll feasible to manufacture in Japan was the country's low cost of labor, combined with the diligence and care of its workers. Much of the doll's wardrobe was stitched together by "homework people," so named because their homes were their workshops. Like immigrant workers in the early part of the century in America, they worked quickly as they were paid by piece. Mattel's efficiency expert, Joe Cannizzaro, marveled at the patience and cleanliness of these seamstresses. "I never saw any dresses—even white wedding dresses—get soiled," he said, "though they were in the homes and on the tatami floors, because everything was so spotless. . . . They were delivered by bike and by pickup truck. They were handled four, five, six times. And they never got dirty." For Mattel, these diligent low-cost workers were well worth the 35 percent import tariff.

The factory workers who assembled the doll came in from the Japanese countryside, willing to work for low wages until harvest time. They lived in company-run dormitories and ate at company cafeterias. In August they quit en masse to harvest rice. They machine-stitched blond or brown plastic Saran strands onto the dolls' skulls and trained them into topknot ponytails and tightly curled bangs. A template covered the doll's face so her pouting lips could be painted, as well as her eyes with their sideways glance and snow white irises. Limbs reengineered by Jack Ryan were fitted to her sockets, and, as Charlotte Johnson had so carefully planned, her clothing slipped on easily.

Dressed in her first outfit, a zebra-striped bathing suit, the new doll seemed to beg for the rest of her wardrobe. For that, Johnson worked with Ruth to create the clothes of girls' daydreams in 1950s America. Besides the wedding dress that would be on dramatic show at Toy Fair, the doll had outfits for attending a football game, playing tennis, and dancing as a ballerina. There was also a puff sleeve negligee and a ball gown with a pure white faux-fur wrap. The Donna Reed television show had premiered the previous fall. Ruth's new doll would feed the fantasies of girls who imagined themselves, like Reed, happily married mothers and wives.

It took Ruth three years to ready Barbie for sale, and then she charged into the doll's marketing. "We were so pumped up by Ruth's enthusiasm, we became believers," said one of the sales representatives who was at the 1959 Toy Fair. "The doll was radically different, but Ruth's logic made sense to us. We thought kids who liked paper dolls would like this." Mattel called the doll Barbie Teenage Fashion Model, trying to downplay her sexuality and to play up, for parents, the idea that many girls would want to be as well groomed as a model. But no amount of ad copy could disguise Barbie's proportions, estimated at 39–21–33 in an adult woman.

In addition, the fashion dolls that Ruth hated glutted the market. Stores were loaded with them and their costumes, unable to sell their inventory and unwilling to add more to their stock. If they were inclined to buy, they were not likely to want a doll that they believed would horrify mothers because of its breasts and sexuality.

As she stood in the Barbie showroom at Toy Fair, Ruth exuded her characteristic confidence. "One of my strengths is that I do have the courage of my convictions and the guts to take a position," Ruth told an interviewer. "I can be very persuasive in getting others to see the light." But her bravado began to seep away as one buyer after another made a cursory tour of the room and took off, leaving few if any orders. "For the most part, the doll was hated," a Mattel sales rep remembered. "The male buyers thought we were out of our minds because of the breasts, and it was a male-dominated business." By the time Lou Kieso, the buyer from Sears, walked into the smoky room Ruth had no idea what to expect.

Ruth gave Kieso her most dazzling smile, shaking his hand and looking him straight in the eye. Showing him around, Ruth emphasized the professional market research Mattel had done for the doll and the television advertising that was planned. Kieso was unimpressed. He refused to take a sample of the doll back to the Sears headquarters in Chicago. He left without placing a single order, as did half the buyers that came through the Barbie display.

Ruth realized that her production projections were a disaster. Twenty thousand dolls a week had been ordered for delivery over the next six months, which seemed reasonable because of the distance of the Japanese plants. She also had planned on selling three or four costumes per doll. Ruth wanted to avoid inventory delays, but now she faced warehouses full of unsold inventory. Panicked, she wired Japan to cut production by 40 percent.

That night, in her room at the New Yorker, Ruth broke down in tears. "She was very upset," Elliot remembered. "I didn't think it would be successful, but she did. This was her dream. She put so much effort into pushing it. She did not cry often, but she cried because she had that heart," he said, pointing to his own. "The doll was like a piece of art for her that held a piece of her heart."

Only Elliot could have understood how much of herself Ruth had poured into the Barbie doll. While he may not have believed in Barbie as a marketable toy, he understood why Ruth did. Over and over, with fierce confidence, Ruth had told those who doubted her idea that little girls just wanted to be bigger girls. She was sure, impassioned, and unshakable because she was not talking about just any little girls. Ruth was talking about one, the girl who, before she married Elliot, had been known as Ruthie Mosko.

Chapter 2

The Tenth Child

I idolized my sister.

Jacob Moskowicz, Ruth's father, was a burly six-foot ox of a man. In 1907 he strode off the boat that brought him across the Atlantic from Warsaw, Poland. Processed through immigration at Ellis Island, he was told to head for Denver, Colorado, where his blacksmithing skills could be used on the burgeoning Union Pacific Railroad. Not liking what he had seen of New York City, Jacob went west.

Jacob left a Jewish community in Warsaw rivaled in size only by that of Manhattan. Warsaw's Jews were bedeviled by the anti-Semitic whims of their Russian overseers, and Jacob had become a target for conscription into the Russian army, where the number of Jewish soldiers far outweighed their proportion in the general population.

Nicholas I started the draft of Jews in 1827 in a scheme to force assimilation and stamp out Judaism, a campaign augmented in the next century by vicious attacks on Jewish communities. Anti-Semitic army regulations made life increasingly harsh for Jews already forced into service and generally impoverished. Jacob fled his army unit while en route to Turkey, and managed to board a ship to America.

Jacob had left a family back in Warsaw and a mountain of gambling debt he could not repay. As he crossed the Atlantic, his thoughts and worries no doubt dwelled as much on his wife, Ida, and the seven children left behind as on what lay ahead in America. Would his eldest children, twelve-year-old Sarah and eleven-year-old Reuben, help their mother enough with the younger ones, Lillian, Louis, Doris, and especially the toddlers, Max and Joseph? And how soon would he be able to bring them all to America?

Jacob journeyed west with a new name, probably given to him at immigration, although some family members say he shortened it to make it easier to understand in a country where he did not speak the language. The thriving and diverse Jewish community in Denver would know him as Jacob Mosko, a tough and enterprising man.

Within two years, first by shoeing horses and then by building carriages and truck bodies, Jacob saved enough money to send for his family. Ida and the children made the crossing in steerage, part of the great mass of eastern European immigrants who flooded into America in the first decade of the twentieth century.

Jacob soon started his own company, supplying truck bodies for the Cohen family who owned the Denver Chicago Trucking Company, destined to be one of the largest moving companies in the country. Jacob's business grew as the Cohens' business expanded. Customers liked Jacob and he had good business sense. He had his own shop, and he moved his family into a modest one-bathroom house at 21st and Gilpen streets. The growing Mosko clan often filled the big park near their house that marked the eastern edge of Denver. By 1915 the Moskos had become a household of nine children with the birth of Aaron and Maurice.

Jacob's strength and temper were legendary. His son Aaron remembered him as "the strongest man I ever saw. I saw him lift people up by the shirt, two people at the same time. He'd pick up one end of a truck body while all of us were on the other end, lift-ing. I saw him lift a car out of a snowbank." According to another story, Jacob once ran his car into a streetcar. In a fury, he lifted the streetcar right off its track. He was proud of his work and a tough taskmaster for his sons who worked with him. They grew up with the threat of getting the back of his hand if they misbehaved.

Unfortunately for the family finances, Jacob sometimes worked as hard at poker as at his business. Sometimes other players came to his house. Other times he disappeared for days at a time. He had a regular game at a Turkish bathhouse, where players brought schnapps, rye bread, and herring, and settled in to gamble, drink, and eat for a whole weekend. Jacob's compulsion for gambling would be carried on in the family. All of his children became gam-blers, some more in control than others, but all influenced by his example.

Jacob's gambling losses burdened his family. Ruth's older brothers and sisters left school to work, to provide support for their mother and the younger ones. Sarah, the eldest, left school at fourteen to work at Golden Eagle Dry Goods, a discount store.

Ida ran the household, cooking, baking, cleaning, and watch-ing over her children and the passel of neighborhood children who played with them. She had a warm nature, but the strain of her pregnancies and life in Denver made her increasingly frail. In the summer of 1916, Sarah married Louis Greenwald at Marble Hall in Denver. Ida stood nearby, pregnant at forty years of age with Ruth, her tenth and last child.

Six months after Ruth was born, Ida went into the hospital for gallbladder surgery. Sarah, the twenty-year-old newlywed, took her baby sister to live with her while Ida recovered. But when Ida came home, the baby stayed with Sarah. Weeks stretched into months, and Ruth never lived in her mother's house again.

There is no record or account indicating that Ida tried to take

Ruth back to her house. It seems reasonable that Ida saw the charity and utility in leaving her youngest daughter with her oldest. They were all family, after all, and Jacob Mosko's household had often been on the financial brink. Sarah and Louie, as he was called, were comfortable financially. The baby would be better off, Ida no doubt reasoned, but the arrangement would leave its mark on the one person who had no say in it.

Ruth vehemently denied that she felt rejected by her mother or that her upbringing led her to always feel that she had to prove herself. She argued that she always knew who her parents were. Elliot remembered that "Sarah and Louie were her parents. They raised her." While Ruth called Sarah and Louie by name, she called Ida and Jacob "Ma" and "Pa," and she thought of them as "loving, indulgent" grandparents. But even when she saw them, they could barely talk to one another. Ida and Jacob spoke Yiddish. Their English was poor and heavily accented, and Ida was hard of hearing. While the children who lived with them had learned enough Yiddish to be understood, Ruth grew up in an English-speaking household. As much as she tried to speak slowly and clearly, she admitted that it was difficult to communicate with her parents.

Ruth's denials and explanations about her biological parents are telling. Ida, her mother, had ten children, yet only one was not raised by her. Only one lived apart from most of her siblings, more than a mile from her parents' house, worshipping at a different synagogue, not playing at the family house, and attending different schools. Sarah, Louie, and Ruth went to the Moskos' for Friday night dinner and holidays, like any relatives, but Sarah rarely hosted her family at her house.

By all accounts, Sarah Greenwald adored her baby sister. She was an uncommonly beautiful child. Ruth would later laugh as she told the story of a woman who approached her when she was in her twenties and said, "Aren't you Ruth Mosko?" When Ruth said she was, the woman said, "But you were such a cute little girl." As Ruth's brother Aaron remembered, "Sarah was just trying to relieve pressure on my mother, but she became attached to Ruth and no way she'd give her back." Sarah also learned, shortly after taking Ruth in, that she could not have children.

The Greenwalds were a family of three, more modern and more affluent than the Moskos. Ruth had a much more comfortable childhood than her siblings, although she resisted being spoiled. "I'm extraordinarily uncomfortable with dependency on anyone," she said in her later years. "I guess I've had this overwhelming compulsion to prove myself all my life." She seemed to be proving herself to the parents who had given her away, the parents who became loving relatives but who would choose not to keep her close.

At the Greenwald house at 855 Garfield in Denver, Ruth was "treated like a queen," according to Aaron. Ruth agreed that she never wanted for anything, but also said, "They never made me feel like I was getting something for nothing." For Ruth, the idea of freeloading would always be intolerable. She looked for the chance to begin working, rushing through childhood as if she owed someone an incalculable debt.

The Greenwalds' one-story house had a small sloped front lawn and was located just blocks from the drugstore that Louie and Sarah started when Ruth was about eight years old. One of the first in Denver, their pharmacy was across the street from Denver General Hospital, in a thriving area of town. The Greenwalds were astute businesspeople, and Sarah worked as hard as her husband. When she was ten, Ruth begged to work at the store. She adored Sarah and wanted to be closer to her, and she began to resent Louie for not treating Sarah as well as Ruth thought he should. Like his father-in-law, Louie was a hotshot at the poker table and often left Sarah to run the business while he went off to gamble. Only Sarah's strong hand kept him from putting the Greenwalds in the same cash-strapped position as the Moskos.

Ruth's school was not far from the pharmacy, so she would come to work as soon as school let out. "I used to love it. I used to wait on trade. I worked the cash register. They had a small soda fountain where I became a 'soda jerk,'" she remembered. She preferred her job to playing with other children and although she had friends she never felt close to them. Later she would recall that she never had the kind of lifelong relationships that many people build. Ruth was often bored by the things that the other children found interesting. She thought many other girls were "sissies," and that girl talk was stupid. She saw herself as a tomboy who preferred the athletic games of the boys. "Boys loved me, and I loved boys," she said. Girls excluded her from their intimate girl-talk sessions, and when she was included she felt awkward.

Ruth also carried a fierce need for Sarah's approval. She tacitly acknowledged Sarah as her mother in this comment from *Dream Doll*, her autobiography: "[Sarah] seemed to thrive on working, so I grew up with the idea that a woman—a mother—with a job was neither strange nor unnatural." For Ruth, the idea of having a job was consuming and exhilarating. Through work she could be closer to Sarah and feel she was paying a debt she felt she owed, even if none was demanded.

In 1933 the Greenwalds expanded their business. They closed the pharmacy and opened a new venture in the Home Public Market, a cavernous stone building with domed skylights and tall windows that extended along California Street in Denver for a whole city block. People streamed inside all day, grabbing wicker baskets and buying fresh meat at the Public Meat Company; fish at Fagan's; and poultry, vegetables, canned goods, and the local brand of Pollyanna breads at the open stands. Sarah ran a lunch counter inside called Greenwald's Soda Fountain.

Despite the Depression that had accelerated since the stock market crash of 1929, hope abounded. Franklin Delano Roosevelt had just been elected president. One of his first acts was to begin the repeal of Prohibition. Seeing an opportunity, Louie opened a liquor store as soon as alcohol was legal, piling bottles high in a front window of the market that jutted into the street.

For Ruth, there was new excitement at the bustling market and an unexpected opportunity for more responsibilities. She wanted to grow up fast, and work was, she said, "what made me grow up. What made me as I am."

Louie excelled at liquor sales, and Sarah's Greenwald's Soda Fountain with its long counter offered the only place to get a sit-down meal inside the bustling market. Ruth got her chance to take over the lunch counter in the summer of 1934. Louie had won a prize from a major distillery for having sold the most bottles of their liquor. The prize was a free trip to Europe. Louie had no desire to go, but Sarah did. She was old enough when she had come to the United States to remember family back in Poland. Ruth was left to run Sarah's business, balancing the money, making bank deposits, ordering food and supplies, and organizing the schedule for employees. "I was busier than a cockroach," Ruth remembered. She loved the work and the dignity of getting paid for it, but one job was not enough. Her brother Joe opened a law practice, but he had worked his way through law school and had no money for a secretary. Ruth had learned typing and shorthand in junior high school and offered to help Joe get started. She went to his office after school every day, keeping her lunch counter job on Saturdays. One summer she added an office job at Frankel Carbon Company. As she put it, she was "busy, busy, busy."

Working with her brother, Ruth started to think about becoming a lawyer. When she graduated from high school she enrolled at the University of Denver, keeping up her work schedule along with studying for her college courses. Another facet of her life was also consuming a lot of time and a great deal of emotion. She was serious about a young man she had started dating in high school, and Sarah did not approve.

Chapter 3

Love at a Nickel a Dance

The chemistry was beyond belief.

Ruth's work and school commitments did not leave her much time for socializing, but she was not oblivious to boys. Her great rendezvous with love happened on Welton Street in 1932 during an unusually warm November. Just turned sixteen, Ruth was cruising downtown Denver behind the wheel of her birthday present from Sarah and Louie: a brand-new three-window Ford coupe. Replacing the Model A, the coupe had elegant styling, with bug-eye headlights on either side of the long vertical front grille, and to Ruth's delight, a pop-up rumble seat in a trunklike compartment just behind the rear window. The "little deuce coupe" was destined to become a hot-rodding legend. The coupe ignited Ruth's passion for cars, perhaps because she was behind its wheel when she saw the man who became her lifelong love.

Ruth was driving past the Home Public Market when she spotted Leonard Phillips, a young man she did not much like, walking with a friend down Glenarm Street. Leonard's mother played cards with Sarah, which was how Ruth knew him. She did not know the tall boy with the massive head of black ringlets who was walking alongside Leonard, but she wished she did. Honking the horn, Ruth tried to attract the boys' attention, but her ploy failed and traffic forced her to move on. After driving around the block, she tried again, waving at Leonard so she could get a look at his friend. "I had to see this guy. I really had to see this guy who was with Leonard," Ruth remembered. She got her look and drove away thinking that she was unlikely to see the cute stranger again.

A week or two later, Ruth's sister Doris invited her to a B'nai B'rith affair on East Colfax Avenue. The Jewish humanitarian organization's fund-raising event was billed as a carnival. When the two young women got there they found simple games on the first floor of the commercial building that had been acquired by the Denver Lodge only a few years earlier. For pennies, nickels, or quarters, Ruth and Doris threw balls at bottles and tried to throw hoops onto rings. As they wandered among the booths they were surprised by Chuck Newman. He was a good-looking young man and, Ruth knew, a good dancer. With Doris's approval she accepted his invitation to go to the second floor for a dance.

After their dance, Chuck escorted Ruth off the floor and over to a group of his friends that he wanted her to meet. Ruth remembered having a moment of shock: "I saw this guy with this oversized head of black curly ringlets, and I looked at him and our eyes locked. It really was that way. I knew who it was instantly. This was the guy I had gone around the block to see." Years later she remembered he was wearing a white T-shirt with a tear in the shoulder seam. Smiling at her, the young man asked her to dance. Ruth recalled that as they twirled around the floor she felt like she was "floating on air." She felt an unmistakable chemistry between them. "It was magic," she said. "I had gone with other guys . . . but I did not have that feeling. No one turned me on like that."

. . . .

The young man who had caught Ruth's eye was Isadore Elliot Handler, though friends called him Izzy. He came from the Jewish neighborhood on the west side of town, an area less affluent and considered rougher than the east side, where Ruth lived. Elliot belonged to a gang of sorts called the Gigolos, mostly Jewish friends and a few Italians. Despite their ethnic diversity, the Gigolos had a good-natured camaraderie. Having played football for North High School, Elliot recalled intercepting a pass and running down the field as his Italian friends cheered, yelling, "Go, schnoz!" Elliot even earned a letter in football, although his father had too little money to buy his son the jacket to go with it.

Elliot's parents were Jews from the town of Matziv in Ukraine. Like Ruth's parents, the Handlers spoke mostly Yiddish. They initially settled in Chicago, but Elliot's father, Samuel, contracted tuberculosis and took his family west to a sanatorium. Denver had clear, thin air that was the only known treatment for consumptives, and Jews from all over the country had been sent there since 1904, when the Jewish Consumptives' Relief Society was founded. The sanatorium, started by a group of immigrant Jewish men from eastern Europe, was free, and though it was nonsectarian, most of the patients were Jewish. Because of the number of tuberculosis patients in Denver, spitting in the streets in the 1920s was forbidden. Elliot remembered his father carrying a handkerchief at all times to spit into. Samuel was thirty-eight years old when he checked into the JCRS, listing his occupation as "painter." He was in the sanatorium only ten days, from May 19 to May 29, 1926, but he and his family never left the city.

The Handlers were part of a small group of Matziv Jews who worshipped at a temple in the back of a building off Main Street, on a creek that fed into the Platte River. Elliot's paternal grandfather in Ukraine had been a rabbi, and he wanted the same for his son. But Samuel Handler was a religious rebel who attended temple reluctantly. On the Jewish High Holidays his wife would plead, "It's a *shonda* for the neighbors for you not to go to shul." Elliot celebrated his bar mitzvah, but he shared his father's religious detachment.

Elliot's passion lay in the arts, and he dreamed of being a cartoonist. He sent cartoons off to newspapers and piled up rejections while he was still in high school. He took the only design job he could find, at a lighting design company. There he had the chance to create detailed drawings for his first original designs. They were not cartoons, but they were creative. Offered an arts scholarship at the Denver Art Institute, he dropped off the football and track teams in his senior year. To make up for the gap between the scholarship and the tuition costs, Samuel Handler volunteered his labor to paint the school.

Elliot remembered being instantly smitten by Ruth's looks even before he met her. She did not know that a couple of weeks before the B'nai B'rith dance he had been at the Mosko house for a crap game organized by her brother Maurice, whose nickname was Muzzy. Elliot and his friends were excited to be with Muzzy, who was an all-city football star and local Jewish hero. When Elliot walked into the house, he noticed Ruth's picture on the mantel and said to one of his friends, "Boy, what a cute-looking sister he has." When Chuck Newman brought Ruth over after dancing with her at the B'nai B'rith event, Elliot recognized her as the girl in the photograph.

Elliot was at the dance with three friends, "all hoodlums," as he later put it, and all standing around in sloppy T-shirts. He did not give them a chance to get near Ruth. Dancers were charged a nickel for charity to enter the roped-off dance floor. Elliot quickly paid for the first dance and took Ruth out on the floor. There was a small band, and as they did the fox-trot Elliot thought, "She's a real cute little gal." Everything seemed perfect to Elliot, but as the first dance ended he realized he did not have any more nickels. He told Ruth to wait on the dance floor for a minute, and frantically borrowed enough change from his friends to keep her by his side for the rest of the night. "We fell in love at a nickel a dance," he said later.

Elliot started driving his father's 1934 Chevy sedan across town to pick Ruth up for dates. They gave the car the ironic name Blue Streak. If it was snowing outside, Elliot would have to stop, jump out, and pull the wipers across the windshield so he could see. When he could not get his father's car, Elliot would hitch a ride on the viaduct that ran from the west to the east side. Then Ruth would let him drive her coupe. In those early days, they could hardly bear to be separated.

Occasionally they had enough money to go to the swank Brown Palace Hotel for dinner, "a fancy joint," as Elliot called it. But it was the worst year of the Depression, and while Sarah and Louie ran steady businesses, Elliot's father was struggling. Elliot worked at the Shockett Lighting Fixture Company, making blueprints and sketching fixtures, but he was also helping out with expenses at home. Happily for him, his job was around the corner from the Home Public Market. He went there frequently for lunch, and though Ruth did not give him free meals, she would serve him twice as much food as she charged him for.

The young couple enjoyed Lakeside Amusement Park, where they could dance at the El Patio ballroom to the Dorsey brothers or Louis Armstrong. There was a lot to do for not much money, including the bumper cars, a Ferris wheel, the Whistling Tom miniature steam train, and the Velvet Coaster, a looping, dipping thrill ride that Elliot enjoyed but not Ruth. Elitch Gardens was another favorite spot. There was a zoo, the Trocadero Ballroom, and another roller coaster for Elliot: the Wildcat. Despite financial hardship, Americans still spent money at the movies in the 1930s. Elliot and Ruth frequented a small movie theater on the west side that charged a quarter to get in and a nickel for popcorn. Gary Cooper starred in *A Farewell to Arms* in 1932, but by 1933, the most popular movie was the ensemble comedy with Danny Kaye and Ben Turpin, *Chasing Those Depression Blues.*

Elliot and Ruth were too love-besotted to be blue. Ruth said that she never felt the same feeling toward another man that she felt toward Elliot; he had a "magnetic" quality that sent shivers through her. "It was an unbelievable experience to just touch him," she remembered, "and I guess he must have had the same reaction because we just couldn't get enough of each other." Despite their strong physical attraction, however, they tried to do what they felt was the right thing. Guided by conscience, they held off being intimate despite how serious they were. Ruth said that more than three years went by before they "went the full route" as lovers. By then they were certain they would be married.

Sarah, however, had other plans. As strongly as Ruth was drawn to Elliot, Sarah was trying to pull her away. She thought Elliot was a poor prospect for a husband. He showed up to see Ruth in the same torn white T-shirt he had worn to the B'nai B'rith dance. Sarah would tease Ruth about it, but there was a serious undercurrent to her jibes. "Doesn't he have anything but that white T-shirt? Is that the only clothes he's got?" She would ask. Sarah worried about Elliot being poor. His father was a house painter who made little money. The Handler household had none of the luxuries found at the Greenwalds'. Sarah did not want Ruth ending up with someone who could not support her. She wanted her surrogate daughter to marry a doctor or lawyer or other professional. Sarah's worries grew when she found out that Elliot aspired to be an artist. She imagined Ruth starving to death in a garret.

Sarah's relentless criticism of Elliot took its toll on Ruth. Sarah told Ruth she was special, and Ruth agreed. Although she was not sure what her future would bring, Ruth knew that she did not aspire to an impoverished life with a struggling artist. After their first year together, Ruth convinced Elliot that they should try to pull apart, that they did not have a future. Sarah sent Ruth to Long Beach, California, where she spent the end of her junior year of high school and part of her senior year living with her sister Lillian and her husband.

The ploy failed. As soon as Ruth returned, she and Elliot were together again. They kept trying to separate, and sometimes they even dated other people. On the second New Year's Eve of their relationship, Ruth passed Elliot on the street and saw another girl on his arm. Her hurt and anger ran deep. Years later she could still remember how jealousy had gripped her. A short time later, she and Elliot were back together again. They could never stay apart more than two or three weeks, and Sarah grew ever more worried.

After her high school graduation in 1934, Ruth enrolled at the University of Denver, announcing her unconventional plan to become a lawyer. She continued to work for Sarah and Louie, but when President Franklin Roosevelt signed the National Youth Administration Act in 1935, providing money to employ young people, she got a job in the chancellor's office as a stenographer. Elliot continued at Shockett Lighting and at the local art school, although he knew his education was mediocre compared to what he would find at the Art Institute of Chicago or the Art Center College of Design in Los Angeles. He dreamed of saving enough money to go to one of those great schools.

The summer after her second year of college, Ruth ran into a girl named Jenny Cohen at a party on the west side. They had met before and Ruth did not consider the girl "her type," but when Jenny told Ruth she was going to Los Angeles for vacation the following week, Ruth was interested. She and Elliot were at another point of trying to separate, and Ruth had enjoyed her time in Southern California. Ruth told Jenny that she would like to go along, and Jenny offered to let Ruth stay with her at her relatives' house. Sarah, of course, was all for the trip. "Maybe now she'll meet a doctor or lawyer and get Elliot out of her system," she told her sister Doris. Doris had lived in Los Angeles when she was in her twenties, and gave Ruth the name of a woman she had shared an apartment with named Evelyn Lee. "She's a swell gal, you'll like her. She works at Paramount Studios," Doris told Ruth.

Los Angeles in 1936 was a city of two and a half million people and just beginning to sprawl. Six years earlier, the sons of the famed planner of Central Park in New York, Frederick Law Olmsted, approached city officials with a plan for hundreds of square miles of parkland. They warned that the people pouring into Los Angeles would bring pressure to pave over the city's natural beauty. Their pleas were ignored.

Instead, the need for Depression-era jobs, the westward march of people displaced by the midwestern drought, and the lack of housing led to desperate choices. The city began deporting Mexicans, some of them American citizens, to the south and sending police to the California-Nevada state line in a futile attempt to stop unemployed hitchhikers from pouring in. Meanwhile, the motion picture industry kept growing. New plants, like the airplane manufacturing facility by the airport, were under construction. Housing tracts were placed in far-flung suburban neighborhoods. To get workers back into the city for their jobs, freeways had to be built. For Ruth, the sleepy mountain town of Denver was galaxies away from the pace and the exotic, exciting character of Los Angeles.

Ruth wasted no time in contacting Evelyn Lee and arranging

lunch with her in the commissary at Paramount. MGM Studios had the largest stable of movie stars, but Paramount was exciting enough for Ruth. When the bulbous-nosed comedian W. C. Fields walked by, she froze. Evelyn assured her that stargazing was easy at a place that employed Marlene Dietrich, Gary Cooper, Cary Grant, Carole Lombard, Fredric March, Claudette Colbert, Mae West, the Marx brothers, Bob Hope, and Bing Crosby.

More out of curiosity than desire, Ruth asked how someone could get a job at Paramount. Evelyn was dismissive. Everybody wanted to work in Hollywood. You needed high-level connections, otherwise getting a job was impossible. "Those jobs are so precious and so hard to get," Evelyn told her, "you just can't get a studio job." But telling Ruth she could not do something was a guarantee she would try. Even though she had had no intention of working in the film industry when she arrived in Los Angeles, Ruth insisted that Evelyn take her to Personnel and let her apply. "I don't remember the application process," Ruth said, "but I remember walking out of the personnel office and I had a job." Ruth became a stenographer at twenty-five dollars a week and a lot of overtime. She had never earned that much money before.

Sarah could not have been happier. For Sarah, Ruth's going to college or on to law school was not nearly as important as her finding the right husband. She would miss her surrogate daughter, but Sarah felt certain that the distance from Elliot would end the attachment. Surely Ruth would meet some eligible new men in Hollywood. Sarah, however, underestimated the sweet, shy young man who still pined for Ruth. He had tried to find a job in graphic design in Denver but, failing that, was working on light fixtures and trying to save enough for art school. "I was very unhappy without her," Elliot remembered, "and I thought, 'the weather's better in California than in Chicago,' where the Art Institute was, so I went to LA."

Elliot found a ride-share for five dollars and arrived a month after Ruth. He knocked on her door, telling her he had changed his mind about Chicago and had come to Los Angeles for the weather. She hid a knowing smile, surprised and delighted to see him. Elliot moved into a long-term room at the Colonial Hotel, near her apartment.

Ruth and Elliot spent an idyllic year in Los Angeles. Two of Ruth's brothers had a car dealership and had given her a re-possessed convertible coupe. The young lovers spent weekends touring the coastline or seeing movies at the two-thousand-seat Orpheum Theatre. In the evenings after work Elliot would come to the apartment that Ruth shared with Evelyn. They would walk about six blocks to Thrifty Drug Store at Wilshire and Western, where they ordered the twenty-nine-cent blue plate special for dinner. On rare occasions they splurged for the thirty-nine-cent special deluxe dinner.

One evening Elliot arrived at the apartment upset and de-pressed. He had just been laid off from his lighting fixture design job. As usual, he and Ruth started their walk to Thrifty's, but depression smothered their usual high spirits. As they stepped off the first curb, Elliot kicked something. He stooped to pick it up and discovered it was a nickel. Neither of them was superstitious, but this time they felt they had received a powerful omen. Ruth said, "That's for good luck. Keep it and you'll get a new job right away." Elliot put the nickel into his wallet, and suddenly his good spirits seemed to return. The next day he got a new and better job at another lighting fixture company. Decades later, he still had that same nickel in his wallet.

Ruth and Elliot's unique partnership established many of its patterns in those early days. She had an optimistic view no matter the situation and kept Elliot's spirits up. She had a boisterous ad-venturism that pulled him along, and he had a quiet, steady, unwavering love for her. At the end of their workdays, there was much to talk, share, and dream about.

Elliot's work as a lighting designer paid only eighteen dollars a week, seven dollars less than Ruth was earning. Despite the lower pay, he had the satisfaction of seeing one of his designs go from drawings to reality. Because his company was doing work for Union Station, the railway terminal being built in Los Angeles, Elliot had his first opportunity to prominently place one of his designs. Union Station was the last of the great railway stations to be built, and Elliot's giant chandelier-like fixtures still hang in the side halls.

Ruth loved working at Paramount, particularly the occasional chance to see some of the stars. She was able to sneak Elliot onto the set of *Thanks for the Memory*, where they heard Bob Hope and Shirley Ross sing the romantic "Two Sleepy People." She became a devoted fan of Lucille Ball after delivering phone messages from her to director Alexander Hall. Ruth also got her first taste of working inside a large company, and she was a sharp critic. She was "appalled at the waste of money and poor management," not only in her department, but companywide. People who worked for movie studios, she decided, would make bad employees since they had such abysmal work habits.

Back in Denver, Sarah worried about Ruth. She had heard about all the time Ruth was spending with Elliot, and she decided it had to stop. Showing up in Los Angeles, she convinced the twenty-one-year-old that she was headed for a miserable life with a man who would end up a starving artist.

Ruth's sense of duty overwhelmed her love for Elliot. She struggled to say no to Sarah but failed. Admitting that Sarah was right, she said a difficult good-bye to Elliot, sold her car, quit her job, and returned to Denver. Once again she worked at the Home Public Market and served as secretary to her brother Joe, the lawyer. She did not even reenroll at college. Instead, she pined for Elliot, making frequent telephone calls to him and longing for her old life in Los Angeles.

As Elliot's birthday approached in the spring, Ruth decided to spend an extravagant thirty-five dollars on a beautiful watch for him. In the thank-you letter he wrote wistfully, "I wish we could get married." Ruth, however, did not waste time on wishing. She wrote, "Why don't we?" He wrote back, "Why not?"

Sarah's strategy had backfired. She realized that there was no breaking Ruth and Elliot apart, and finally she gave in. By the time Elliot returned to Denver, an extravagant wedding was being planned. If Sarah's surrogate daughter was getting married, Sarah and Louie would spare no expense.

Ruth and Elliot married on June 26, 1938, at the posh Park Lane Hotel just outside the center of Denver. One hundred and forty guests came to the hotel, which overlooked Washington Park and provided a spectacular view of the Rocky Mountains from the glass-enclosed ballroom on the top floor. After the ceremony, guests were treated to an elaborate dinner with dancing.

Ruth walked down the aisle carrying a white Bible and gardenias. She had borrowed her dress from her friend Charlotte, who had recently married Chuck Newman, the young man who first danced with Ruth at the B'nai B'rith fair where she met Elliot. The white satin gown had long sleeves, a simple round collar, and a full skirt that swept the floor. Ruth wore a white halo hat to hold a long, plain white tulle veil. The dress fit her perfectly, accenting her figure, as curvaceous as a Hollywood starlet's. Elliot looked happy, if uncomfortable, in a rented tuxedo, his thick dark hair combed straight back in the style of the day.

For the ceremony, Ruth wore a tin wedding ring given to her by her brother Max and his wife, Lillian. Jewish custom dictated that she not use a ring with jewels. Soon after the marriage, Elliot bought Ruth a simple gold wedding band, which they both agreed looked better than the tin one. Elliot took the tin ring and put it in his wallet, where it stayed.

In the wedding photo, Jacob and Ida flank the newly married couple. Ruth's parents wear restrained smiles, but Sarah, Ruth's matron of honor, sitting next to her father, looks ecstatic. She had put her doubts aside to stage the perfect wedding, and nothing would ruin the day for her. Samuel and Freida Handler, Elliot's parents, may not have been as pleased. The two families, Jews from different parts of the old country, never got along.

After the wedding, Ruth and Elliot drove away in a new Chevy coupe, bought by her siblings. The newlyweds felt they had outgrown Denver and were heading back to start married life in Los Angeles, where they had been so happy. Even though they had both given up their jobs in LA, Elliot had no doubts about their plan. "I just loved that little girl," he remembered, "and everything we did was just right."

Chapter 4

Ruth and Elliot and Matt

*So-called impulsive decisions are very often the
ones that turn your life.*

Now that Ruth and Elliot had formalized their relationship, Ruth
lost no time in testing its bounds. As they drove across the Arizona desert, she asked Elliot to change his name.

Ruth had been introduced to Izzy Handler, only later learning that his middle name was Elliot. Secretly, she hated the name
Izzy. Long before she met Elliot, Ruth's older brother Maurice,
nicknamed Muzzy, had come to pick her up from Sarah's house
to drive her to their parents' house. As they arrived, two police
officers pulled up behind them and accused Muzzy of a driving
violation. Ruth remembered the officers being "quite nasty" as
they questioned her brother. When Muzzy told them his name,
one officer asked snidely, "What was that . . . Izzy?"

Given the atmosphere of the time, the officer's comment was
not surprising. Throughout the 1920s and 1930s a rising tide of
American anti-Semitism washed over the country. Even as Jews
became more upwardly mobile, their admission to universities,
professional schools, and the upper reaches of corporate America

was restricted. Henry Ford used the *Dearborn Independent*, a weekly Michigan newspaper he'd bought, to spread anti-Semitic propaganda. Ford claimed that German Jewish banking interests fomented World War I. The Ku Klux Klan had reached the pinnacle of its power in the late 1920s. From 1924 to 1928 the Klan's leadership took over the Colorado state government, further fanning anti-Jewish fervor. Governor Clarence Morley, elected in 1924, and many local elected officials were Klan members. By 1930, when Ruth turned fourteen, Jews were scapegoated for bank failures that set off the Great Depression. As jobs became scarce, anti-Jewish restrictions in job advertisements became commonplace.

In Denver's close-knit Jewish community, Ruth was aware of anti-Semitism but had not experienced it. She had been shocked and frightened by the police officer's threatening tone with her brother. As she and Elliot drove through the dry, brown landscape toward Los Angeles, she told Elliot that his nickname reminded her of the hateful incident. His middle name was "beautiful," she said, proposing that he become Elliot Handler. He was surprised but compliant. "She felt pretty strongly that it was too Jewish," Elliot remembered. "She liked my middle name, and I did not like 'Izzy' either." They were immigrants' children, still somehow strangers in their own land, still trying to find their place. Unconsciously, they were moving away from their roots and edging closer to assimilation, heading toward a storybook realization of the American dream.

Back in Los Angeles, the young couple stayed in the William Penn Hotel on Melrose Avenue until they could find an apartment. Ruth returned to her job at Paramount. Elliot went back to Beranek and Erwin Lighting Fixture Company, and began classes at the Art

Center College of Design. Eventually, they found a tiny, swelter-
ing, roach-infested but affordable studio on Melrose.

Months later, on a Sunday drive, Ruth spotted a new building
and told Elliot to stop, even though she thought it looked out of
their price range. The apartment at 5142½ Clinton Avenue in Hollywood seemed huge by comparison to where they were living.
Half of a two-car garage was included in the $37.50 monthly rent.
Even though the rent was 30 percent more than they were paying
and they would have to buy furniture, they took the apartment
on the spot.

Later in her life, Ruth read a great deal of meaning into taking
the new apartment, as well as other milestones she identified in
her life. She believed in "predestination," focusing particularly on
her most impulsive decisions as evidence that "there's some kind
of plan for each of us." It was just as true that Ruth was a person of
action from a very young age. She spent far less time deliberating
than deciding and moving forward. If mistakes were made, she
quickly grasped her errors, corrected them, and moved on. This
pattern would repeat itself throughout the early years of building her business. Her penchant, even impatience, for action would
lead to her greatest successes, but it would also lay the trap for her
most devastating failure.

Settled into their new apartment, Elliot had a new dream. The
Art Center had opened the possibilities of industrial design to
him. At the time, new materials were being discovered, present-
ing unique opportunities to design products. Prior to 1931, the
only man-made molded plastics were Bakelite and Catalin, used
to design and manufacture casings for clocks, radios, telephones,
and colorful jewelry. But then two different companies discovered
a polyacrylic that was water-resistant, crystal clear, and shatter

resistant. DuPont called this product Lucite, while its competitor Rohm and Haas dubbed its Plexiglas.

In 1936 the Army Air Corps decreed that Plexiglas was the only plastic sheet material approved for use in military planes. Ninety percent of the material was being sold for aviation, destined as a replacement for glass in windshields, gun turrets, and radar domes of airplanes used in World War II. Elliot's teacher at the Art Center had a different idea, assigning the class the job of designing consumer items from the new material.

Elliot was full of ideas for Plexiglas, which was not only clear, but could be buffed to a high shine. As Elliot looked around the young couple's apartment he imagined everything from furniture and lamps to small items such as ashtrays and bowls made from the material. He began sketching. When Ruth looked at his ideas she began to plan. If Elliot made samples, she told him, she would find a way to sell them. He was willing, but there was a problem. He needed equipment that was available only at school. With other students in line, Elliot did not have enough time to complete his schoolwork and produce his own projects. Ruth had an answer for that too. "Let's buy our own equipment," she told her husband.

If there is an entrepreneurial gene, Ruth had it, but she also had something more concrete: her memories of Sarah. "Sarah was my role model," Ruth told an interviewer years later. "She was the responsible person in that marriage. She held things together, made the decisions, took care of the money. I guess that's why I never thought it strange for a woman to take the business lead in a marriage." Ruth had an ethnic-based rationale for her assertiveness in business as well. Jews from Poland, like her family, had suffered from anti-Semitism and life in a ghetto. Men and women had to work together to make a living. Ruth believed that was why she and Elliot did not see anything unusual about women working and running things.

Ruth took charge of providing Elliot what he would need to make the first products that she would sell. It was the beginning of a stunning partnership of creativity and commercial acumen.

The Handlers bought the necessary equipment on an installment plan from Sears for two hundred dollars, and set up shop in their half of the garage. Elliot sanded and shaped the wood molds for the Plexiglas sheets. When they were smooth enough to produce the surface he wanted, he heated the plastic in the kitchen stove and then rushed it out to the garage to press into the molds. The garage, already cluttered with his drill press, sander, and saw, was soon littered with wood shavings, plastic bits, and wood dust. The tenant whose car shared the space grew annoyed and complained to the landlord. He gave Ruth and Elliot an ultimatum: move their shop or move out of the apartment.

The young couple still owed money on the equipment, which they would soon have no place to house. While their worldly wealth was a bit of savings and a car, they had the irrepressible optimism of two people barely out of their teenage years. Elliot offered to quit school, but Ruth pushed the gamble much further. Elliot would quit his job, collect unemployment, and make his designs in a shop she would find and outfit with a new oven. In her grand vision, she would then sell all that he made.

In her biography, Ruth professes absolute confidence in Elliot's talent. His fertile creativity and consumer-oriented imagination were evident, but he was often too introverted to order dinner in a restaurant. "I've always been the shy, stay-in-the-background type," he said. All of Elliot's brilliant work would have gathered dust in his shop save for Ruth's belief that she could sell it, even though she had no sales experience. She had been a store clerk and an office assistant, and she intended to keep her job at Paramount.

But she was as creative as Elliot was in his design work and full of ideas for marketing.

They found a former Chinese laundry to rent with about 200 square feet of space. It cost fifty dollars for six months. They were so broke that Elliot's friend Seymour Green remembered going by in the morning to drop off eight dollars to get them through the day. He helped Elliot paint the new space, but they had to water down the blue calcimine powder so much that it ended up being nearly white.

Elliot asked Harold "Matt" Matson, a tall, strong Swede who had worked with him at the lighting company, to build an oven for the new shop. It weighed about four hundred pounds and sat on narrow steel legs. Seymour and Elliot's brother Al rented a truck to bring it to the shop, but as they unloaded it the oven slipped and one leg scraped Seymour's ankles, leaving him screaming in pain. Ignoring his distress, Ruth yelled, "What the hell are you doing? You bent one of the oven legs." She later apologized, but it was not the last time Seymour was the focus of her anger, even though he was volunteering his time. Tensions ran high as the Handlers launched their new business.

In her off-hours Ruth schemed about which shops to cold-call with Elliot's designs. She was eager to take on a challenge Elliot would not consider. She said, "I soon realized that I would have to do the selling. My husband is a brilliant artist and creator, but he's also shy and introverted . . . I am just the opposite." Their differences seemed to prove the old axiom "Opposites attract," but there was much more to their relationship than that. In a time when society expected women to be subservient to their husbands, Elliot was willing to give Ruth absolute freedom to satisfy an almost innate entrepreneurial drive. "We made the jump. I quit and she kept working. She liked Paramount all right, but she stopped talking about movie stars. Being a secretary was not enough for her."

Ruth had her target store picked out: a swanky Danish modern gift shop on Wilshire Boulevard called Zacho's. Ruth loaded a beat-up suitcase with Elliot's bookends, trays, cigarette boxes, hand mirrors, and candleholders made from a combination of wood and Plexiglas. Cutting out from work one afternoon during her lunch hour, she marched into the store's quiet, intimidating luxury. With her thick, shoulder-length brown hair swept off her forehead and a starlet's figure, she forced a broad, nervous smile as she approached the haughty salesclerk.

The woman insisted on inspecting the items before calling the owner, Mr. Zacho. After having a look, he told Ruth in heavily accented English that he wanted to meet Elliot and see their workshop. Panicked, she imagined this elderly man walking into the dilapidated Chinese laundry they had converted into a shop. "If he sees the crummy place . . . we'll lose him forever," she thought. Zacho saw her reaction and reassured her that, coming from Europe, he had seen many small, nondescript workshops. Still, Ruth was nervous. She told him to come on Saturday, not wanting Elliot to be alone when Zacho rejected them, as she felt certain he would.

On Saturday, Zacho arrived at the small storefront in the 4000 block of Olympic Boulevard near Normandie Avenue, which they had named Elliot Handler Plastics. Zacho shook Elliot's hand, took a quick look around, and said he wanted to place an order. Ruth and Elliot were stunned. Elliot realized he did not even have a paper or pencil. Tearing a corner off some brown packing paper, he scratched out the details, his shaking hand grasping a pencil stub. For Zacho, the $500 order was trivial, but for Ruth and Elliot it represented the incalculable affirmation of their dream. After Zacho left, they shouted and hugged. They had made their first sale.

Ruth worried, however, about their revenue and expenses. She was beginning her learn-by-doing business apprenticeship. If they bought polyacrylic sheets at retail they might not make a profit, so they tried to buy wholesale from the suppliers. DuPont did not return their calls. The representative they contacted at Rohm and Haas, Jerry Young, said they were too small for a wholesale deal. He did not, however, forget them. A few weeks after he met Ruth, he called to give her a lead at Douglas Aircraft, a big customer for his company.

Douglas had asked Young to recommend a company that could design a promotional gift product. The company wanted a novelty item to give to helpful officials and special customers, and to reward employees. It had die-cast a handsome miniature of the DC–3 airplane and it wanted it incorporated into the design. The finished product was meant to be displayed in an office or home library.

Before proceeding, Douglas wanted to have a meeting to discuss what it was looking for. While Elliot would have been the best one to talk about its design ideas, Ruth knew he would be too intimidated to trust with such a large potential customer. She could not rely on him to make the pitch for what could be a huge account. Instead, she took an afternoon off work and met with three male executives at Douglas in a large corner office. She listened carefully, trying to hide her ignorance of design, as they described what they wanted. Exhilarated, Ruth walked out with a deal. Just as she was sure that she had done a good job handling the meeting, she was also certain that Elliot would come up with something to satisfy their new customer.

Elliot decided on a simple, elegant clock, notably modernist at a time when Picasso and Braque were large influences. He turned a sheet of Plexiglas about ten inches high on its side, and bent it around, stopping a few inches before the ends met. The sheet was wider in the front and narrowed as it curved to the back. On the front face, he placed airplane rivets in a circle for the clock numbers. On the back edge, he balanced and attached the model DC–3, its nose facing forward, its wings spread wide as if it were going to fly past the clock face.

Elliot's clock and a simpler bookcase design were immediate hits with Douglas. Now Ruth had a large enough order to get wholesale prices on Plexiglas from Rohm and Haas. Filling the Douglas order became a family affair. Elliot's brother Al, home from the army, helped. Ruth borrowed fifteen hundred dollars from Sarah for materials, which she paid back as soon as the revenue from their second big sale came in. The profit went toward renting another, bigger space at 4916 South Western Avenue. Meanwhile, Elliot was increasing his production of giftware, and Matt Matson came to work with him on fabrication. The business's stationery read, "Elliot Handler, designer and fabricator in Lucite and Plexiglas."

Elliot needed the new space. Infected with sales fever, Ruth frequently skipped out of her job at Paramount to land new clients like RKO Studios and a company called Enka. Al Handler went back to Denver, where he made suggestions for products and secured orders from a local company, Daniels and Fisher.

Elliot showed a special ability to spot trends. Costume jewelry was the rage in the late 1930s, and Elliot began designing a few pieces. In 1940 he made a tiny woman's hand clasping a vial that could hold some water and a flower bud and could be pinned on a woman's blouse or blazer. It was a hit, and he began producing distinctive pieces from Plexiglas, including pins in the shapes of cuckoo clocks, sabers, hearts, and scissors. Ruth's distribution expanded as well, and Elliot's jewelry soon appeared in stores all over Los Angeles.

Ruth struggled to get bank credit to buy materials. They had expanded to make fruit bowls, powder boxes, coffee tables, breakfast trays, coat hangers, and special order furniture. Their cash flow continually lagged behind delivery, and they had to borrow from Sarah and some of their friends, especially Seymour Green, Elliot's old roommate and best friend. Louie Greenwald had lent them a hundred dollars in September 1940. In October they had borrowed three hundred dollars to buy a car. In November Sarah gave them a loan of five hundred dollars, paid off two months later when Douglas made a payment of $1,399.77. Their finances were either up or down but never stable.

The young couple also had a problem far more worrisome than cash flow. Ruth was pregnant with their first baby, and there were complications. She started hemorrhaging, and the business suffered from her need to rest. In February 1941 Elliot sent a letter to the state tax board explaining his failure to pay sales tax on time. Evidently, he had forgotten to put a stamp on his payment and pleaded not to be penalized. "Until recently," he wrote, "my wife has taken complete charge of my books and office work. However, during the latter part of December she became very ill and has been in bed since that time." He went on to explain that he had been busy moving the business and had been selling wholesale until the previous month, so he had no experience with sending sales tax reports. He begged his way out of interest and a penalty totaling $4.28. Either way, the Handlers' balance sheet was running precariously close to the red.

Entrepreneur Zachary Zemby, a Russian Jewish immigrant, noticed the pieces in several stores. Intrigued, he found out the name of the designer. One day in early 1941 he showed up unannounced at Elliot's shop. He would end up to be a savior for the fledgling business owners.

Zemby arrived at Elliot Handler Plastics just after Ruth had been confined to bed for two months, not even allowed to go to the bathroom. Sarah and Louie had moved to Los Angeles in time to help out, and Ruth had quit her job at Paramount. A financial success in jewelry, Zemby had the money and the financial backing to grow a new business. As soon as he met Elliot, he asked, "Would you like a partner?" Zemby took over the marketing, sales, and management where Ruth left off. As the country was preparing for possible entry into World War II, metal was in short supply. The new partners agreed to use ceramic, wood, and scrap Lucite for the jewelry they produced. With Ruth miserably sidelined to bed rest, the men agreed to call their business after their names: Elzac.

On May 21, 1941, Ruth gave birth to a healthy baby girl she named Barbara Joyce. Elliot had to borrow sixty-five dollars to pay Dr. Paul Steinberg for the delivery and to get Ruth out of the hospital. The Handlers' checking account had only $14.97 and a pending deposit of $84.75. Luckily, Zemby had thrown himself into the new business, and the partners were starting to make money. Elzac expanded to a new shop on Western Avenue, north of Slauson. Zemby brought in three partners, all immigrants like himself, to keep the capital flowing as the demand for costume jewelry boomed.

Elzac grossed nine hundred thousand dollars in its first year. Zemby wrote cheery copy for retailers, selling frivolity to a country finding its stoicism in the days leading up to Pearl Harbor. "Two saucy penguins, papa and son. Two winged pigs, mother and daughter. Be sure your stock has these Elzac caprices." The penguin pins sold for $2 retail, and $1.25 more for matching earrings. A bunny pin boasted "ears pricked up in green Lucite." Elliot designed them all.

After the bombing of Pearl Harbor by the Japanese on December 7, 1941, followed by the United States' entry into World War II, Elliot decided against enlisting because of his growing family. He devoted himself to Elzac, which struggled to keep up production in the face of inductions, enlistments, and the demands of war plants. They developed a line production system so that unskilled labor could be used to work on a single component of the final product. Workers were allowed to sit down so that the elderly and handicapped could be hired. Since war plants required proof of citizenship, Mexican workers flooded Elzac, both men and women, who had not yet been legalized. The manufacturing plant took up four floors and the basement of two adjoining buildings. Wages were on the scale of war-related plants, and the partners used noncritical materials for tools and dies, carefully avoiding any criticism that they were interfering with the war effort.

Machines churned away in the basement of Elzac, mixing clays that went into tile molds for delivery to electric and gas kilns. Upstairs, women hand-painted novelty figures and ceramic jewelry, while others attached leather, hair, or wood trims. By 1943 the company had three hundred employees. Elliot worked long hours, both designing new products and spending time on increasingly bitter intracompany disputes. His three new partners came from Russia, Hungary, and Romania. They brought not only conflicting tongues, but also differing ideas about running Elzac. To add to his stress, Elliot also had worries at home.

Ruth tried to settle into her role as a first-time mother; then in 1942 she became pregnant again. This time, however, she miscarried. Determined to have a bigger family, she was again pregnant in the summer of 1943. She chafed, however, at being a stay-at-home mother with two-year-old Barbara. She did not like housework or cooking, and the meals she prepared were abominable. A can of cream of mushroom soup slathered over French toast, with canned peas and tuna on top served as dinner. Her traditional "matzo brei, matzo soaked in eggs and fried in a pan with slices of kosher salami and onion," was one of Elliot's few favorites. Ruth wanted to get back into business.

Bored and tense, Ruth was also afraid to exercise, as she feared another hemorrhage. "I was fit to be tied with staying home," Ruth said. "I hated it. I couldn't stand it. It was awful." She felt unattractive and uncomfortably distant from the business world she and Elliot had shared. When he seemed to be spending too much time with an attractive blond at Elzac, she complained, the only time in their marriage that Elliot remembered her voicing such an objection. In the evenings, Ruth listened in frustration as Elliot became more and more disgruntled about his job. She wanted to manage Elzac, but as pregnancy progressed she could barely crawl out of bed.

On March 22, 1944, with her weight ballooned beyond endurance, Ruth took Barbara on a bus ride from Pico Boulevard and Motor Avenue to Manning Avenue and back. "We sort of went around in circles and the streets were very bumpy," Ruth remembered. "That bus bounced so bad, and I kept saying, 'Bumpy bus, bounce baby brother out,' and Barbie would laugh and we had a good time." That night Ruth's son, Kenneth Robert, was born. He weighed more than ten pounds. Elliot was relieved and overjoyed. Elzac, with its two million dollars in sales and feuding owners, faded from his mind as he held his little boy for the first time.

Despite his size, Ken was dehydrated and had a slight infection. The doctor recommended holding off on the bris, the traditional Jewish circumcision. The Handlers had planned to have the ceremony at the hospital two days after the birth since Ruth wanted her mother and father there. The Moskos, having just celebrated their fiftieth wedding anniversary, had come to Los Angeles to see their grandson. But Jacob, still headstrong and impatient, refused to wait for the baby to convalesce. With Ruth in the hospital, Elliot drove his in-laws to the train station for the ride back to Denver. As soon as they reached home, Jacob headed straight to an all-night poker game. In the middle of a hand, he dropped dead of a heart attack.

All the family except Ruth, still too weak to travel, attended the funeral. A day later, Ruth's brother Joe wrote her a long letter about the sad events. There was a large crowd and "Pa was fixed up beautifully," he told her. In the traditional Jewish manner, the family entered a seven-day period of mourning, or shivah. Joe found it good to "sit around and talk," although he confessed that the family's davening, the recitation of prayers, was weak. He told her that their mother had received Ruth's wire and understood why she could not come. "Ma was comforted," he told her, that their father had seen Ruth's new son. Joe closed with some good news in the family: another nephew had been born. But as Joe finished and posted his letter, another tragedy was unfolding. By the time Ruth received the mail from her brother, he called her with horrible, unbelievable news. Their mother was gone as well.

The day after Jacob's funeral, his children had been sitting discussing Ida's future. She sat nearby, too deaf to understand what they were saying. As they argued over whom she should live with, Doris looked over at Ida. She told her she looked tired and suggested that Ida go upstairs and rest.

As Joe told Ruth in another letter, Ma had been so upset at the funeral that it had taken six people to restrain her. When she had gone upstairs to rest on the day she died, Joe had sat with her for an hour. "She kept talking about you and Babsie and your new son," he wrote Ruth. "She was so glad that Elliot was doing so well and that you did not have to struggle. She told me how pretty your home was." Ida also told Joe that if anything happened to her she wanted all of her money to go to their brother Muzzy, whom she felt needed the most help. "She was content when I told her that we would follow her wishes." Joe went to lie down in the next room, but he did not go to sleep. No sound came from Ida's room.

A few hours later, when Joe checked on her, she had passed away. "I can't describe the shock. We haven't gotten over it," he wrote. "So many tears were shed we can't bring up any more." Jacob and Ida were together fifty years, and now they were together for eternity, Joe assured Ruth.

Ma had raised ten children, Joe said, including Ruth, even though she had been raised apart. "We must make a double effort to stick together. We must avoid petty differences and arguments." He was reminding her of the strong Mosko bond, a bond that Ruth would never abandon.

Just as Ruth missed the chance to be raised with her siblings, she was robbed of the chance to grieve with them. Whatever her feelings about the parents who had not parented her, a piece of her past had disappeared. It is unlikely, however, that Ruth engaged in introspection or prolonged remorse. She believed in moving on. Action was her antidote to despair. A few months after Ken's birth, claiming to be fed up with being a stay-at-home mother, she went back to work. When she wrote her autobiography fifty years later, she left out any mention of the circumstances surrounding Jacob's and Ida's deaths. To her, it was as if they had simply disappeared.

Harold Matson laid the groundwork for Ruth's return to work. He was as unhappy at Elzac as Elliot. Matson had been running the factory and fending off the conflicting demands of the partners for several years, and he was tired. Elliot came home one day and told Ruth that Matson had quit. She said to Elliot, "Let's go see him," recalling later that it felt like "something hit my head." Standing in Matt's garage, Ruth asked him what he planned to do. He said that he wanted to make gift items and hoped to use some of Elliot's designs if he could get permission. Elliot agreed, and Ruth offered to sell what he made, suggesting that he start with picture frames. She had noticed dozens of Austin Photography Studios all over the Los Angeles area and decided they were the perfect outlet for frames. "For some reason, I knew I could sell them picture frames," Ruth remembered. "It seemed so natural to me that I did not hesitate for a moment in informing Matt what he was to make." Ruth had no idea what marketing meant, but she had been paying attention to what was in the marketplace and what she thought was needed. She felt that this "compulsive intellectual process" formed her identity in the business world.

Elliot helped decide which picture frame designs Matt would use. They also worked together on a name for the new company. They tried various combinations, finally settling on putting "Matt" together with "Elliot" to form "Mattel." Ruth said she never thought of insisting that her name be included. She said her name was too hard to incorporate, and she did not mind being left out.

Elliot went back to Elzac, and Matt began making the sample Lucite frames. Just as she had predicted, Ruth got her first big order of several thousand dollars from Austin Photography. Metal had been restricted because of the war, so the shop was delighted with Elliot's Lucite designs. Mattel seemed to be off to a great start. Thrilled with the order and anxious to present it to Elliot and Matt, Ruth turned on the car radio to find some upbeat music to underscore her happy mood. That was when she heard that the president had ordered a freeze on the sale of all plastic materials for any use other than the war effort. Scrap materials were included.

Sitting with Matt around the Handler table that night, Elliot came up with a new design using flocked wood for the frames. With Sarah tending the children, Ruth headed out the next morning to convince Austin's buyer that the wood frames were even better than the plastic ones. She was also determined to put her housebound years behind her. She wanted to return to the adrenaline highs. She wanted to get back in the competition and the dizzying gamble of building something she owned. This time she had more experience. This time it would be bigger. This time she would not leave or let someone else take over her company.

After showing the buyer the alternatives Elliot had developed, Ruth left the store with an order twice as large as the first. Mattel was in business. They moved from Matt's garage to a larger space and began to expand production. "Yes, it was Elliot's designs," Ruth said later. "Yes, it was Elliot's name. Yes, he was very much a part of it in my mind. But I actually started Mattel."

Chapter 5

A Working Mother

I'm the most independent person I know.

The small sign over the door read, "Mattel Creations." Austin Photography's picture frame order had forced Matt and Ruth to move the company from Matt's garage to rented space at 6058 South Western Avenue. Matt worked out of a converted garage on one side of the low-slung brick-and-stucco building, while at the other end a small office faced the street. Inside, the frameless windows broke the bare and dingy plane of the walls. White wide-slat venetian blinds were haphazardly drawn. If the little shop looked rough at the edges, its saleswoman/manager-in-chief did not.

Only a few months after delivering Ken, Ruth had lost most of her pregnancy weight, as much from being on the move as from any diet. She liked trim-fitting suits that showed off her figure. She styled her hair carefully and favored siren red lipstick for her sales calls. With her lightning smile, direct gaze, and firm handshake, she represented Mattel as if it were a manufacturing concern with a thousand employees.

The Austin order, however, showed that the new business was

tenuous. Ruth, seasoned from her giftware experience at Elliot Handler Plastics, had done a careful estimate of unit costs and thought she had set a good price for the order. But renting the building and ordering materials had put her close to the red. She did not believe Matt could help with the finances and had left him to handle the manufacturing. She would have to be the one to figure out how to save some money.

Elliot's design called for intricately carved wood frames that could be made only with special equipment used by furniture manufacturers. Ruth went through the telephone book, finding a number of small companies that might have the equipment. Leaving Ken with a babysitter, she loaded Barbara in the car to look for the machines and skilled craftsmen she needed.

She drove from one company to another, trying to keep her daughter cheerful as she dragged her in and out of the car. Ruth walked into one company where a large dog that was lying on the floor jumped up and attacked Barbara. She was not hurt, but it was a horrible experience for Ruth and her three-year-old. Her arduous searching, however, paid off. Matt got the equipment to make and assemble the frames, but they were bulky, which drove up delivery costs. With finances tight, delivery threatened to eliminate any profit. Once again, Ruth decided to handle the problem herself.

A truck rental company was next door to Mattel. Although she had never driven a truck before, Ruth decided to rent one so she could deliver the frames herself. Besides her inexperience at driving the big truck, Ruth was only five feet two inches tall and weighed 104 pounds. Reaching the gears and brakes was a challenge, especially since the gears operated in the reverse from those of a car. The men at the rental agency looked stunned as she attempted, without initial success, to back out of their lot. Arriving downtown at Austin's, she discovered that the delivery had to be made in a narrow alley. It was noon and a lunchtime audience of warehouse workers watched in amusement as Ruth struggled to align the truck with the loading dock. "I was frightened and determined and thoroughly embarrassed," Ruth remembered, but she maneuvered the truck into place and convinced her bemused audience to unload it for her. "I felt like a stupid ass, but I got that goddamn truck. I was gutsy. I made it work," she said.

Ruth neglected to add that she drove the truck in a dress and heels, at a time when many women had not even learned to drive a car. She was back in her element, thriving on the high wire of a business start-up. Her husband, however, was miserable. His partners at Elzac had little creativity. They wanted to repeat the same designs, while Elliot longed for originality. He saw costume jewelry as a changing market where women wanted surprise with new and unexpected designs.

Where Ruth looked at a product and thought about the customer and where to sell it, Elliot looked at material and thought of what product to create. He began to play around with the scrap wood and some plastic in Matt's shop. Most people would not have seen a use for the small scraps, but Elliot decided to fashion dollhouse furniture. His first piece was a chair, its frame shaped by one piece of Plexiglas ingeniously turned and twisted to form the legs, sides, and back. A small piece of wood was glued on for a seat. "If he can make it, I can sell it," Ruth said. Elliot followed her suggestion to design a full dollhouse line.

By July 1944 Elliot was fed up with his partners. He called Ruth from work, and she could hear the tension in his voice. "Ruth, I gotta get out of this place. I've asked them to . . ." Elliot hesitated, but Ruth instantly knew what was going on. They had talked about it many times. "Did you ask them to buy you out?" Elliot was hesitant. "Yes, I did. They told me they'll give me ten thousand dollars," he said.

By that time Elzac had more than three million dollars in annual sales, and Ruth estimated that Elliot's share of the net worth was between seventy-five thousand and a hundred thousand. She also knew he could demand several times his share, but she said, "Will they give it to you now?" "Yes," Elliot replied, "but . . . ten thousand dollars?" "Take the ten thousand dollars and run," Ruth told her husband, knowing he would not want to fight for more. Ruth wanted them to work together again. "We'll put the money in Mattel. We need you here full-time because we've got to design new products."

On October 16, 1944, Elliot signed the papers giving him $9,500 dollars in cash, $2,500 for a side business called Beverly-craft, $3,900 dollars in cancellation of debt, and permission for his partners to keep all of his designs. They may have thought that Elliot got the worse end of the deal, but a year later Elzac went out of business.

Ruth achieved her goal of getting Elliot to Mattel, but nine months later his efforts to forestall military service finally failed. Elliot had stayed out of the army by claiming he did war work at home. In December 1943 he had written to the Selective Service Board that he was engaged in war-related design engineering work with the "Advance Plastic Engineering Company." If this company was an offshoot or subsidiary of Elzac, there is no record of it. The army accepted the claim, however, and Elliot was not ordered for duty at Fort MacArthur until June 11, 1945. By then the allies had been victorious in Europe. Victory with Japan would come by the end of the summer. Elliot was sent to Camp Roberts, a few hours north near the California coast. He had no worry of being sent overseas, but he began writing anxious and, in his words, "whining" letters, anyway.

The heat was terrific, Elliot wrote Ruth. The recruits were about to start seventeen weeks of basic training with full packs, rifles, and steel helmets. "Oy!" he moaned. The camp was rough. He missed her terribly. To forestall lovesickness, he let himself dream about her only two nights a week.

The Handlers worked at keeping their business partnership intact. Elliot began to send Ruth sketches for new dollhouse furniture and, after basic training, could come home on weekends. These weekends gave them more time to work on the business, as well as time together. "Listen, toots," he wrote, "if your red-headed cousin is hanging around when I get my next pass you tell her to get the hell out." They were apart for their wedding anniversary. "Tomorrow will be seven years, darling," Elliot wrote. "I would love very much to be in your arms." After their next weekend together, a smitten Elliot wrote, "Our weekend sure was heaven! Those Saturday nights with you are something a guy doesn't forget very easily. After I become a civilian . . . we should have weekends like that more often. I can dream, can't I?"

Elliot's friend Seymour Green had enlisted four years earlier. He remembered Ruth picking him up at the station just after Elliot was sent away. "I was gone for four years of hell in the worst places in the world," Green said. "All Ruth could talk about was how rough it was for Elliot, who was just a few miles from home, and how hard it was in basic training. I had to laugh. It was all right for me to get shot at, but Ruthie's man was another matter. She really loved her Elliot."

By the end of 1945, Ruth wanted Elliot out of the army and working full-time at Mattel. Her hand is evident in the letter her accountant, Irving Feiger, sent on November 30, 1945, to the commanding officer of Company B, Eighty-seventh Battalion, at Camp Roberts. Elliot had an undisputed talent, but Mattel was hardly the powerhouse described, except perhaps in Ruth's mind.

"Prior to the time of induction of Private Elliot Handler into the Armed Forces, [Mattel] was rapidly expanding to a position of leadership in the field of plastic fabrications due in our opinion to the creative ability and imagination of Private Handler," Feiger wrote. "The fact that Private Handler is not able to take an active part in the management and operations of the partnership and to give his ability in designing and creating new products is working a serious hardship on the business and threatens its future successful operations." Once the letter was sent, Elliot began to push for a discharge hearing.

Meanwhile, his dollhouse line had grown, but Ruth was dissatisfied with the distribution. A local jeweler had taken the pieces into some ladies' clothing stores on consignment, but the sales were not good. In January 1946 Ruth decided they needed national distribution, and to get there she knew she would have to go to New York City, the toy center of the country.

At the time, Barbara was three, and Ken was less than a year old. The Handlers had paid just under ten thousand dollars for a house in a lower-priced section of the tony Cheviot Hills neighborhood. Elliot was at his army post during the week, but the house was large enough for Ruth to have a live-in housekeeper. She also relied on her sister Sarah, who had moved to town with Louie, for help with the children.

It seems Ruth felt little compunction about leaving the children for her trip to New York, even though during the week she and Elliot would both be gone. These early years managing the fledgling Mattel company would set a pattern for her family life. Despite later protestations that time was diligently set aside for the children, neither Ruth nor Elliot could have accomplished Mattel's growth over the next decade without putting most of their time into the business. Ruth always claimed that being a mother and wife came before being a businesswoman, but her actions spoke otherwise. At times she admitted as much. "When it came to being a good mother, those things like knowing how to cook and keeping a good house and spending the time with my children and all that, I was not really a very good mother, because I had so much on my mind that it was hard to fit it all in." She and Elliot did try to reserve the weekends and holidays as family time. Barbara has memories of going shopping with her mother on Saturdays, but also remembers that "She worked all the time. She was always doing something." Ruth was following her passion, even if at times it took her far from home. Her daughter, more high-strung and volatile than her little brother, would increasingly resent her for it.

Ruth set off for New York in February 1946. Everything was new and confusing. Her only previous travel had been between Denver and Los Angeles. She had never been east at all.

Due to war restrictions, she could not get an airplane reservation. Train tickets were also scarce, and Ruth did not even know what to ask for. She stood at the ticket counter and asked to be put on the Union Pacific line to New York City, only to be told that there were multiple lines and she would have to change trains. She probably ended up on the Union Pacific's City of Los Angeles for the forty-hour ride to Chicago. She slept on the bottom bunk of a double-decker sleeper car. In Chicago she changed trains, perhaps for New York Central's Twentieth Century Limited and twenty more hours on the rails. When she arrived at New York's Pennsylvania Station, Ruth did not even have a name to call. Paying what seemed an exorbitant fare, she took a cab to the Hotel Lexington. She spent the next day or two wandering around 200 Fifth Avenue, where toys were sold wholesale and where those working in the toy trade got together. Ruth was an attractive young woman alone in a building full of men, and as she told a colleague later, "I had a lot of offers but not to buy toys."

The Toy Building, as it was known, was a skyscraper devoted to the display and sale of toys. Ruth wandered the long corridors, which looked to her like a huge merchandise mart. She was not sure how to find the right place to sell Mattel's dollhouse furniture. Then, as she approached the end of one hall, she saw a man standing outside one of the storefront-type offices, staring at her. Waving her to come closer, he asked whom she was looking for. As Ruth approached, she saw dollhouse furniture in his window. She thought the metal furniture looked sterile and unimaginative, but at least she had found a contact.

Vic Goldberg took Ruth by the arm and pulled her into his office. After looking at her line of doll furniture, he told her he had a partner, Ben Senekoff, and that she should join them for dinner that night.

Ruth met Goldberg and his girlfriend, Minyan, at a club called the Latin Quarter. She remembered how amused she was that Minyan, whose name Ruth had never heard, had the typically Jewish last name of Goldstein. After Goldberg and his girlfriend drank a quart of Scotch, Minyan poured her heart out to Ruth about how poorly Goldberg treated her. He had told Minyan to meet them at the club, rather than pick her up, which Ruth thought rude. The couple had also been dating for fifteen years and were committed to each other, but did not live together. "I was not yet sophisticated," Ruth said. "I was getting a whole new insight into a relationship."

Back at their office, Goldberg and Senekoff said they sold to Sears and to Firestone Tire, which also retailed toys, and they showed Ruth piles of invoices to prove it. Later, when she discovered that those were their only two clients, she felt conned. She had, however, contracted for Mattel's first sales organization.

Ruth was gone less than two weeks, but Elliot wrote her several letters. "The house is mighty lonesome without you," he wrote. "Bobby [Barbara] was very blue the first day . . . Kenny calls for Mommy . . . he keeps expecting you to walk in the door. He's been a good boy, except he just doesn't want to go to sleep anymore." He told her that Bobby had a cold, then shared some information about the business. After doing anything but allaying her concerns about the children, Elliot closed with, "Darling, don't worry about things at home." He wrote again two days later, fretting that she would catch a cold as she frequently did, and speculating that she was missing the kids. Elliot wanted her home.

Ruth returned triumphant and full of plans for Mattel's expansion. She was "thoroughly proud of herself," as she wrote in her autobiography, where her trip is chronicled without any reference to how her family fared during her absence. Only later did she realize that her new distributors were more interested in selling their own line of dollhouse furniture than Mattel's. Sales were still good, however, and the letter to the army led to Elliot's discharge from his job as a supply clerk in March 1946.

Ruth and Elliot were riding high. They expected 1946 to surpass the previous year, when they had made thirty thousand dollars on a hundred thousand dollars in sales of dollhouse furniture. They would do well in the future, but never in all their years of business together would they enjoy as high a return as in Mattel's first full year.

Chapter 6

Uke-A-Doodles

We learned through product how to run a business.

When Elliot called from New York in March 1947, Ruth could hear the panic in his normally calm, soft-spoken voice. Due to the time difference, he caught her at home before she left for Mattel. As he told her what had happened, Ruth knew she would have to drop everything to help. Their first big toy was about to be stolen.

Even though the children were still so young, Ruth had arranged her life so that she could be a full-time working woman. In later life, responding to an interviewer's question about how to manage a career along with being a wife and mother, Ruth talked about her need to get out of the house and her gratitude for having work. "The urge was so strong in me that I got up early and did what had to be done. I took care of the children or anything else." Elliot, unlike many men of his generation, offered some help around the house. He would not fry eggs, but he did make toast. He would not change a dirty diaper, but he would change a wet one. Still, Ruth recognized that she carried the bulk of responsibility at home. "I always said that if a woman is going to make it she has to work twice as hard, three times as hard, be available at all times to be a mother, wife, and to the business. It did not occur to me that work had to be divided more evenly." She also did not believe that most women belonged in business. She did not believe they were willing to "give themselves totally" as she did the minute Elliot explained the crisis.

Mattel had recently hired and quickly lost their sales representatives, the Caryl brothers, over the marketing of a unique toy, the Uke-A-Doodle. Elliot had created the toy design and the playful name. Like millions of Americans, he and Ruth loved to listen to Arthur Godfrey. In the years before television, when entertainment came through radio's disembodied voices, Godfrey's show had more listeners than all others. Elliot and Ruth rarely found time to listen to his daily show, but they loved his wildly popular weekly evening program, *Arthur Godfrey's Talent Scouts*. Talent agents would bring performers to the show, including singers Tony Bennett and Patsy Cline, and the comedian Lenny Bruce. Godfrey, anticipating *American Idol* by more than half a century, used an "applause-meter" to pick the winner.

Amiable and informal, Godfrey kept his studio audience laughing and applauding with his corny jokes. His loyal listeners made his show top-rated on radio and his name ubiquitous. Anything that evoked Godfrey had broad appeal, even his ukulele, which he played with abandon at unpredictable moments.

Elliot saw the potential for a toy instrument and designed a miniature version of Godfrey's ukulele. The blue-and-coral-colored toy came packaged with floral stickers for decoration; a small pick for the four strings; and an expensive, colorfully decorated specialty box. The suggested retail price was $1.49. The plastic strings were not melodic, but neither was Godfrey. Fans could pretend to be a radio star or a down-home string-plucker.

A few months before Mattel began producing the toy, Ruth

began thinking about distribution. Mattel was just two and a half years old. She had done most of the sales and distribution, starting with its dollhouse furniture. After the success of 1945, a company that made more detailed furniture at a cheaper price had over-taken Mattel. Shifting from dollhouse furniture, Mattel rushed a Birdy Bank and a Make-Believe Makeup Set to market. Working bruising hours and keeping to only five employees, they ended 1946 with a profit. Ruth realized that to grow would require a national sales organization. There was a baby boom in America, and after the war years the nation hungered for toys. After poring through toy trade magazines, she began to hire sales representatives around the country.

In the Midwest, she settled on the Caryl brothers, who had offices in the crucial New York market. They were set to sell the Uke-A-Doodle, but Ruth decided she could also make some sales on her own. Three months before the March 1947 Toy Fair, without consulting her new distributors, Ruth took samples of the Uke-A-Doodle to Butler Brothers' Los Angeles office. The wholesale giant, based in Chicago, franchised the chain of nearly three thousand Ben Franklin retail variety stores. They also acted as jobbers, or middlemen, buying large quantities of toys and then supplying different stores around the country.

Ruth returned home elated. Butler Brothers' headquarters had approved a huge order based on the enthusiasm Ruth had generated in the Los Angeles office. When she called the Caryl brothers, however, they were furious. How were they supposed to sell to the giant chain, based in their own hometown, now that Ruth had gone directly to Butler? And did she not realize that Butler was both a chain and a jobber? She had agreed to ship the toys at jobber prices to all the Butler stores. That was just stupid, they told her. Butler should have done the shipping, or Ruth should have charged for delivery. The Caryls quit on the spot.

In her autobiography, Ruth claims she offered to pay the Caryls a commission on sales she had made that shipped into their territory, a tacit admission that she had overstepped in cutting her own deal. Butler Brothers was a major target for the sales force she had just hired, and her action no doubt undermined the Caryls' faith in her. Although they might have negotiated a more lucrative deal with Butler, Ruth insisted she had done the right thing. "I think we were very wise. I think [the Butler order] got us going." She never acknowledged that by cutting her own deal she was angling to keep the commission for herself. The incident was an early indication that Ruth loathed admitting mistakes and had a strong sense of her own rectitude. She was also protective of the bottom line. The Uke-A-Doodle set the stage for many of Mattel's great toys and for Ruth's emergence as the no-holds-barred guardian of the company's finances.

Without the Caryls to cover New York, Elliot made plans to go to Toy Fair to scout for a new sales team. He arrived with a recommendation to meet Al Frank, whom he quickly hired, along with Frank's sales organization. Frank showed Elliot around Toy Fair. As the two men evaluated the potential of the latest products, Elliot saw a display that shocked him and ran to a telephone to tell Ruth what he had seen.

A competitor from Los Angeles, Leo White of Knickerbocker Plastics, was showing the Uke-A-Doodle in his sales office and was quoting lower prices. White had scraped the Mattel name off the sample, knowing that he could fill orders because the toy was easy to produce. The customers who were writing big orders to Mattel told Elliot that they could get a better price from White. A price war ensued as the two toy companies tried to underbid each other. Back in Los Angeles, Ruth was left to figure out how to reduce the cost of production. The pricing plan had called for a retail charge of $1.39. The wholesale price was half of retail.

Mattel's toy sat in a beautiful multicolored printed setup box that was expensive to produce, but the price kept falling, finally settling at $0.98.

Back in Los Angeles, Ruth heard from Elliot every hour, his calls more furious and worried as the bidding grew hotter. He was getting a ton of orders, but he was getting them at a lower and lower price. Knickerbocker Plastics was a huge company compared to Mattel. Having seen the Uke-A-Doodle selling well in Ben Franklin stores, White had bought several to display and to give to his engineers so that they could begin tooling for production. Confident that Knickerbocker could make up in volume what they were sacrificing in price, White perhaps realized that the owners of the fledgling Mattel company were too naive to know that toy ideas were stolen by competitors all the time.

Ruth was furious. She realized Mattel had to ramp up production and cut costs in a hurry. She had the jump on Knickerbocker, as her toy was already tooled. If she could flood the market, she hoped to keep the Knickerbocker ukulele off store shelves.

She started with Art Sugarman, the manufacturer at Peerless Plastics. He ran an injection molding shop and had extended her credit to produce the first ukuleles. He agreed to up the volume and give her a price break, but it was not enough. If she could not cut the toy price further, she would go for the packaging. Ruth begged the box company to switch from the expensive two-piece box to a one-piece fold-over. They were not interested, reminding her that her small company already owed them money. Ruth grabbed the phone book and began calling every box company listed. After tense hours of waiting, only one young man, Eddie Myers, showed up at the company door.

Ruth told Myers the truth. She told him that Mattel had to get the price way down and that they did not have credit or money, but they did have a lot of big orders coming in. According to Ruth, "he got very thrilled with the whole thing" and agreed to get the boxes. Years later, Myers told her that when he returned to his factory they wanted to know about Mattel's credit. He told them that he would personally pay for the account if Mattel did not. Ruth never forgot his generosity and faith in Mattel. "As our company grew," she said, "our loyalty to Eddie remained firm. The larger we grew the more we bought, the more Eddie got. He eventually ended up owning that box company."

Ruth won Myers over with the instinctive, dynamic sales style that she had used to build the company to that point, and that would save her, financially and emotionally, time and again. Just as characteristic was her fierce loyalty to those who supported her in the early years, though it would be weighted by a less attractive style that demonized those who thwarted her. There would be a fair number of each in a life of dramatic highs and lows.

By the time Elliot returned from New York, Ruth had everything in place to put out a cheaper version of the toy. She had pressed everyone linked to the company into service. Sam Zukerman, who with the Handlers had founded their local synagogue, Temple Isaiah, helped set up their books and establish their business plan. He agreed to take dozens of Uke-A-Doodles into his garage, pressing his children into service to pack them for shipping.

Orders still poured in, but Ruth could not be sure the company would make any profit. She was operating off loans both from family and from her new bank, Bank of America. After bringing a suitcase crammed with orders to Union Bank and finding resistance to her business plans, she switched banks. She told the bank officer that she expected to do about a million and a half dollars in volume. He looked at her in astonishment and told her there was no way she could make that happen. Even though he ended up giving Ruth a third of what she had asked for, she did meet her goals. The next time she needed money, the loan officers at Bank of America responded more positively. She was on an aggressive quest for cash, the biggest problem she faced in building Mattel.

Supervising five paid employees, Matt raced to fill orders, all the while worried about the ten thousand dollars he had invested in the business. He had left Elzac because of the stress, and Mattel was turning out to be even more stressful. He had been a workingman his whole life; he could not afford to lose his investment. He also did not have complete faith in Ruth, and she had little respect for him. She still resented his attitude when she had taken it upon herself to drive the truck to deliver the Austin Photography frame order. He had been certain she would fail.

Ruth thought Matt was stupid. She also believed he was trying to test her, a feeling she had had about other people as well. She thought people egged her on and enjoyed watching her attempt something that seemed impossible to do. Believing others were anticipating her failure, Ruth felt the need to prove herself.

Ruth was showing the chip on her shoulder, but her assessment of Matt hastened his departure from Mattel. He had been in the right place at the right time to help her back into the business world, but he could never survive in any company she ran. Her hiring would be marked by searches for the best, the brightest, the most aggressive and resilient people in every part of the company. When she found Matt at his desk, with his head buried in his arms, she did not work hard to dissuade him from giving up his share of the business. Sarah and Louie had recently sold their businesses in Denver and moved to the Westwood section of Los Angeles. Ruth suggested to Matt that they might be interested in buying out his share of Mattel. Matt jumped, according to Ruth. Louie bought Matson out for fifteen thousand dollars, five thousand more than Matson had invested. There is no record of the transaction. According to Ruth, neither she nor Elliot ever heard from Matt again.

Over the next decade Mattel would sell eleven million Uke-A-Doodles. The toy had yielded not only twenty-eight thousand dollars in profits its first year, but also some crucial business lessons and some casualties. Harold Matson was gone. Sam Zukerman, the public accountant who helped Ruth with the books and early business plan, felt taken. Ruth had promised him that he would be a partner, and in exchange he had worked for several years at a reduced fee. In 1948, when Ruth was ready to incorporate, Zukerman drew up the papers for her and included his name as they had agreed. But Ruth had changed her mind and his name was struck off. "My father was the kind of man that if he shook your hand that was it," Zukerman's daughter remembered. Zukerman never worked for Mattel again.

On the marketing side, Ruth learned that she had been foolish to bring the Uke-A-Doodle out in advance of Toy Fair. By selling it to Butler Brothers she had made it easy for competitors to get one of her toys and copy it, a practice she learned was common in a business that relied on a constant stream of new ideas. She would never ignore Toy Fair again. Instead, she set about conquering it.

Chapter 7

Music Makers and Sour Notes

In the toy business we found that you constantly
have to create new products.

W"Why can't you be like other mothers?" Barbara screamed at Ruth before storming off once again from the dinner table. The Handlers made dinner together a priority, but they could not mandate the mood. In the modernist house that Elliot had designed on Duxbury Circle in Beverlywood, tensions between work and family often ran high.

In 1951 the Handlers had moved into the upscale enclave, not quite as posh as Beverly Hills, but a far cry from their first Murphy-bedded apartment. Elliot's artistic sensibilities played out in every room. A grand piano sat on one side of the living room for Ken. Nearby, a handmade cone-shaped corrugated flue was suspended over the round fireplace, its copper surface the focal point of the room. A wall of plate glass windows overlooked the swimming pool and garden-enclosed patio. The downstairs playroom had a soda fountain for the children. A real sycamore tree with chirping mechanical birds rose up two stories, growing inside the curved stairwell that led to the expansive second floor. The house was featured in magazine spreads. Guests found it astonishing, a livable work of art, but for Barbara it was another expression of what was wrong with her young life. She told Ruth that she wished she could live in the plain middle-class house of a nearby relative. In a way Barbara could never understand, the middle-class home she longed for was part of her problem. Those homes were filling up with Mattel toys, making her parents rich and making Barbara feel ever more different from her peers.

Mattel grew phenomenally in the late 1940s and early 1950s. Ruth and Elliot made five moves to bigger and bigger facilities. Ruth took the title of executive vice president in 1948, always careful not to encroach on the male dominance expected at the time. Elliot was president, at least in name. As Ruth said later, "You know, I always acted as president from the day we started." As Elliot created brilliant results with new products, Ruth handled everything else.

The business increasingly claimed Ruth's time, and Barbara's protests grew louder. "Oh, how I hated my mother being in business when I was young," she recalled, "and even when I was a teenager. Remember, this was at a time that women only worked if they absolutely had to work. I used to think my mother was loud, talked like a man, and was homely. All of my friends' mothers were home most of the time. I kept wondering why we were so different. I did not want my mother to be different." Barbara's complaints and accusations often left Ruth in tears as she tried to go to sleep. She felt rejected by her daughter and helpless to change.

Ruth was different from other women of her era, and her attitude toward family was a large part of what set her apart. She saw herself as an outsider, often describing herself as a loner and someone who did not have many friends. "I loved being unique. The very thing that my daughter fought in me was the thing that I prized. I did not seek to be unique in my appearance, in the way I carried myself, but I was. Everybody knew me; I knew nobody."

Ruth took pride in acting outside the norm. She worked with many men, a reason she believed she was a source of gossip for other women. She said she did not care if people talked about her. If they resented her power and ability, that was their problem. She did not feel she had anything in common with the women who stayed home to be mothers. They talked about babies, babysitters, clothes, and hairdressers. For Ruth, "that was the world's biggest bore. I couldn't talk business to them, and I was living, eating, and breathing business. I never was very good at talking about my kids, and I can't stand people who talk about their kids."

Occasionally, Ruth allowed intimacy. She admitted needing friends once in a while and missing having someone to talk to. But she chose people who were also unusual in their own way and served her purpose at the time. When the children were young, Ruth had only one friend, a woman named Trudy, whom others shunned. "Trudy was everything wrong," Ruth recalled, "and I approve of people who are less than righteous. I like people who are not perfect, who're just full of faults. I can get very close to those kinds of people." Trudy held Ruth's interest because she flirted, swore, and never censored what she said. "She really did not give a shit about anything," Ruth said. With Trudy, Ruth felt that she could be herself.

Ruth's maverick spirit fueled her drive and her risk taking in the early years of Mattel. If she was not like other women, she was free to be anything she wanted, and what she wanted was the ever-greater thrill she was getting as she propelled Mattel's growth.

With the company on the financial ledge and Elliot insisting on creative freedom, Ruth devised an unorthodox manufacturing approach. She lacked the capital to buy equipment for making toys from all the different materials Elliot wanted to use, but she was determined to bring his ideas to market. She recognized his ability to know what toys would appeal to children. "He was, unquestionably, the best toy designer in the entire world. I mean that without any reservations," Ruth said. Elliot would sketch his idea, and then work with the engineers, toolmakers, and manufacturing people. To support him, Ruth developed a corps of subcontractors who manufactured in metal, plastic, rubber, paper, cardboard, and any other material Elliot wanted to use. This unorthodox method was the first of many decisions that would set Mattel apart from the competition. Other toy companies were confined by the expensive equipment they owned to making only plastic toys or to rotocasting for making dolls. With the subcontractors, Mattel did not have to invest any money in equipment, and they realized the added benefit of flexibility to meet the industry's demand for new products.

Elliot had been right about the popularity of the Uke-A-Doodle. Building on the musical toy theme, his next big idea seemed even more perfectly timed. He designed a tabletop baby grand piano with seventeen keys. Unlike any made at the time, it had raised black keys for sharps and flats, and allowed children to play a reasonable imitation of a scale. Red with yellow legs and priced low at three dollars, the piano taxed all of the Handlers' growing design and manufacturing skills.

Ruth was proud of this second major toy from Mattel, and the response at the 1948 Toy Fair was enthusiastic. The toy industry "went nuts over it," according to Ruth. Orders were strong. Then the buyer for Sears, Roebuck at the time, Ralph Leonardson, came into the Mattel showroom.

Ruth called Leonardson "Mr. God himself" and said he frightened her for years. Sears was the biggest buyer and could make or break a toy. Ruth expected Leonardson to be as enthusiastic as the other buyers when he inspected Mattel's toy piano, but instead he refused to place an order. Ruth pressed him for a reason. He explained that they had made a mistake by combining incompatible materials. They were going to have numerous problems with breakage in shipping, and he did not want to be bothered with it. "You're never going to solve your quality problems on this one," he told them.

Ruth was confident about Mattel's testing. They had already thickened some areas of the piano where the steel bars were fastened, and she tried, without success, to convince Leonardson that he was wrong. Ruth soon discovered, however, that Leonardson knew his business. "We shipped over a half million," Ruth recalled, "and for our little 'cockamamie' company, that was a bunch. We figured out that we lost about $75,000 on the ones we shipped. We lost about a dime a piano because of breakage, and we learned an important lesson."

Ruth admitted mistakes rarely. Setbacks were lessons. Bad judgments always had a kernel of good judgment in them. Her belief in herself—despite her lack of education, training, or experience—seemed boundless, except when it came to her personal life.

Barbara, now in grade school, was growing up increasingly belligerent and spoiled. One babysitter remembers her as a "brat," who was hard to get to sleep and whose mother was cold and imperious. "I got along very well with adults, but I did not like going there. Ruth was nasty. She acted like she was so important. Elliot was the opposite and very henpecked." Once, Barbara put a cat under the sheets of the Handlers' friend Seymour Green when he was sleeping at their house. "He chased me down the street. I was really a brat," Barbara remembered. "But then I don't really think children are ever brats; I think I was angry."

In her papers, Ruth kept a torn scrap with a little girl's careful script on it. "If you were a nice mommy you would make up and tuck me into bed, that's if you were a nice mommy." Barbara wanted something Ruth could not give. Focused and driven, Ruth struggled to show the gentle, loving demeanor that Barbara craved. As a result, every decision became a battleground. The aviator Charles Lindbergh's baby had been kidnapped and killed in 1932, and the notorious tragedy still haunted Americans, especially the wealthy. When Ruth insisted that their chauffeur take Barbara to school, the young girl erupted. She wanted to walk with her friends. She longed for a sense of normalcy, for a life like her peers.

Ruth struggled to cope with Barbara's resentment, at sea about how to respond. Leaving the business was out of the question, so she shouldered her guilt. There were other stresses that roiled the household however, especially between the siblings. Barbara's brother, Ken, had a calmer spirit and more unconventional tastes than his big sister. He had a tense relationship with Barbara and was closer with Ruth.

Ken showed an early love for movies and music. He had the gift of perfect pitch and a beautiful ear for language. On a trip to Hawaii when he was six, he sat down at the piano in the hotel lounge and played the "Tennessee Waltz" even though he had never had a piano lesson. But while Barbara liked all the latest trends, Ken seemed trapped in a time warp. He gravitated to opera and music from the early part of the century and avoided rock and roll, the new music emerging in the late 1940s. He was writing movie scripts before he was ten and going to movies with subtitles. Creating a list of old movie theaters in Los Angeles that had closed, he used *Cue* magazine to write in the movie that he thought would be playing if the theater were still open. He studied theaters in New York City, seeing what movies they were running and creating a fantasy movie run for a similar theater on his Los Angeles list.

Ken saw his parents and sister as living in the mainstream, while he, as he put it, "dribbled along some obscure tributary." Barbara had a sharper assessment, reflecting lingering resentments. "I've never been close to my brother, Ken. When we were growing up he hated my music, and I couldn't believe a kid his age was listening to opera. My brother is eccentric and he thinks my mother is God. My brother never likes the restaurants other people like or the places other people like. He always has to like something different." So it seemed to a conventional person, but Ken was possessed of his father's fertile and creative mind. He was a nonconformist by nature and well aware of how the rest of the world viewed him. "I was a nerd, a real nerd. All the girls thought I was a jerk." He took a dim view of his sister's interests. "My sister was a conform freak," he told the author of *Forever Barbie*.

Tensions at home and the pressures of family life contrasted with the fulfillment Ruth found at work. Business "turned her on" more than anything else. "Every time we had a major success in the business it was a new high and a new experience," she said. "This experience of power had to be the most exciting of all the experiences." And as the business grew, so did Ruth's power.

The financial debacle of the toy piano unexpectedly opened the door to Mattel's next huge success. In 1949 a man named Ted Duncan came to see the Handlers to show them a modernized music box he had spent three years creating in his garage. A former musician and music arranger for some Hollywood studios, Duncan was also a part-time tinkerer. He collected Swiss music boxes, but he was often frustrated that his children broke their delicate mechanisms. He wanted to create a more durable music box and had devised a two-inch rubber belt with pinhead-size knobs. He spaced the knobs so that as the belt was turned, their tips would pluck a dozen stiff piano wires mounted on a metal comb. This "chime bar" made from a zinc plate was small enough to fit inside a variety of toys.

Swiss music boxes sold for five dollars or more, putting them in the luxury toy category. Duncan's idea was a low-priced, durable box that would play continuously as it was cranked. Duncan had tried to interest a number of companies in his idea without success. Ruth and Elliot were the first to see the potential. Elliot designed the toys that would hold the music box mechanism, starting with an organ-grinder's hurdy-gurdy music box and then a jack-in-the-box, one of Ruth's few toy ideas. They asked Duncan to work with a trusted foreman in the factory, Paul Blair, on the toy's engineering and mass production.

Paul Blair was a black man who had found a tolerant workplace at Mattel. Where other factory floors were segregated by race, Mattel's production line not only employed mostly women, but included many ethnicities. Blacks, whites, Asians, and Mexicans worked side by side in close quarters. Ruth claimed that she never thought about the racial makeup of her workforce, but she knew the sting of anti-Semitism, and that may have played some part in her attitude. "We hired black and brown people; it did not matter to us," Elliot remembered. "Our families weren't racist. One of my first managers was a black guy, a very capable mechanic. We were very liberal. We were Democrats." Others took notice of Mattel's unconventional factory floor. "A tour of your plant is like walking through the United Nations," read a letter from the Los Angeles Conference on Community Relations. "People of different races, various religious faiths, handicapped people, elderly people, all working as a unit. You have set an example that might well be followed by business people everywhere." In 1951 actress Loretta Young gave the Handlers the annual Urban League award for their nondiscriminatory practices.

Ruth and Elliot recognized Blair's talent as a manager and an engineer. They trusted him to find the best approach to producing the small box that Duncan had conceived. They were confident that the product would be a success, and they were pouring money into development, but it was not enough. The toy required a major investment in equipment and tooling, and Ruth could not get the bank to lend the money she needed. She and Elliot flew to Denver to ask her sister and brother-in-law Doris and Harry Paul for a loan. They had already borrowed another twenty thousand dollars from Sarah and Louis Greenwald. The Pauls agreed to lend fifteen thousand dollars. Ruth told Harry, "If something happens and we don't make it, we'll work the rest of our lives to pay it back." He said he knew that.

But the toy had problems from the start. Duncan and Blair were at odds about how to make the music box, and the Handlers had to choose between the two. When they sided with their employee, Duncan was incensed.

Duncan not only sued the Handlers, he spent his own money to order materials and tried to prove that Blair's manufacturing scheme was wrong. Ruth claimed that after spending thousands of dollars, he failed, but she shaded the truth. While Mattel's music box would be many times more successful, Duncan, who held the patents, perfected his own idea. The Duncan Voice Box was used in four million toys in the four years after Duncan introduced it at the 1954 Toy Fair. Due to the settlement of his lawsuit, he also collected a hundred thousand dollars a year in royalties from Mattel. Ruth claimed not to "begrudge" the money, but she felt Duncan had betrayed her. Ruth believed that not only had he fought for control of the product, he had lied about whom he had shown the idea to before the Handlers.

Duncan had peddled the music box to Mattel's archrival, Knickerbocker Plastics. Leo White, the same man who had stolen the Uke-A-Doodle idea, had encouraged Knickerbocker to work on producing Duncan's music box for months before Mattel's jack-in-the-box launched. When it did, Knickerbocker made a knockoff. But this time Ruth decided to fight. Mattel sued Knickerbocker, winning a judgment that forced their rival to destroy all inventory, cease manufacturing, and pay Mattel fifty thousand dollars. Ruth's legal fees totaled as much as the fine. She did not care, she claimed, just as she claimed that she wished the relationship with Duncan had worked out better. But she was not given to forgiving and forgetting. She had put the toy industry on notice that Mattel would fight for its products. She never spoke to Ted Duncan again.

The music box was a hit. Children created music at their own pace by turning the crank. If they stopped turning, the music stopped, unlike the Swiss music boxes over which a child had no control. Ruth and Elliot coined the term "play value" to describe the amount of involvement a child had with a toy. They considered the music box to have superior play value compared to other toys, and the toys that were built around the mechanism brought a steady stream of revenue for years. "We were developing a principle with the music box that we tried to stick with for the rest of our toy career," Ruth explained. "If you develop a basic mechanism or a basic concept, you develop one or two or three items around that concept at the initial introduction, and then year after year you add new products around the initial concept."

Elliot continued to dream up new ideas for the adaptable music box mechanism. It was placed in eighteen different toys including a revamped Uke-A-Doodle, the chuck wagon pull-toy that played "Oh! Susanna," the Musical Merry-Go-Round that played "Farmer in the Dell," and a variety of musical books. Almost overnight Mattel had become the largest manufacturer of music box toys in America.

The Handlers had staked everything, including borrowed funds from family and employees, on the music box. The gamble paid off. Nearly seven million dollars' worth of music boxes were sold at retail that first year, and two million dollars more the next. In 1952 the *Saturday Evening Post* called it "the million-dollar music box." *Kiplinger's* magazine, calling Ruth and Elliot "The newcomers to the toy business," noted that they had built a brand-new 60,000-square-foot factory in the Los Angeles airport tract and employed six hundred female factory workers. In 1949 the Handlers started holding annual company picnics, and by July 1952 they were treating seven hundred employees to ice cream every time another million toys rolled off the production line.

Ruth was proud of the relationship she and Elliot had with their employees. As owners they were relaxed and informal with everyone, from the maintenance staff to designers and engineers. They spent time on the production floor, sometimes pitching in on one of the lines. Everyone called them by their first names. If an employee was more formal, Ruth thought something was wrong. "We knew every single person," Ruth remembered. "We knew their names and they knew us. We had a lot of group events and we had a lot of fun."

At Mattel, Ruth minded community and public relations. She invited the press for lunch and factory tours. She tried to buy materials from local businesses, gave thousands and then tens of thousands of toys away to sick and needy children every year, and made sizable charitable contributions. She sent Blinko the Clown, with his trademark two-and-a-half-inch eyelashes and whiteface, to Santa Monica Hospital to entertain kids confined to wheelchairs or bed. He played songs from the Mattel Musical Library, using a music box called the Lullaby Crib. The local paper ran a picture of smiling, delighted children. At the Handler home, by contrast, Barbara and Ken had grown blasé about new toys, so much so that Elliot could no longer use them as a built-in test market.

"We work twenty-four hours a day," Elliot told a magazine in-terviewer, adding, "We *worry* twenty-four hours a day." In the same article, Elliot is described as "the brains behind the creative end of the business, while his lovely wife, as in so many families, sees to it that the bacon gets into the Handler ice box." Ruth did take care of the household, but she did it with hired help. Elliot needed her to run the business as much as she needed to run it. He was still taciturn and shy, in "his dream world" as Ruth would often say. "He can sit in a crowd with everyone talking and hear nothing, until all of a sudden he snaps out of it with an idea," an assistant said. Ruth, by contrast, never seemed to stop moving or voicing her excitement and plans for their next business move.

In later years, Ruth and Elliot would both portray themselves as having a balanced home and work life. Work, they would say, was never discussed at home, and every weekend was reserved for the children. These recollections were somewhat revisionist. As with so many company founders, the business became the Handlers' most demanding child. Owing money to family added an emotional element to the business stress. Ruth and Elliot owed money to the Pauls and the Greenwalds. Ruth had promised to pay Harry Paul back within a year. Once the music box was launched, about a year after Harry Paul gave the loan, Ruth called him. She told him the toy was doing well and she offered him a choice. She told him she could send him a check with interest for the money or he could buy a fourth of Mattel. He asked her what she would do. "I'd buy into the business," Ruth replied. Harry agreed. Mattel stayed in the family. The Pauls and the Greenwalds owned 25 percent each, and Ruth and Elliot owned the rest.

Harry Paul was wise to follow his sister-in-law's advice. In 1949 she had not been able to get the financing she needed to build the company. Three years later, net sales were $4.2 million, and earnings before taxes were a modest but respectable $238,000. Ruth was thirty-four and poised to make the biggest business deal of her life.

Chapter 8

Gambling Everything on
Mickey Mouse

In true Handler fashion, we went for it.

At the moment Ruth was entertaining dreams of building the biggest toy company in America, Walt Disney offered her the chance. In 1955 the ABC television network started seeking advertisers for a new program called *The Mickey Mouse Club.*

The Mickey Mouse character, which made its first appearance in a cartoon called *Steamboat Willie* in 1928, was conceived by Walt Disney. Disney turned the scrawny, wide-eyed anthropomorphized mouse into a franchise. By the mid-fifties, the internationally recognizable Mickey had starred in cartoon strips and motion pictures, and his image appeared on myriad pieces of merchandise. In 1929 a local movie theater in Ocean Park, California, started a club for kids on Saturday mornings where they watched Mickey Mouse cartoons and played games. Soon, thousands of such clubs around the country bore Mickey's name.

In 1950 Disney ventured into television programming. His first hit was the program *Disneyland,* which started on ABC in October 1954. By then, the age of television had arrived, with national broadcasts and color televisions coming onto the market. Disney's show, an extended advertisement for the Disney theme park, was the first ABC series to hit the top ten in ratings, beating out *Arthur Godfrey's Talent Scouts*. Within six weeks, Walt Disney began developing a second show, this one highlighting the popular Mickey Mouse Clubs.

Robert E. Kintner, president of ABC, was known as a tough, uncompromising competitor in his industry. When he thought he had a winner he went all out, and he was high on Disney's *Mickey Mouse Club* idea. Kintner wrote Disney that he had talked with advertisers and advertising agencies about the pricing and the character of the new show. He felt they were enthusiastic. "They expressed the belief that the program could be outstanding in television program structure," he wrote Disney. "That it could enable advertisers to expand to the children's group without the criticism of using 'guns and killings' and that with your touch it should be the outstanding daytime programming on all television."

Kintner was right. Media historians often argue that *The Mickey Mouse Club* marked the modern era of children's television. For the first time, networks recognized that a children's market existed. Children's programming became more than just a tool to get a family to buy a television. Kintner's vision, however, had one big problem. To produce the children's show he and Disney wanted would be enormously expensive. Advertisers were hard to find for children's shows, which was why most programs were reruns of old cartoons or movies like *Hopalong Cassidy*.

ABC was also in a weak financial position. To put on a show five days a week with music, songs, cartoons, children's news features, adventure serials, guest celebrities, and a young cast called the Mouseketeers was unprecedented. Disney would have to find twenty advertisers to pay a minimum of five hundred thousand dollars to advertise in the first year of the show. Kintner proposed

an entirely new advertising scheme with four fifteen-minute seg-
ments in each hour-long show, with each sponsor getting three
minutes in each segment. The plan would yield fifty thousand
dollars per week in revenue, but Kintner was not willing to take
just anyone's money. "Advertisers would be limited to those which
appeal directly to children; primarily, cereals, candy, soft drinks,
toothpaste, and similar products." Not surprisingly, Kintner left
toys off the list. No toy manufacturer had ever advertised year-
round. Even cereal companies, who spent more on advertising,
had been slow to move from radio to television.

Up to that time, toy companies, including Mattel, bought television time only for the ten or twelve weeks leading up to Christmas. Wholesalers and nationwide stores like Sears were the main
advertising target, and trade journals were used to reach them. Toy
companies also targeted parents with catalog advertising aimed at
the Christmas market. Television was seen as an advertising frill
that might give the final push for parents to buy toys that were
already stocked on store shelves.

Television advertising was pricey. Ads targeted audiences
who could afford television sets. Most advertisements were for
cigarettes or cleaning aids. The first toy ad on television was for
Hasbro's Mr. Potato Head. The ad went up in 1952, when two-
thirds of American TVs were owned by families with children
under twelve. The toy grossed a healthy four million dollars in its
first year. But most toy companies kept their television budgets
small. Mattel spent more than most, a little over a third of their
$150,000 advertising budget for the year. Concentrated in big city
local markets, the advertisements by toy companies consisted of
the local children's program host enthusiastically demonstrating a
company's toy and telling kids how much they should want one.
Did this style of advertising work? No one knew.

At the same time Disney was working on the *Mickey Mouse*

Club shows, Elliot was looking beyond music boxes for Mattel's next big toy. He loved the idea of the old West. For several years, the family had been vacationing at a dude ranch outside Tucson, Arizona. Elliot would don a cowboy hat, plaid shirt, and cowboy boots and ride into the desert to chase coyotes. *The Roy Rogers Show*, starring the amiable "King of the Cowboys," was a so-called kids' western, but Elliot loved it. Within a few years, the adult westerns *Gunsmoke*, *Bonanza*, *Wagon Train*, and *Maverick* would be filling the nation's television screens.

As Elliot cast about for the right toy, an inventor named Ken Frye came to Mattel with a replica of a paratrooper's machine gun. With one pull of the trigger, a child could fire fifty shots, the sound punctuated by the bursting of Mattel's Greenie Stik-M-Caps. The rapid firing reminded the toymakers of an extended burping sound, and so the gun was christened the Burp Gun. Interestingly, a lightweight portable submachine gun used by the Chinese during the Korean War, which had ended only a few years before, had the same name.

The Burp Gun that showed up at Toy Fair in 1955 after a year of development was true to Elliot's love of realistic toys. His ability to reduce an adult product to a child-size replica had inspired his unique baby grand piano. His later guns, the Fanner 50 pistol, a Colt .45, and the Winchester rifle were accurate reproductions. The Fanner 50, true to its name, could be drawn with one hand and its hammer fanned with the other hand as cowboys did in the movies. Its handle looked like bone, and the holster and belt were made of real leather, since Elliot felt that the plastic of the time was too cheap looking. Ruth discovered how realistic the guns were on a trip to New Haven, Connecticut, to get permission from the Winchester Repeating Arms Company to use its name on the toy rifle. Picking up the replica to demonstrate, she pointed the rifle at the head of one of the vice presidents. He hit the floor in panic. Mattel was given the rights.

The Burp Gun made the later Winchester rifle look tame, and the Handlers were aware of objections to violent toys. Elliot said, "Our guns are the type the kids see on TV. If they can't buy one, they're going to put it together out of pieces of wood or coat hangers or something." Ruth had a more detached response: "People make wars; we don't." Her world had a narrow focus. Events were good or bad relative to their effect on Mattel or her immediate family. If Elliot wanted to make guns, Ruth would defend his ideas and figure out how to make them work. "My husband is a very gentle man, and has no cruelty or meanness in him," she said. "He felt that if children did not have toy guns they would use sticks anyway. He saw nothing wrong with them playing like they were soldiers and cowboys and Indians."

As marketing plans were being made for Elliot's Burp Guns, Ralph Carson from Ruth's advertising agency came to see her. His firm, Carson/Roberts, had only six employees, and Mattel's budget, though small by most standards, was important to the up-and-coming agency. Carson thought the advertising he was about to propose would be beyond Mattel's reach, but he also knew Ruth could be bold. He turned the meeting over to Vince Francis, a West Coast sales representative for ABC. Well dressed and charming, Francis explained ABC's unprecedented move into a new Disney children's show. ABC planned to run the show in a time slot normally reserved for local stations. They believed the Disney brand was strong enough to guarantee that 90 percent of homes with televisions would carry it. *The Mickey Mouse Club* would reach almost every child in America five days a week, Francis declared.

Francis then got to the bottom line. Disney was asking for an unheard-of commitment: payment that could not be canceled for a full year of advertising. Toy manufacturers had always considered year-round advertising wasteful. The toy industry was cyclical and heavily dependent on Christmas, when 80 percent of sales were made. Factory downtime was an industry hazard, so much so that some companies often used their excess production capacity for non-toy-related products.

Ruth handled the downtime problem by reaching out for government money. Shortly after moving into their 60,000-square-foot plant in 1951, Ruth competed for a large contract to assemble complicated electric controls for army tanks. Her engineers retooled the equipment, and she met her million-dollar payroll despite toy orders slowing to a crawl after the flurry of Toy Fair. But she did not like it. Mattel had a brand and a mission, and that was toys. Any toy company that could figure out a year-round sales strategy would have a huge advantage over its competitors. She listened intently as Carson and Francis argued that twelve-month television advertising could increase and even out sales.

Everyone in the room that day also had a young family. The postwar baby boom was touched off by war veterans like Carson and his partner, Roberts. They and the Handlers recognized that the Depression and the world war had left families hungry to give children what they'd never had. And everyone agreed that Disney was a master at reaching children.

Francis took about half an hour to explain the idea. Elliot and Ruth listened with excitement. As soon as he was finished they turned to each other and agreed that the idea made sense, but Elliot suggested asking Yasuo Yoshida, Mattel's controller, to give them his opinion of whether Mattel was financially able to commit to the deal. "Yas," Ruth asked him when he joined the group, "if we spent a half million bucks on television, what do you think would happen if it didn't work?" Yoshida took his time before answering, then offered that Mattel would sell more product. Ruth impatiently agreed but wanted to know what would happen if the advertising were not a great success. Would Mattel be broke? "I don't think you would be broke," Yoshida replied. "I think you would be badly bent." His answer was good enough for Ruth to sign on to the plan. Less than an hour had passed since Carson and Francis had arrived. "It was the easiest sale ABC ever made," Ruth said. She had committed half a million dollars, which was the entire net worth of Mattel.

Yoshida also pointed out that failure would mean a shaky credit record, but Ruth was not deterred. She instructed Carson to draw up a contract for three commercials. The first two were for long-standing products, the jack-in-the-box and the Cowboy Ge-tars, another popular crank music toy. The third commercial would introduce the new Burp Gun.

The Mickey Mouse Club was not set to air until October, but the Burp Gun had to be previewed at Toy Fair in March. Buyers had not seen anything like it. Not only did it look like a real sub-machine gun, it fired like one. Ruth had set up a 16-mm projector to play the commercial Carson/Roberts had put together for the toy. She and her sales reps ran through an enthusiastic explanation of Disney's new *Mickey Mouse Club* concept and the advertising scheme. The television ads, they argued, would have the guns flying off shelves by Christmas. Mattel encouraged buyers to order their whole year's inventory up front. It worked. Based on the success of Mattel's other toys and the growing Disney brand, orders soared. For once, Ruth thought she would have a full year of production, even allowing for canceled orders. Instead, she ended up with chaos.

Due to the strong volume of orders, Mattel had heavy production schedules and shipped more product than usual, earlier than usual.

Stores were full of Burp Guns, but they were not selling. The public did not know how to use the new toy. The television ads were not running yet, so consumers had yet to see the gun in action. Buyers started to panic as the toys sat on the shelves, and they began canceling future orders. Account representatives called Mattel, arguing that they had been shipped too many Burp Guns and wanted to send them back. Stores were canceling all of their September, October, and November orders, and Ruth panicked. She stopped production as quickly as she could, but Mattel still had large unsold quantities of the gun. "Things got pretty bleak around our place in the fall," Ruth remembered. Hopes lifted at Mattel when *The Mickey Mouse Club* started in October and the first ads were on television. After the first week, however, sales were still down.

Each week, Ruth and Elliot watched *The Mickey Mouse Club* in dismay. They were proud of the commercial Carson/Roberts had developed for the Burp Gun. On screen, Cary Carson, Jack's young son, stalks around the furniture in his living room, submachine gun at the ready. Rear-screen projection makes photos of herds of wild elephants appear on the walls, but when the boy fires his Burp Gun, the film runs backward and the elephants retreat. As he reloads, an announcer explains how the gun works and where the extra "ammunition" is stored. The advertisement invited every watching boy to hunt elephants in African jungles with "his trusty Mattel Toy Burp Gun."

At the end of the commercial, Roberts tagged on a new logo: a cartoon of a boy with a crown on his head, waving from his seat in the center of the letter *M*. The tag line "You can tell it's Mattel— it's swell!" filled the screen as the announcer repeated the slogan. Ruth paid $2,500 for the ad, but it did not seem to do any good. *The Mickey Mouse Club* was a huge success, dominating its time slot, but Mattel's toy sales were still in the tank. Carson/Roberts suggested taking out newspaper ads to remind parents to watch the Mattel television commercial. "It was a desperation move," Cy Schneider, who worked at Carson/Roberts, said. "We started to believe the gamble had failed."

Ruth was in a miserable mood as she left Mattel for the Thanksgiving holiday. When she returned, however, she said, "It was like the roof was going to blow off the place with excitement." Over the holiday, after six weeks of television advertising, Burp Guns had flown off store shelves. Telephones were ringing, telegrams were arriving, and the mail began to fill with orders. Buyers were begging to reinstate canceled orders and to place new ones. Ruth's staff tried calling the stores who had been pleading to be relieved of their stock, but they no longer had any guns. Like the other stores, they wanted to get more. It was too late to start up production, so employees raided the storage area for guns that had been rejected as not up to par. They were repaired and sent out.

President Dwight Eisenhower's grandson David received one of the repaired guns at the White House. Mattel sent another to a California hospital where a journalist had promised it to a sick child. By Christmas Ruth had shipped one million Burp Guns at four dollars each, matching her entire previous year's sales volume for all her toys. "By Christmas," Ruth said, "there was not a Burp Gun in the country. That was the *Mickey Mouse Club* show. You can imagine how those buyers came prepared to our next Toy Show."

As Mattel raked in the orders, Louis Marx, the founder and owner of the Marx Toy Company, the biggest toy company in America, appeared on the cover of *Time*. He declared that Marx toys had spent only $312 on advertising in the previous year. Toys just were not sold on television, and they never would be, he claimed. The story went on to describe other big toy companies and their sales strategy. Mattel was too small to be mentioned, but not for long.

. . . .

Ruth not only changed a supply market to one that stirred demand, she changed the key consumer from parent to child. Toy advertising on television altered the family dynamic. No longer would parents buy only what they thought was best for their children. Over time, children's opinions, shaped by television ads, would drive where parents spent their toy money. Years later, Elliot told *Time*, without apology, "We feel it's up to the parents to handle the child." It is unlikely that parents whose children were begging for toys they saw on television found comfort in Elliot's pronouncement.

Retailers were also unhappy with Mattel. Ralph Carson told a reporter that retailers were irked because television advertising undercut their influence in the industry. The ads forced them to buy what Mattel advertised. "It used to be store buyers dictated what toys would sell, but Mattel reversed that."

The sales power of television led Ruth to consider expanding the company's on-air presence. By 1959 she asked Carson/Roberts to create a show called *Matty's Funday Funnies*, a cartoon show hosted by the animated characters Matty Mattel and Sisterbelle. The show's cartoons, *Casper the Friendly Ghost*, *Little Audrey*, *Herman and Katnip*, *Baby Huey*, and *Buzzy the Crow*, were huge hits, but Ruth was most delighted by the sponsorship deal she cut with ABC.

Normally, sponsorship contracts ran for thirteen or twenty-six weeks, and were renewed on October 1 of each year. Ruth, however, had negotiated a contract with ABC for fifty-two weeks in the Sunday 5 p.m. time slot. She insisted on the extra weeks so that the ads would be carried through Christmas. At the time the deal was signed, ABC's chairman of the board and vice presidents were happy about the contract. Sunday afternoons were normally a hard sell. Their subordinates, however, were worried. Another bigger deal was being negotiated that might rely on the time slot Ruth had won. By the middle of the year, ABC realized their problem. Their big new show, *Wide World of Sports*, was set to run on Sunday afternoons starting in October, but Ruth was holding that time slot until the end of the year. Ruth's contract was worth much less than that of the new show, and Carson called to tell her that ABC was willing to "do a lot" to get her to move to another day. "I was tough then," Ruth said, "and I knew I had them just where I wanted them. We got Friday night primetime in trade for Sunday afternoon, and what a difference it made to us! And we got it at the same cost as the other, although it was normally so costly that we could not have afforded it." The new television deal resulted in a major jump in sales.

Other toy companies began to copy Ruth's aggressive use of television advertising, and as they did, advertisements on television changed toy development. Designers now had to consider how a new toy would look in commercials, and how to display it to highlight the differences from competitors' toys. And the speed of television drove a major change in Ruth's sales and manufacturing method.

Ruth became one of the first real experts at sales forecasting and control after analyzing the progress of Burp Gun sales. Never given to modesty, she called her post-television sales innovation "marketing genius." In many ways she was right. "We were on the air six times and nothing happened," remembered Ralph Carson. "Then the Mattel people came back from a long weekend and . . . the place was filled with orders and reorders. That was when we realized the pipeline in this business is six weeks long." Why had it taken so long for Mattel to learn that the television commercials were driving sales? Ruth set her management team to investigate the problem. The answer was simple.

After a parent bought the toy, the sales information had to travel from the store to the jobber's representative who sold to the store, to the factory representative who sold to the jobber, and finally to the manufacturer. In large chain stores such as Sears or Ben Franklin, the chain of communication was even more difficult to navigate. Ruth realized that she could not be dependent on those outside Mattel to get her timely sales information, so she hired a new set of employees, the "retail detail." Their job was to travel around to stores, setting up attractive Mattel displays and measuring how fast Mattel toys were selling. If they saw a need for more toys or an overstock, they contacted the regional Mattel sales representative, who called the factory. Instead of a six-week lag time, Ruth now had sales data in a day or less.

Ruth's genius lay not only in developing the method for collecting the data, but in analyzing the information to forecast sales and control production. Three years after the first Burp Gun commercial went on the air, Mattel had grown from four million dollars a year in sales to fourteen million. Marx Toy Company, with sales of fifty million dollars, was still far ahead. But not for long.

Chapter 9

The Woman and the Doll

I could only relate to them as a leader.

Most mornings, Ruth left the house in Beverlywood at eight fifteen, driving off with Elliot in her pink Thunderbird convertible. She still loved cars, and Mattel's phenomenal success in television advertising in 1955 allowed her to indulge herself in what she chose to drive. Convertibles, among other products, had been imbued with a sexual cachet, thanks to the marketing genius of the psychologist and corporate consultant Ernest Dichter. He made a business out of analyzing people's motivations to buy products, rather than diagnosing their neuroses.

Dichter had the broad, welcoming smile of a car salesman. With a deeply receding hairline accenting a high forehead, black-rimmed eyeglasses, and a neatly folded pocket handkerchief, he wore his intellectualism like a salable product. Dichter packaged himself as the answer to American retailers' greatest question: how do we sell more product? Dichter sold himself to the American consulate in Vienna as an émigré who would transform American business practices, and he set out to prove his claim.

Manufacturers eager to beat the competition gave Dichter large contracts for his unique skill.

Ruth first approached Dichter when Barbie was going through the design and production phase leading up to the 1959 Toy Fair. Besides her work on Barbie, Ruth sought ways to assess how Mattel toys were received. She knew parents had some concerns about Elliot's toy guns, and there were strong critics inside Mattel who thought that going forward with the anatomically adult Barbie was a huge mistake. Ruth had lost track of the number of people who had told her that mothers would never buy the doll for their daughters. Television commercials were being prepared, and Ruth had to figure out how to position the doll to get past parental objections.

Ruth loved Dichter's iconoclastic genius, along with what he promised. If Ruth's fellow toymakers underestimated anything about her, and they often did, it was her competitive drive. She liked to win, and she intended to do so with the Barbie doll. Part of her strategy included bringing the guru of new marketing to Mattel's aid.

Dichter was attracting enormous public attention as the evil genius who was the master of manipulated marketing. An inflammatory and influential book by Vance Packard, *The Hidden Persuaders*, had come out in 1957. The book's cover copy, "The attempt to control our subconscious mind," captured Packard's central argument. His theme fit with the conspiracy theories of the time. Packard tapped into the angst of Americans who believed that communists might be holed up in government offices. Cold war hysteria had turned into paranoia, lending Packard credibility when he pointed his finger at Dichter as a purveyor of mind control.

Packard's book succeeded in making Dichter not only more famous, but also more in demand by corporations. Ruth saw Dichter, like herself, as a rebel entrepreneur, unapologetic about ideas and methods that were outside accepted practice. He was a fellow groundbreaker, and her relationship with him would be another turning point for Mattel and for the toy industry.

A Viennese Jew, Dichter had set up his psychologist's office across the street from Sigmund Freud, but fled the country in 1938 as the Fascist threat became intolerable. In one of his first assignments for his American employer, Compton Advertising, Dichter researched Ivory soap by conducting long, free-form interviews with a hundred people about their most recent experiences with soap. Besides these "depth interviews," as Dichter called them, he would ask people to pretend they were a particular brand of soap, a "psychodrama" technique that helped him develop his idea that products had personality and images.

Dichter pioneered what would later commonly be called branding. His 1939 soap report concluded that Ivory soap "had more of a somber, utilitarian, thoroughly cleansing character than the more glamorous personalities of other soaps such as Cashmere Bouquet." He went on to help market Chrysler cars with a similarly sexual slant. "Individuals project themselves into products. In buying a car they actually buy an extension of their own personality." Sedans, he said, were like wives, "comfortable and safe," but convertibles were like mistresses, "youthful, beckoning." Dealerships quickly moved convertibles to the front window.

Influenced by his Freudian background, Dichter pioneered motivational research. He called it "qualitative research designed to uncover the consumer's subconscious or hidden motivations that determine purchase behavior." Armed with the certitude that he could uncover what others failed to see, he told the cigarette industry that consumers found in smoking oral satisfaction comparable to breastfeeding. Domineering and always the center of attention, he pronounced that phallic-looking lipstick packaging was more attractive to women, and that necktie manufacturers should contrast an old, limp tie on an older man with a "smooth, colorful, erect and manly" tie on a younger man. He had hit on the idea of turning "sex into sales," founding his own Institute for Motivational Research in 1946 in a castlelike mansion over the Hudson River.

When Mattel entered a market, Ruth believed, it had to be in a bigger, better, more explosive way than its competitors. She wanted Dichter to give her a marketing blueprint for Barbie. She also wanted to conduct a study on toy guns to convince the public that they did not promote violence in children. Willing to pay whatever it took to get the best talent, she agreed to a hefty twelve-thousand-dollar contract with Dichter's consultancy for a report on Mattel's toy guns, holsters, rockets, and the soon-to-be-unveiled Barbie doll.

Dichter was in such great demand that he could not handle every account. But he took Mattel for himself. No one had ever explored the motivations behind children's choices of toys. Ruth later claimed that Dichter's results about guns were "reassuring." The 357 children he interviewed saw toy guns as props in make-believe games, and they liked the feel of the gun and its sounds. The gun was a "tool in the learning process." But Ruth left out the more controversial parts of Dichter's findings, although it is easy to imagine that they gave her a good laugh, considering the focus her all-male product development team had on making guns. "Big guns are like penises," Dichter wrote, and children were relieving psychic tension as their knowledge and bodies were growing and experiencing the pressures of the adult world.

In analyzing Barbie, Dichter interviewed 191 girls and 45 mothers. He asked, is Barbie "a nice kid, friendly and loved by everyone, or is she vain and selfish, maybe even cheap? Does she have good taste or is she a little too flashy?" Mothers, it turned out, hated the doll, but not their daughters. "He interviewed girls about what they wanted in a doll," Dichter's wife said. "It turns out that what they wanted was someone sexy looking, someone that they wanted to grow up to be like. Long legs, big breasts, glamorous."

Not all of Dichter's girl interviewees felt the same. Some said Barbie looked "snobbish," "sharp," and "too glamorous," but he had been hired to find a strategy for sales, not to remold the doll by committee or appeal to the minority view.

Everyone seemed to agree on Dichter's brilliance, but not necessarily as Dichter packaged it. Marvin Barab, who took over Dichter's contract when Mattel hired him in late 1959, remembered, "He was one of the most brilliant men in marketing. Notice I did not say psychology. As a researcher he stunk. He did not believe in real quantitative market research, like defining the scope of activity or determining the weight of preferences. But you wanted to pick his mind because he was so creative. He could take a minor point you overlooked and give a brilliant lecture on its importance to marketing."

Dichter suggested enlarging Barbie's breasts. He also encouraged Ruth to market her with a simple idea. Girls needed a way to convince their mothers that Barbie and her many outfits would teach them to be ladies—and well-groomed ladies at that. Barbie would be an educational tool for mothers. The sexual overtones of the doll would be downplayed by emphasizing the way her outfits could help girls learn to accessorize.

Armed with Dichter's research, Carson/Roberts began to plan television commercials. "Watching children play with the doll, we concluded that little girls saw Barbie as the young woman they wanted to be someday," wrote Cy Schneider, one of the ad men working on the television campaign. Ruth, of course, agreed. She had always believed that the doll's play value rested in girls' fantasies about growing up. Carson/Roberts brought that idea, literally, to life, creating a commercial that cast the doll as a real person. Every variation of the Barbie commercial was then tested on children. The result mesmerized girls.

Barbie debuted on television in March 1959, not as a doll but as if she were a teen fashion model. For toy advertising, this was uncharted territory. Only once in the sixty-second commercial was Barbie even called a doll. Instead, the plastic toy was simply Barbie, a girl who swims, dances, parties, and changes clothes. Carson/Roberts, who also represented Max Factor cosmetics at the time, treated the doll like a model. "No cosmetic or hair-grooming commercial ever put more attention to detail or was photographed with more style and flair," wrote Schneider. "Special techniques were developed to make Barbie look glamorous under hot lights and through the eye of the camera. Filming a close-up of a beautiful woman has its own set of problems, but when the model's head is the size of a quail's egg, enormous difficulties arise." Dolls were frozen overnight so they wouldn't melt under the lights. Hair and fashion stylists stood at the ready to do touch-ups as the filming went on.

Carson/Roberts commissioned a special song in the style of Connie Francis's rich-toned, lyrical pop tunes of the 1950s. The lyrics made the Mattel sales pitch clear: "Someday I'm going to be just like you, 'til then I know just what I'll do . . . Barbie, beautiful Barbie, I'll make believe that I am you."

At every Toy Fair since 1955, when the Burp Gun launched, Mattel built on its successful entry into television. "Remember the Burp Gun" was the rallying cry in 1956. By 1959 Mattel had announced a million-dollar annual budget for advertising. In the weeks leading up to Toy Fair, Ruth announced that an extra $125,000 would be devoted to Barbie's launch. But it was not enough to attract the buyers who still worried over Barbie's breasts and overt sex appeal. Orders fell short. Ruth flew home after frantically cutting back production, even as the television ads blanketed the country. After all, if the dolls were not on store shelves, it was unlikely there would be much demand. Due to Ruth's new methods for pinpointing sales, she knew the doll was languishing.

Competitors in the toy industry reveled in Mattel's apparent failure with Barbie. One Mattel employee who joined a smaller company prior to Barbie's debut remembered a conversation with the company president's wife. "Can you believe what that crazy Mattel did? They went on TV and expected moms to buy whore-looking dolls for their kids." Many people inside Mattel kept similar views to themselves.

For Ruth, the spring of 1959 was grim. The Barbie doll had failed to catch on the way Ruth had hoped, and the doll's namesake, her daughter, Barbara, was determined to leave home prematurely. Only eighteen years old, Barbara announced her plans to marry Allen M. Segal after she graduated from high school. She had started dating him the previous year when she saw him at an insurance company where she worked. She knew him from Hamilton High School, where they both had been students, but he had gone into the navy and she had lost track of him. According to Barbara, he was "rough, tough, and very macho." Ruth and Elliot were not happy that Barbara was marrying so young, but they went ahead with plans for a big August wedding. "He was very romantic looking in his sailor suit," Ruth remembered, "but she needed him like she needed a hole in the head." But Barbara was headstrong. "I used to wonder why they did not put up a bigger fight," Barbara said, "but I guess they knew that if they did, I would have married him anyway." Ruth was also distracted by Barbie's fate after Toy Fair.

As schools began to close for the summer, however, Mattel got calls from buyers wanting Barbie dolls. For Ruth, it must have felt like the roller coaster of the Burp Gun all over again. After Toy Fair, she had remained conservative with the orders for Barbie dolls sent to her Japanese manufacturers. "In the toy business," Ruth said, "you live or die with the quality of the projection you make. Your lead times are very long, and the commitments you make very early influence how many you make or ship and whether you get stuck with what you do." She was trying not to get stuck with Barbies when suddenly she had the opposite problem. The demand skyrocketed as the effect of the television advertising, free time for summer play, and the novelty of the doll propelled girls to pester their parents for Barbie. "The industry was just going frantic with demand for Barbie," Ruth remembered. The buyers who had been uninterested at Toy Fair were now clamoring to get the doll. Little girls wanted to play at being big girls, just as Ruth had guessed.

Barbie would become an international phenomenon, the best-selling doll in the world and one of the best-selling toys of all time. Worldwide sales would be counted in breathless increments. As one *Fortune* article in 2003 claimed, "A new Barbie doll is sold approximately every three seconds." Girls in America would own not one Barbie, they would own two or three or ten or more, with many wardrobe changes for each of them. Sales would be counted in the billions. The doll's one-word name recognition reached the heights of Chaplin or Kennedy.

Mattel would go public on Barbie's tiny plastic triangular back, and her apparel market, if adult-size, would have made Mattel the fourth largest clothing manufacturer in America. Ruth predicted that Barbie would be a kind of Rorschach test for little girls' imaginations, and she was right. By 1963 the *New York Times* wrote of "the revolutionary idea that little girls today are viewing their girl dolls increasingly as themselves and not as their babies." But Barbie also became tinder in the fiery arguments over sexism, gender roles, and feminism that burst out in the second wave of the women's movement in the 1960s. For better or worse, Ruth realized her own vision and created both a controversial icon and a money machine. Besting her doubters, she had given girls something she believed they wanted, maybe even needed, and they had proved her right.

Mattel would not catch up with demand for Barbie for three years. A glowing *Los Angeles Times* article in September 1959 began with a quote: " 'I'm a little lost in the home—I'm just not efficient,' says Mrs. Elliot Handler." The reporter seemed to think that Ruth was being apologetic, but that seems unlikely. She was stating what had been true since the day she got fed up with being a wife and mother in 1944. She left homemaking behind the day she told Harold Matson that she would sell the picture frames he made in his garage.

Fifteen years later she was executive vice president of Mattel, overseeing twelve hundred workers, twenty million dollars in sales, and the consolidation of five plants into one enormous 250,000-square-foot building in an area south of Los Angeles soon to be named Hawthorne. When pressed by the *Los Angeles Times* reporter for insight into her motivations as a businesswoman, Ruth said, "If I had to stay home I would be the most dreadful, mixed-up, unhappy woman in the world." She had never been so candid or introspective in print before, but Ruth was riding high enough to be clear-eyed about her choices.

That fall, Barbie dolls were available in twenty-two varieties, and their ranks were expanding. New clothing lines were being planned. There was talk of other dolls, perhaps a male version, which girls were already writing to Mattel to request. With the doll's success, Ruth could expound upon her original vision of

Barbie, and no naysayers were left to contradict her. "Little girls dream of being curvaceous, dreamy, exciting. They want—some day—to have gorgeous clothes, be chic and look like movie stars," she said. She saw nothing wrong with encouraging such fantasies. After all, she loved chic clothes and had been fascinated with Hollywood since her days at Paramount.

Ruth insisted that Mattel did not have an agenda. They were not setting trends but following them. Barbie's figure simply reflected the idealized female of the 1950s, albeit a male ideal put forth by male-dominated media. But Ruth was not political or prone to dwell on the root of cultural standards. If girls were being told they should wish they were busty blonds, Mattel would profit from that message.

Although Ruth rejected sexist norms in her business life, she still felt the conflict of challenging conventional ideas about women. She might never have started working again after becoming a mother, or accomplished what she had, if Elliot had not given her permission. But when a friend asked what she would have done if he had said no, Ruth stopped and thought for a long time. Finally, she laughed and said, "I probably would have done it anyway." Later, hearing that story, she changed her mind. "I'm not sure," she said. "In those days I was brainwashed enough in my head through the world around me, if he had said 'no' I might not have done it. I might have been a very miserable person, and we might have lost our marriage eventually."

For his part, Elliot had always followed a simple formula. "As long as she's happy, I'm happy," he said. Ruth was happy as a businesswoman and, more than that, as a business founder. She possessed the defining characteristics of successful capitalists who turn ideas into profitable businesses. Consumed with the struggle and challenges of building their business, they have time for little else, not family, not friends, not introspection. Ruth told one interviewer that her career took "a willingness and a capacity to try to slot your private life into your total existence so that it interferes as little as possible with your business life."

Ruth had no interest, time, or patience for debates over the political or social impact of products such as the Barbie doll or toy guns. She had hired Ernest Dichter to tell her how to sell the most Barbie dolls, not how to make the doll a proxy for an emerging feminist vision of women. She had no desire to dictate the fantasies girls played out with Barbie. If the Dichter and Carson/Roberts focus groups and interviews showed that girls wanted to pretend the doll was going to parties or shopping, getting married and dressing up, that was fine with Ruth. She trusted that if she got the doll in girls' hands, they would have a richer fantasy life. As tens of thousands of dolls were bought around the country, mothers began to reconcile themselves to the doll. "She was such a tomboy before," one mother wrote. "Now I've been able to get her to wash her face and comb her hair." Ruth's controversial idea, Dichter's unprecedented focus groups, and Carson/Roberts's unique commercials had all been vindicated.

As Ruth made plans for the new decade, she knew she was sitting atop a behemoth that would require all her attention and still-developing business skills. Back in 1957, after the *Mickey Mouse Club* commercials had put Mattel on a trajectory to go from five million to fourteen million dollars in sales in three years, her general manager, Dave Menken, had a suggestion. He had grown concerned about the rapid rate of growth of Mattel, yet when he spoke to Ruth about his concerns she brushed him off. Elliot had been pushing to expand product lines, and Menken felt the company was not equipped to handle the expansion. Ruth did not seem to understand his worries over the coordination of divisions or the chain of supervision. He told Ruth that it would help her and the company if she got some formal business training. He suggested she take a course for business executives at the University of California, Los Angeles.

Ruth showed up on the first day of class to find fifty men as her fellow students—no women. They were presidents, executive vice presidents, and chairmen of large companies. As she took her seat, Ruth felt ill at ease, not sure that she belonged in a class where she was certain the other participants had obtained the formal business education that she lacked. "I was hiding a great big inferiority complex," Ruth said, "and at first I had a tough time with it. I sat there with those men, listening to their educated discussions of all the subjects relating to business management, and I realized how little I knew." Soon, however, as she read about organizational theory and the formal concepts underlying the work she had been doing instinctively, Ruth said she felt "like a person on a desert who found water." She checked extra books out of the school library. She felt she could not get enough of this new world of business ideas.

Gradually her insecurities faded. She realized that while the other students had a great deal of education, they had far less business experience than she did. Most of them were not entrepreneurs, but executives who had been hired to run ongoing concerns. "They walked in with their classy education," Ruth remembered, "and they did not really know what the real world was. Well, I knew what the real world was like because I had been there and I had done it."

During one class, the professor talked about the challenges of managing employees. He presented a case study involving a woman who had worked in an office for ten or fifteen years. She had a great deal of institutional knowledge. She could be counted on to provide valuable background on clients and company history that was otherwise undocumented, and she knew where to find everything. Newer employees often came to her for help, but she was crusty and unfriendly. She frequently refused to follow her supervisor's instructions or fulfill his requests, falling back on her standard retort that things had never been done the way he was suggesting. She was hard to manage and resisted change, the professor concluded, asking the class to tell him how they would handle such an employee.

As the professor went around the class asking each of the members to give his opinion, the answers focused on reforming the recalcitrant woman. Students said, "I'd talk to her about it," or "I'd counsel her," or "I'd have the personnel department work with her." Finally, the professor said to Ruth, "Well, what would you have done?" Ruth had been growing increasingly impatient as she listened to the other students. Her reply was curt: "I'd have fired the son of a bitch forty-five minutes ago." The story of the case study and Ruth's answer became a legend within the program. Years later, recent graduates who met Ruth would tell her that it was still being repeated.

One night Ruth took home a book on organizational theory from her course and studied it at a desk in her living room. While Elliot slept, she sat up most of the night outlining the ideas that impressed her on a separate piece of paper for each chapter. It was a method for studying and remembering information that she used throughout her life. She focused on those ideas that would show her how to improve Mattel. She was struck by the idea that she could not reach her goals if someone was blocking her access to the people she needed to supervise. As she read, she understood how a resistant manager could prevent her entire operational plan from succeeding. Dave Menken, who insisted on having the personnel, financial, production, and engineering departments all report to him, was in Ruth's way. She had only the marketing department and Menken reporting to her. "I realized I could not function with a 'general manager' reporting to me," Ruth said, "because I had to get to the various parts of the business myself."

Ruth thought about taking some of the departments away from Menken, but the more she read the more she realized that she could not demote a man with that much power. He would protest. If he stayed he was not likely to be effective and would hurt the organization. Ruth laid out a new organizational chart for Mattel. On it, personnel/industrial relations, finance, production, marketing, and certain other departments reported to her. She laid out all the subfunctions reporting to each department. Research, design, and engineering reported to Elliot, and she created a dotted-line relationship connecting her to them. When she finished, there was no place for Menken. She decided that he had to go.

When Elliot woke up the next morning, Ruth pulled him to the table and made him sit down. She showed him her new organizational plan, announcing that they had no choice but to fire Menken. Elliot studied the paper for a few minutes before agreeing. Ruth said the decision was hard to make. "This was a good man," she said, "a very talented man, a very loyal man, and a man that I liked very much who was doing a pretty good job. Yet it had to be done. So if people say I'm tough, I guess when I had to do it, I did it and it was the correct decision at the time." Ruth was in full operational control of Mattel.

In December 1959, as Mattel readied to move into its giant new plant, Ruth was feeling expansive. She started a new charity program, agreeing to give toys to the police department in Los Angeles every year, which they would give away door-to-door in needy neighborhoods. The *Los Angeles Examiner* had agreed to follow the police and take pictures, and Ruth was delighted by the children's faces when officers came to the door dressed as Santa Claus.

Mattel gave Ruth other reasons to smile. After consolidating her control of the company, she had built a team of hard-driving vice presidents: Clifford Jacobs for marketing; Seymour Adler for operations; Robert Mitchell for industrial relations; Ted Horowitz as treasurer; and the flamboyant, brilliant, and quixotic Jack Ryan for research and design. Elliot still held the title, if not the function, of president, and Ruth had added an important outside role with the Toy Association in addition to her job as executive vice president.

Ruth remembered how proud Abe Swedlin of the Gund toy company acted as he gave her the news that she was being named as the first woman on the Toy Association board of directors. The following year he proudly told her that she was being named the first woman vice president of the board. For the first time in the association's history, however, a second vice president, who was male, had been appointed. By tradition, the vice president succeeded to the presidency. "They did not dare let me become president," Ruth said. "They didn't have the guts." She admitted being both annoyed by the slight, as well as proud to be an officer and the first woman. She found the board meetings fun and stimulating, quickly growing comfortable in the all-male milieu but aware of the gender discrimination she encountered. "[For women] it was not a glass ceiling in those days," Ruth said. "It was concrete. The ceiling was there, and the walls were there. I had instance after instance in which it was made known to me that I was a fluke or a quirk. It gave me a lot of self-doubt. I had all kinds of mixed feelings. It also gave me a feeling of power, strangely enough."

Ruth's rise in a corporate world dominated by men made her a target. Behind her back, they called her loudmouthed and profane. They resented her grandiose pronouncements, such as her claim that Barbie was "the greatest phenomenon that ever hit the toy business." Although Ruth was arguably right, they found it hard to forgive a woman who lacked modesty and self-effacement.

An attractive woman who liked to dress for men's admiration, Ruth also freely spouted the most indelicate expletives. She strode into rooms as if she expected to take over. Most of the men she worked with had never seen a woman like her. She had been running Mattel for fifteen years, and her ambition was still manifest. She believed in her instinctive marketing talent, her originality, and her willingness to operate outside the norm. She saw herself as a leader, one who related to people in a special way. "I can motivate people in a way that is superior to just about anyone else," Ruth said. "We got our people so highly motivated, Elliot with his great ideas and his sweetness and warm personality, and me with the power of my own convictions and my ambitious drive and warmth toward people." Ruth believed that she, Elliot, and their executive team were poised to build the company by tens of millions of dollars.

At times, Ruth referred to Mattel's meteoric rise from its origins in a seedy garage as a happenstance, saying, "We didn't know what the hell we were doing." But after 1960 there could be no denying that every decision was intentional, planned, vetted, scrutinized, and approved by Ruth.

Chapter 10

Soaring in the Sixties

Life changed the minute we went public.

Just before the 1964 Toy Fair, Mattel executives squeezed into a small company conference room to look over the toy a rival company hoped would compete with the Barbie doll. The Hassenfeld brothers, whose toy company would later be renamed Hasbro, were serious competitors for Mattel. The solvency of Hasbro was riding on the muscular physique of an eleven-and-a-half-inch toy that executives swore never to call a doll.

G.I. Joe, "America's Movable Fighting Man," had twenty-one movable parts with which to throw grenades, wield a flame-thrower, or storm the barricades of Mattel's success. His face was an artist's composite taken from the pictures of twenty Medal of Honor winners, or so the advertising falsely claimed. No matter— the martyred President Kennedy had been a war hero, and millions of veterans were also fathers of little boys who wanted to play soldier. Doll toys for boys had never worked, and so Joe was advertised, to the music of "The Army Goes Rolling Along," as a "soldier," a "frogman," and a "fighting man," never as a doll. Joe came with costume changes and fighting accessories. The lesson of Barbie and her wardrobe had not been lost on the Hassenfeld brothers. Elliot called it the razor/razorblade theory. Once customers bought a razor, they had to keep buying more blades.

Executives at Mattel had been hearing rumors about the supposed blockbuster toy for weeks. They hovered around the table where the doll had been placed, and Jack Ryan, head of the design team, slowly took off each piece of Joe's clothing. Ruth was the only woman in the room.

G.I. Joe had mannequin-like joints. Unlike the sleek but relatively immovable Barbie doll, Joe had a rotational joint at his shoulder, upper arm, elbow, and a ball-like wrist joint. His heavily muscled upper body was divided from his hips by a large stomach ball joint. Each leg was jointed at the hip, and even his ankles were flexible. His head swiveled on a thick neck, and his look was impassive, if not stern.

Ryan made a big show of taking off the doll's cap and dog tag. Then his camouflage jacket. Then his combat boots. No one said anything. The doll's engineering was impressive. Joe's clothes showed the detail that Mattel's Japanese seamstresses had perfected with Barbie's tiny snaps and stitches. Hasbro had, for the first time, gone to Japan for the manufacture of Joe's clothes. Everyone could see that a military-themed doll would appeal to the boys' market.

Finally, Ryan tugged off Joe's pants. The molded hip piece, separately jointed from just below the stomach to the legs, had a nondescript U-shaped crease in the front, and a vertical crease suggesting buttocks from the rear. Not a word came from the Mattel team as it evaluated the strange-looking nude doll. Breaking the silence, Ruth barked out a laugh. With a dismissive wave of her hand that flashed her large emerald-cut diamond ring, she declared, "Why, he ain't got no balls!" There was a breathless pause in the room before everyone started laughing. It was "hearty, good-natured, confident laughter," recalled Joe Whittaker. "As it finally subsided, I noticed a few pairs of eyes locking, quiet smiles, a nod or two of the head."

Whittaker was new to Mattel, but he knew its culture was unique. He had been hired into product planning at a time when Ruth was focused on building professional systems in an industry that operated fast and loose. Toys, like fashion or movies, needed constant innovation. It was a fad business, where designers often guessed wrong about the next big thing. People might buy the same brand of soap year after year, but every Christmas they expected new and better ideas in toys.

Ruth sent her hypercharged team into an animated discussion of G.I. Joe's chances in the marketplace. Joe Whittaker sensed the change that Ruth's brash comment about the doll's anatomy had made. In a tribute to her at an awards ceremony years later he said, "Was it really a transcendent moment? Probably just in the imagination of a kid straight out of B-school, but I first sensed at that moment what they already knew: and that is that it was we, we at Mattel, we in that room, we had the balls, and the will and the force of corporate personality to mold and shape and positively remake an entire industry in our own image. . . . That is *exactly* what we did for the entire decade of the sixties. We were golden and what we touched turned to gold."

The decade started with Mattel going public, selling 350,000 shares over the counter at ten dollars each. Ruth would use the money to expand operations, mostly in the United States and Japan. She and Elliot spent months doing due diligence meetings to prepare for the stock offering.

Ruth acted as spokesperson and did all of the talking after Elliot made a brief introduction. One of these meetings was in Chicago. A day or two before the big event, which the stock market analysts were going to attend, the venue was suddenly changed. Ruth was told that women were not allowed at the original location. On another occasion, Ruth and Elliot met two men from a Wall Street firm who were to escort them into a New York club. They went up in an elevator as a group, but when they got off, one of the men took Elliot's arm and led him in a different direction from Ruth. Ruth was taken through the kitchen and garbage area and down some back halls, finally arriving at the meeting room, where about twenty men were waiting. Even though she was the key speaker to this group of stock analysts, she had to be sneaked in because women were not allowed on that floor of the club.

Despite the indignities, Ruth found it a heady experience to be the only female operating in a world of men. She felt it was a form of power and that she was ascending business heights she had never envisioned. She said she got her "kicks" and a great deal of satisfaction from being the only woman. "It gave me power over them," Ruth recalled. "It gave me a feeling of self, and I don't know if the word was 'pride'? I think so."

Rather than be intimidated by the treatment given her because of her gender, Ruth coped sometimes by embracing it, sometimes by letting it roll off. Discrimination, she told a woman manager at Mattel, "was the price you paid for being ahead of your group." As with so many other parts of her life, she tried to turn the negative into a positive. Some men felt she used her sexuality, turning on a big smile and calling them honey. Men who tried to make her feel powerless only succeeded in making her feel more powerful. She had done everything they had and more, and she had done it against the odds that said women could not succeed.

As for other women, Ruth was willing to give them a fair shot. "She was not particularly mentoring of women," remembered Sandy Danon, who started in management as a fashion cost estimator in 1968. "She was ruthless and saw herself as one of the guys, [but once you were hired] you had the opportunity to reach higher than you ever could. She wanted you to be entrepreneurial, be at the forefront before anyone else. We were thinking two to three years ahead. We did not know the meaning of 'it can't be done.'"

Discrimination did exist. When Danon discovered pay differentials between women and men, she protested and won increases of 25–30 percent. Ruth believed that most women did not want business success as much as men did. Where a male executive was catered to when he came home, a professional woman still had to do the catering and not act, as Ruth put it, "like she's doing her family a big fat favor." Yet if women wanted the opportunity, Ruth would not stand in their way. By the late 1960s, Mattel had more women executives than any other toy company.

Ruth recognized her unique place in the business world, speaking of her life as "a woman's story," but she had little interest in what her rise to power meant for other women. Any feminist tilt to her rhetoric was tempered by her insistence that she always had her husband by her side. She credited Elliot with tolerating the sexist treatment she sometimes received so that they could achieve their business goals, although it often sounded like he was simply oblivious. She claimed that neither of them was trying to "cure the evils of the world." Ruth was just following her instincts. "She would have made a great trial lawyer," Josh Denham, an executive who was close with her, remembers. "She asked very penetrating questions. She had a female instinct for when you were putting her on, and she wouldn't tolerate b.s. She'd just stop listening. She had the most perceptive, gut feelings of what would work or not of anyone I'd known." Ruth used a joke about her success that was all the more humorous because no one who knew her would give it any credence. "I got here by sleeping with the boss," Ruth liked to say.

. . . .

For busineſſ practiceſ, Mattel looked to Procter & Gamble, considered a model for its superior way of developing new products and marketing them. Ruth aimed to create generalists who could manage product lines by being at the center of a wheel-shaped organizational model. These leaders were charged with understanding Mattel's markets and their consumers so that they could quickly respond as new products were ready for distribution.

To find the best and the brightest, Ruth recruited from the top business schools. New employees from Berkeley, Stanford, UCLA, Harvard, and Columbia were given written tests. Thirty engineers might be brought in for a weeklong interview process in which they were pitted against other hopefuls. No other toy company had such an aggressive recruitment process.

Candidates would arrive at the big, gray industrial building in Hawthorne, with trailers set on the outside to expand the space. A river of water flowed out of the production area. The headquarters of the building was tiny. A new headquarters was not built until the mid-sixties. Most offices were cramped cubicles, and prospective employees would encounter a charged atmosphere in every department. To an outsider, Mattel must have looked like a classroom without a teacher. Pat Schauer, who worked in sales, remembered, "It was racy. People were throwing around lots of sexual double entendres. There was lots of joking, throwing things over the cubicle walls, playing games."

Depending on their job interest, prospective employees might be given design projects to complete or a marketing package to prepare. They were given the Activity Vector Analysis test to see if they were "creative and volatile enough," in Ruth's words. This test became known as the Mattel V or claw, because the points of a V were used to plot "achievement," "power," and "affiliation," meaning feelings and collaborative style. Successful applicants scored high on achievement and power, which were the top two points of the V, and much lower on affiliation, which was the bottom point. "It was a measure of how aggressive you were," remembered Frank Sesto, who became chief tool engineer. "They wanted hard-charging people."

What Ruth wanted were people like her—candid, competitive, uncompromising, and tough. "You did not just go through a wall," executive Josh Denham explained. "You were expected to knock it down." Ruth was willing to let her team try new things. Boyd Browne, who started in 1959 as a manager for safety and security, had ten jobs in sixteen years at Mattel. "I came from RCA, where everything was by the book. At one level you had one pen, one desk. At another level you got a shared office, then an office with a half wall. At the top you got an enclosed room. Mattel was the opposite. Whatever had to be done, you did it."

Browne remembered doing an experiment to test security. He went to the docks, loaded four boxes of toys into his car, and drove away. After seeing how easily inventory could be stolen, he wanted to issue badges for everyone and secure the gates. "I went to Ruth, but I was scared to death, and I told her the story. 'Yes?' she said. 'What's your point? If you think it's the right thing to do, then go do it.'" At that moment, Browne understood that Ruth was telling him that his job was his responsibility. "If you wanted to do something that was good for the company, go do it, but you had responsibility and would be out if it was not good. You could take risks and move up the ladder." In Ruth's company, you were more likely to get fired for underspending than overspending.

Sandy Danon, who started as a fashion cost estimator, remembered that "People were scared of her. She'd rip them apart. She'd say things like 'I'll cut your balls off' if they did not perform as she expected." But Ruth also encouraged Danon, advising her to let slights roll off her as she herself had learned to do. Those, like Danon, who made it at Mattel, felt like they were in a company army. "We were Mattel brats, and we were in it for life," Danon said.

The high energy and pressure made Mattel a stressful place to work. People were surprised when Tom Kalinske, who would eventually become CEO, got married. Few people in marketing were married. "The place was so exciting," Danon said, "home was boring, the divorce rate was high." There were a lot of affairs going on in the company and a lot of partying. People were competitive even when they were supposed to be relaxing. Working in Ruth's shadow, they did not relax. "Her approval was always on our minds," said Lou Miraula, who worked in marketing. He remembered one of her early pieces of advice: "Lou, when you see another salesperson working, you watch and see how you can do it better."

In the mid-sixties Miraula went to Ruth's office with a huge order from Kresge, one of Mattel's top customers. He expected her to compliment him, but instead she said, "They did not buy this toy or this one," pointing to the list. She did not want stores to cherry-pick Mattel's line, buying only the best-selling toys. She wanted shelf space, and at every sales meeting, Cliff Jacobs, who headed the department, would remind his team of Ruth's expectations. She expected every order to be comprehensive. She wanted salesmen to sell every item Mattel had. "She kept the pressure on," Miraula said, adding that he felt wary of her power. He never felt she cared about employees personally. But other employees felt quite different. Several referred to Ruth and Elliot as "parents." "They were my second set of parents in the business world. They were my role models. Ruth always asked about my personal life with real kindness in her tone," Joe Whittaker remembered.

Even as she expected top performance inside the company, Ruth supported outside entrepreneurship. Fred Held, working in operations strategy, had a real estate business that Ruth encouraged. Marvin Barab had a business publishing family campground directories. It had just started to take off when he had his interview for Mattel. He told Ruth about it. "Will it interfere with toys?" she asked. When he said it would not, she told him it was not a problem. Sometime later, when Barab was having lunch with her, Ruth asked how the publishing business was going. "It's going too well," Barab replied. "I'm up against the wall because all my value is in accounts receivable and I need money for more printing." He explained that Sears and Montgomery Ward owed him fifty thousand dollars, and Rand McNally would not print more directories for the upcoming season unless he came up with twenty-five thousand dollars. Ruth told him to meet her back at her office. When he got there she called her contact at the Englewood Bank of America. "Jules," she said, "I have an executive who has another business and he's cash short, and I want you to help." Barab kept his publishing company and, after six years at Mattel, he left to run it full-time.

If applicants did not have what Ruth called "the entrepreneurial personality," she classified them as NMM, or "not Mattel material." Those few who made it through the gauntlet of tests and questions and competition were hired. Ruth ended up with a brilliant bunch of combatants. "She hired people for their attitude of 'nothing can stand in our way,'" remembered Fred Held, who was hired into Mattel management in 1962. "She wanted young people who could take over a hundred-million-dollar division in five years. The Mattel way was to believe nothing is impossible and creativity is king." In interviews nearly fifty years later, these employees were strikingly creative and energetic. Many were still inventing and starting businesses. They were full of the curiosity and entrepreneurial excitement that had made them good Mattel material in their youth.

Management employees were always on the hot seat. Ruth was always asking opinions and challenging assumptions. She liked to work off hard data using scientific tools. She created measurement instruments that became the standard in the industry. According to Joe Whittaker, Mattel invented "an entire language for the industry, which soon learned of A prices and EBDs and Magics and W reports and TLPs. It was not merely the gospel, it was practically the alphabet according to St. Mattel."

The Toy Line Projection (TLP) listed every product with its stock-keeping unit number, or SKU, and information on sales revenue, product experience, gross margins, tooling, and advertising. "Ruth was the master of the TLP," Tom Kalinske said. As Mattel executives moved on to other companies, the TLP concept moved with them.

Ruth also worked with her top executives to create the W report, or weekly sales and shipping report, a demand-and-supply document that was two to three inches thick, written by hand, and copied on old-style copy machines. The W report listed every product, with its detailed production and sales history. Ruth would flip through it with her thumb and say, "That's not right," catching errors that were sometimes as small as pennies on the dollar. "She had an unerring ability to find *one* mistake in this document. She had a sixth sense to zero in on the mistake. If one number was suspect, what about the others? She would find minor but critical mistakes. Her mind worked by finding the flaw in the plan," Joe Whittaker remembered. "She'd go to Palm Springs," said Fred Held, who helped create the report, "and mark the W report up with her lipstick, then the first person she saw when she got back really got it if she found a mistake. She would ask questions the executives couldn't answer. She really understood the numbers." Boyd Browne said, "If there was a phony number, she'd catch it." Her facility with numbers made it ironic when, years later, after Ruth had left the company, a talking Barbie was programmed to say, "Math class is tough."

To be *successful*, Mattel had to come up with fresh designs every year. Developing and producing each new design usually took three years. Production schedules were tight, because products needed to be out in time for seasonal buying. Most products were on a one-year production cycle, which meant that it was crucial to get the initial pricing right. Ruth instituted strict product planning and controls, and stayed in close touch with managers as the product moved toward distribution. "I was good at controlling how many of a product was made against what the product would generate in sales," she said. And she had a genius for taking her experience from one product and applying it to the next.

"We're a company that's just man killers," Ruth said to Frank Sesto early in the 1960s as she discussed the stock options she was giving him. "This is something you've earned," she told him. "I hope you make money on it." Her hopes were being more than realized. The *Los Angeles Times*'s headlines from the early 1960s tell the story. In December 1960: "Toymaking Business Booms in Southland, Sales Now Holding Up Year-round." In August 1961: "Toy Company Plans $900,000 Addition, Second Major Expansion Since Moving to Hawthorne 18 Months Ago." February 1962: "Mattel Hikes Dividend Rate." October 1962: "Mattel Named Outstanding Growth Company in Nation."

In 1962 Ruth's advertising budget was $5.7 million dollars. Sixty million toys would carry the little crank music box that had gone into the jack-in-the-box a decade earlier. Business was so strong that a second stock offering was planned for April. Ruth and Elliot decided to go to New York for the event, and Harry and Doris Paul, now wealthy partners, came along.

The two couples were at the Waldorf-Astoria hotel when they received a call from their brokers, who wanted to see them right away. They were told that there was no way the offering could take place. The stock market had dropped precipitously and was expected to keep going down in a Wall Street catastrophe later dubbed Blue Monday. "You wouldn't want what you could get for your stock," they were told.

The four had been having a great time in New York and were full of anticipation about the big event. Their previously high spirits made the cancellation of the offering even more disappointing. They walked down the street from the Waldorf to a restaurant for dinner, but no one had much to say. Harry had bought Doris an expensive wristwatch that day, and she asked if she would have to give it back.

As they were walking back to the hotel, a homeless man came up to Elliot and asked for a quarter. Elliot, normally so kind and gentle, told the man to go away, saying, "I've got troubles of my own." When they heard his response, Ruth, Harry, and Doris broke out laughing. "We rolled all over the sidewalk," Ruth remembered. "We knew we had lost all perspective."

Ruth and Elliot did not have to worry. By 1964 their total personal assets were worth more than forty million dollars, with thirty-seven million in stock. They had made generous stock transfers between 1962 and 1967 to relatives, the City of Hope, the United Jewish Welfare Fund, Temple Isaiah, UCLA, and other charities.

Ruth considered public service a way of life. "That was our training, our background," she said, "the Jewish ethic." When the war in Israel began in 1967, Ruth was president of Mattel, but despite her overwhelming schedule she called the head of the local United Jewish Appeal, to which she had been a generous donor, and asked what she could do to help. He invited her to come down to their offices on Vermont Street as soon as possible. When Ruth got there he told her that the telephones were ringing incessantly, and they were overwhelmed with questions and offers of aid. He asked Ruth if she could take over the telephone operations and manage the requests. "Do something," he said, "so we can get it off our backs and function." He arranged a place for Ruth to work and she plunged into the job. "It was major, but I was accustomed to doing things like that," she said. She set standards for what donations would be accepted, set up a team to answer and screen calls, and within a few days was able to leave a well-functioning operation in someone else's hands. "That's what I call public service. I felt very good about it," she said.

In August 1963, Elliot opened trading on the floor of the New York Stock Exchange. Mattel was being listed on both the New York and Pacific Coast exchanges, and as part of the ceremony Elliot bought the first hundred shares at $48.50 each. Three years earlier, at the initial offering, shares had sold for $10 each. "We just sat there," Ruth told a reporter, laughing, "and we couldn't believe that anyone would pay that much for our stock."

All around, life was good. That same year Barbara gave birth to their first grandchild, Cheryl Segal. Ken, like his sister, had also married shortly after leaving high school the previous year. In retrospect, Ken's out-of-character rush toward convention may have masked the raging conflict that would mark the tragedy of his life. At the time, however, Ruth's children seemed settled and happy. She was free to build on her success.

At one lunch Ruth and Eliot were having with their brokers in late 1963, the group kept getting interrupted. A young runner repeatedly rushed into the dining room to whisper to a broker.

Finally Ruth asked what was going on. Mattel stock was on the rise. The Handlers' shares had gone up twenty million dollars while they were sitting there. At the time, Elliot earned a salary of $67,500 and Ruth $52,000. They controlled 54.5 percent of Mattel's stock, then worth about forty-four million dollars.

Success had grown alongside the Barbie franchise. The 1960s saw a series of milestones for the doll, all carefully considered in terms of play value and protecting the brand.

Barbie was joined by a growing group of friends. First came her boyfriend, Ken; then Barbie's friend Midge and Ken's friend Allan, then Barbie's little sister, Skipper; soon followed by Barbie's sister and brother, the twins Tutti and Todd. Francie, Barbie's cousin, was introduced as an adult doll with a slimmer and less shapely and voluptuous body. Francie's smaller size had brought about a debate inside Mattel. She required different-size clothes, meaning the creation of a whole new wardrobe line. All the other female friends of Barbie could wear Barbie's clothes. Ruth worried that stores would not stock enough clothes for Francie or display them as well as they did the Barbie line. She also worried that consumers might have a negative reaction when they discovered that Francie could not wear Barbie's clothes. The difficult decision to bring out Francie, however, did pay off and showed Mattel that there were new ways to expand on the Barbie franchise. This held true in design as well. Jack Ryan invented and patented bendable legs, which appeared on Barbie in 1965, and swivel hips for Barbie. Bendable arms, however, could not be successfully engineered.

Ruth felt that Barbie should not have a specific personality. "Barbie should be used for every little girl's personality," she said, "and through Barbie each little girl could project her own personality." She said Mattel was not trying to make a beautiful doll, because she believed that would limit its play appeal. As new Barbies were developed, however, Ruth's concern was increasingly ignored. Barbie grew more model-beautiful with age.

Ruth and Elliot's life seemed to grow more beautiful as well. On paper, since most of their stock could not be sold, they were wildly rich. In 1965 they moved into a double-size penthouse apartment that they designed in the new Century Towers East in Century City. The next year Elliot bought his first Silver Shadow Rolls-Royce. From the balcony of their penthouse, Ruth and Elliot looked down at the sprawling city of Los Angeles and the Hollywood Hills beyond. Ruth could imagine that in every house where there was a child, there was also a toy from Mattel.

Chapter 11

Toys, Money, and Power

*Once we got the taste of growth, we felt we
could do no wrong.*

At Mattel, Elliot was still coming up with new ideas, but he had a top-notch research and design team of nearly two hundred people to work on them. They had expertise not only in engineering, but in chemistry, sculpture, music, and fine arts. With a $1.5 million budget that kept growing, they jumped on every challenge. Part of their industry could be attributed to Ruth's hiring process, but the unusual personality at the head of research and design also set the tone.

Jack Ryan had not been an easy catch for Mattel. He graduated from Yale with a degree in electrical engineering, and the Handlers met him when he was thirty years old. Ryan had a randy, eccentric, and flamboyant side that found full expression after he pushed for a royalty-based deal with Mattel that made him a millionaire in short order. Ryan was schooled to work on the complexities of telecommunications systems, power stations, and missiles. Elliot and Ruth convinced him to apply his knowledge of math and physics to toys. While his counterparts were inventing the integrated circuit, Ryan was engineering Barbie's appendages.

Ryan's personal indiscretions were legion and well-known. He held parties at his five-acre Tudor estate in Bel-Air, which he had had raised off the ground in order to dig a moat and put in a draw-bridge. He carried the castle motif into his bedroom, which he decorated from a King Arthur movie set. The toilet was a throne with a pull cord for flushing. He liked to show off his tree house, complete with crystal chandelier; his mansion's thirteen bath-rooms; and the grottos, pool, waterfalls, and lagoons that graced the property. At least one employee thought that when guests came over, Ryan hid his ex-wife in a black-painted dungeonlike room with shackles on the wall, but she actually lived in a sepa-rate wing of the house. He did not try to hide his coterie of mis-tresses and UCLA student assistants or his proclivity for all kinds of debauchery.

Ryan was on the short side—one employee called him "gnome-like"—but he had piercing, squinty eyes. Possessed of an outsize ego, he had a fanatical need both to be in charge of everything and to take all the credit. Ryan also had a mean streak. One employee referred to the R & D department as a "sadistic" place, where Ryan never missed an opportunity to belittle an underling. His brother, whom he hired, often took the brunt of his brutishness. Ryan would order him to get coffee or harangue him in front of others in the department.

Marvin Barab, who worked under Ryan, endured numer-ous humiliations, the most memorable being at a party at Ryan's palatial house. "I was there with my wife, wearing a business suit. Ryan said, 'Jump in the pool and race me.' I said, 'You've got to be kidding,' and Ryan shot back, 'I'm not kidding at all. Get in.' I handed my wife my wallet and jumped in. He was wearing a bath-ing suit, and he won, of course." Barab quit the day after another humiliating episode with Ryan, and although he had a good relationship with Ruth and Elliot, neither tried to stop him.

Elliot and Ruth were willing to overlook Ryan's excesses, and they generally acceded to their top staff in personnel matters. As long as Ryan did not embarrass the company, they did not seem to care what he did, even when he was an irritant. He precipitated a fierce rivalry with Seymour Adler, the head of production and engineering, that had the two men vying for Ruth and Elliot's approval. Occasionally, Ruth would decide that Ryan's department was underperforming, and she would lash out at his behavior.

Ryan liked to hire attractive women as office assistants and secretaries. One day Ruth attacked him, saying, "If you'd put more attention to your job than hiring pussy women to decorate the department, we might get something done." Ryan shot back, "Well, I'll worry about my department if you just worry about marketing." Elliot, who heard the exchange, jumped out of his chair. "That's no way to talk to her," he admonished Ryan. But Ruth hardly needed a defender. Most employees were in awe of her. "I never saw her do it, but I heard she threw things and yelled," remembered Fred Held. "She'd ask a question and lean in to someone and stare in their eyes. I was her darling and could do no wrong, but that was not true of everyone." Ryan was one of the few who stood up to her, protected by his talent and Elliot's approval of his work.

Even the lack of an ethical compass did not sink Ryan. Barab remembered going into the toy archives shortly after he transferred to Ryan's department. He stumbled on a box with a doll in it that looked like Barbie. Scanning the notes, he saw that it was a German doll that predated Mattel's creation. At that time, Barbie's connection to Bild-Lilli was being officially denied because of a dispute with Greiner & Hausser (G & H), the successor to O & M Hausser, the German company that created Lilli.

In 1960 G & H filed a U.S. patent for the "doll hip joint" used in Lilli. They then licensed the rights exclusively to Louis Marx's company for ten years. In 1961 Marx sued Mattel in the U.S. District Court for the Southern District of California, claiming that Mattel had infringed the hip joint copyright by using it for Barbie. Claims and counterclaims flew back and forth as Mattel denied that Barbie was a direct knockoff of Lilli.

It was around this time that Barab found the Lilli box. "I showed the doll to Jack Ryan," said Barab, "and I said, 'This looks like Barbie.' He said, 'So?'" Ruth had given the Lilli doll to Ryan to take to Japan years earlier. Then Ryan spoke as if reciting a nursery rhyme, "'Plagiarize, plagiarize. That's why God made your eyes. Now, put it back.'" Ryan's words never made it into the court case. The suit was dismissed on all sides. The next year Mattel purchased G & H's Bild-Lilli copyright and its German and U.S. patent rights for three lump-sum payments worth approximately $21,600. In exchange for an additional payment of $3,800, the agreements also provided that upon the expiration of Marx's license in 1970, its marketing territories would transfer to Mattel. By the early 1980s, as Barbie continued to bring in millions of dollars for Mattel, both G & H and Marx went bankrupt.

In 1962 Ryan was juggling seventeen new engineering concepts that could be applied to a variety of toys. He worked behind the locked and restricted confines of his R & D department, where a special key card was needed for entry. Elliot had pioneered the idea of incubating new toy ideas rather than waiting for inventors to show up at Mattel's door.

At the uniformed guard's desk a sign read, "You must be signed in at the R & D turnstile and escorted by an R & D employee for entrance into the model shop with a striped badge." Inside, Ryan had a supersecret section for preliminary design, which only Elliot and two other top executives could enter. Every paper, no matter how slight the marking, was sent to the company's in-house Document Disintegration Service for shredding when it was no longer needed.

Inside R & D, staff competed to come up with the next big idea. Employees loved the pace and excitement in the creative space, but joy and resentment sometimes made a volatile mix. One Christmas, Ryan gave out rock-hard frozen turkeys. After a few rounds of spiked eggnog, employees started whacking one another with the birds in a zany but painful free-for-all. "Next Christmas," said one of the engineers, "we got chits good for a turkey at the supermarket. It was safer that way, for them and us."

Despite his strange ways, Ryan was an in-house genius, exactly what Elliot had in mind when he created the department. "I remember going to Jack about making a knitting machine for girls," Tom Kalinske, then a production manager, said. "He drew very fast, and it took him about thirty seconds to invent Knit Magic and Sew Magic." Another young manager, Fred Held, remembered Ryan as "the pied piper of inventors who got the most out of his team. They did not care if he took the credit." The *New York Times* called him "Mattel's real secret weapon."

Derek Gable worked for Ryan in preliminary design and remembered the toy business as "fascinating, fast-moving, and intriguing. There was such a thirst for innovation, and thousands of new ideas every year. Ruth and Elliot let people make mistakes. It was so much fun." Creativity was part of the fun, as were stock options, profit sharing, retirement contributions, and Ruth's willingness to move and promote people based on their interest and talent. She called the team she put together in the 1960s her "young tigers," and the ever-growing company gave them room to roam and experiment. Brilliant eccentrics like Ryan added to the charged atmosphere. And since toys were at the center of everything, the tigers, and often everyone else, got to play.

Gable had an idea one day about drag racing, an increasingly popular pastime. He devised a toy car with a string attached so that it could be turned into a drag racer. Another designer had the same idea, but he used a flywheel. Elliot said, "Let's have a race." Later that week all the departments assembled to cheer on their favorites.

Ryan pushed for such competitions. Children and the R & D staff were also invited to play with new toys, under strict vows of secrecy. Their feedback was carefully noted. When groups of five- to six-year-olds were testing Baby First Step, an eighteen-inch mechanical doll that walked and danced in place, the doll's panties kept falling down. "I wonder why they don't sew them to the dress," one little girl said to her friend. Her recommendation became reality. "Our best toys are the ones the engineers can't leave alone," Ryan told a reporter. In 1962 he bragged to *Time* magazine, "We're right out on the frontier of technology." He was also quick to polish his reputation with the press. Ryan would eventually claim credit for inventing Barbie, much to Ruth's annoyance.

But Ryan had more than the success of Barbie to hang his laurels on. In 1960 Mattel had introduced another unique smash hit, the Chatty Cathy talking doll. Elliot had again conceived the idea for a revolutionary sound mechanism. He tasked the engineering staff to come up with a device that did not require batteries or winding up. He wanted to add to the play value by keeping the doll's speech unpredictable, and he suggested they think about a pull-string. The resulting doll was twenty inches tall, a round-faced toddler with a three-inch vinyl turntable-type record in her stomach operated by a pull-string at the back of her neck. She could say eleven phrases, spoken by voice actress June Foray, which rotated randomly from "Tell me a story," to "Will you play with me?" to "I love you." She came with a storybook and sold for ten dollars, a relatively low price at the time. Like Barbie, Cathy had outfits that could be bought separately, and like the Uke-A-Doodle, Cathy's pull-string voice mechanism was used for other hugely successful Mattel toys, including the educational See 'n Say preschool toys.

One of Ruth's core business principles was insistence on superior quality control. "She was relentless in terms of product quality," Frank Sesto said. "She understood that she had to go to quality control people directly to find out the truth. She would find me on the floor and say, 'Take me to the line and show me what's going on.'" With Chatty Cathy, Sesto had to deliver bad news. Even though the doll was successful, he had found a quality problem that would require shutting down the line for a month. Hundreds of thousands of dollars would be lost. Ruth did not hesitate. She would not ship a product that did not meet company standards.

Cedric Iwasaki, an engineer in the quality control department, recalled one incident. He had worked on the standards for Barbie's legs to ensure that parts with impurities or water marks were rejected. He was overseeing the quality control inspectors as they watched the rotocasting of Barbie's legs. Plastisol had to be injected into molds, and the legs were popped out at the end of the process. Ruth came along the line, surprising Iwasaki, who had yet to meet the big boss. She began thumbing through a box of legs, and then said, "Uh-uh, these aren't good enough. Shut down the line." Iwasaki rushed over. He knew that the gospel of production was to avoid shutting down the line at all cost. "What's wrong?" he asked. "Look at these dirt marks," Ruth replied. Iwasaki protested that the legs met the specifications. "Well then, change the specifications," she replied.

Quality control extended beyond the shop floor. Ruth told a reporter, "We spend a fortune on quality control and every toy is guaranteed. Our rate of return on defective goods is less than one-half of one percent. We repair and return anything turned into us." Toys had to pass a thirty-inch drop test on concrete, with each toy dropped six to ten times from different angles. They were put into a "torture chamber" for forty-eight hours that simulated the motion and temperature of a freight train.

The introduction of Ken came after thousands of letters entreating Mattel to give Barbie a boyfriend. The first Ken dolls, named for Ruth's son, hit stores in 1961, again facing naysaying buyers, who did not believe boy dolls would sell. But Ruth remembered that Barbara had played with paper girl *and* boy dolls. Maybe the success of Barbie could overcome the history of poor sales for boy dolls. First another anatomical minefield would have to be crossed.

Ruth felt the design team lacked "the guts" to give the Ken doll even the suggestion of male sex organs. She saw herself as ahead of her time, arguing that there should at least be a bulge that would suggest realism. Charlotte Johnson, Barbie's clothing designer, agreed with Ruth. Despite ordering prototypes with varying degrees of bulge in the crotch, the male designers resisted all but the barest hint of a penis. Underwear was painted on the nearly flat surface of Ken's genital area and buttocks. As Ruth predicted, he looked unrealistic in the zebra-stripe bathing suit that was his first piece of clothing. Ruth's son, Ken, who was fifteen at the time, resented the flat-crotched doll that bore his name. Ruth did not blame him, knowing that it embarrassed him.

What Ruth did not know was that Ken felt something deeper than self-consciousness. He felt shame and anger. Deep conflicts about his sexuality, which would come to light later in his life, no doubt fueled his reaction.

For the research and design department, however, the main issue about Ken's anatomy had nothing to do with emotions. They just thought about whether his physique would help or hurt the company. On that point, Ruth was willing to acquiesce. "They decided it was better for Mattel if he was neutered, and that was the end of it," remembered Marvin Barab.

As the Barbie line expanded, first with Ken, then with relatives and friends, like Midge and Skipper, sales went into the stratosphere. The *Wall Street Journal* called Barbie a "cult" and "something approaching an industry." Ruth called the phenomenon "the Barbie complex." Licensees and subsidiaries of Mattel had been contracted around the world to make clothes and accessories for the Barbie line, to publish a fan magazine, and to make child-size clothes with the Barbie brand. Ruth built the brand through more and more aggressive television advertising, raising her budget by a million dollars a year in the early 1960s. She knew her money was well spent. Ninety-three percent of girls aged five to twelve recognized the Barbie name. None of her competitors could boast that level of brand recognition. The results showed. Mattel's revenues were $26 million in 1963, cementing its place as the largest toy company in the world. Two years later its revenues had soared to more than $100 million and three years later, to $180 million.

Ruth felt confident that she had earned her place and her salary. She said, "Anyone can manage the upside cycle of hit toys. The secret is managing a product down its life cycle properly." She made product sales forecasting and inventory control Mattel's top priority. She proved that a company with one to two hundred unique products each year could still be managed just as professionally as one where the brand's entire yearly responsibility was a new deluxe size of detergent. Her "retail detail" people went into stores, arranging company displays, checking in with buyers, and seeing how Mattel toys were selling. She built and guarded the resources given to R & D, even in lean years, and recognized the importance of thinking internationally both in manufacturing and in sales. Mattel aggressively diversified operations around the world. They acquired Dee & Cee Toy Company in Canada in 1962 and, later, the Hong Kong Industrial Company.

Mattel's extraordinary success through the sixties gave employees and shareholders spectacular returns on their shares of company stock. There were occasional setbacks, however, and calamities. A labor strike slowed sales for the first quarter of 1964. The opening of new factories in Los Angeles, Canada, and New Jersey, and a new headquarters in Hawthorne also drained revenue that year. The New Jersey factory was a bad idea, with communications problems dooming the bicoastal experiment in production. It had to be shut and sold two years later. Earnings were disappointing, and when handlebars on the new V-RROOM! bicycles began collapsing, so did the stock price, dropping three dollars in 1965. As Ruth predicted, the stock price bounced back the next year. Still, some analysts grumbled that Ruth and Elliot were not up to the task of running such a large company. Shareholders, though, were happy. Mattel joined the Fortune 500 in 1965, and Ruth's business life continued to seem charmed. She said she was getting her "kicks" from her growing power. "You don't need things that people turn to like drugs and soul-searching," she said. "All that stuff is for people who are not having the kind of trips I was having. I was having power trips that were headier than any conceivable artificial stimulant could be."

As Toy Fair was set to start in 1968, the *Wall Street Journal* predicted another year of bright prospects for the toy industry. There were "more kids, a flock of new products, greater affluence, improved marketing techniques and a somewhat tighter rein on expenses." Ruth had assumed the title of president from Elliot the year before, and he became chairman and chief executive officer.

As the *Journal* suggested, Ruth assured investors that despite advertising expenditures growing from $11.5 million to $12.7 million, "our budget is only slightly more than increased costs." She was relying more heavily than ever on the idea of driving demand through a hard sell of the Mattel brand. Ever since the first *Mickey Mouse Club* commercials sent the Burp Gun into stratospheric sales, Ruth had been building advertising and sales promotion. She loved that side of the business, and had always been the one who did the talking for Mattel and oversaw the advertising budget. In 1968 a record fourteen million dollars had been budgeted for television program sponsorships, newspaper and comic book ads, and large magazine ads in *Life, Good Housekeeping, Parents*, and *Jack and Jill*, which would reach one hundred million people. "We expect the effect of the combined activities to create an unprecedented demand for Mattel products," Jack Jones, the vice president for advertising, told the *New York Times*. His comment was not exaggerated. "No matter what we touched," Ruth said, "it turned to gold."

Ruth also announced an innovative marketing program. A new Barbie, flexible at the waist and knees, had been engineered by Ryan. Girls who had older models of Barbie dolls could trade them in for the new model for $1.50. As with every Barbie initiative, the demand far outstripped expectations. Girls swarmed stores, wanting to swap their old dolls for the new one, which had a hot pink two-piece bathing suit with a white plastic flower on the bottom. It was another banner year for Mattel and for Ruth. When the *Los Angeles Times* announced its annual awards, Ruth was named as one of its twelve Women of the Year.

As Ruth and Elliot looked forward to the 1970s, Mattel's trajectory seemed unstoppable. A 1967 Shearson, Hammill & Company research memo predicted that by 1970 sales would be $175 million. The Handlers were still in their early fifties. Their children were grown and out of the house. Ruth no longer had to worry about how her success might be affecting them.

Nothing had diminished Ruth's competitive drive or Elliot's creative desire. "It was more important for us to be successful than rich," Elliot remembered. "We enjoyed the fact that people liked the toys. We wanted to be successful in the marketplace, to be accepted. We did not want to get stagnant. We wanted to grow."

Joe Whittaker, who had cut his teeth on the G.I. Joe competition, recalled, "In the 1960s we could do no wrong. Perhaps that led to being willing to take more chances. Because Mattel was so successful, Ruth and Elliot felt comfortable to take chances. I think they *needed* to take chances . . . to carry out their dreams, to wrench an entire field of endeavor into the modern era." A toy buyer for a large Chicago-based department store chain summed up the thinking of the industry at the end of the 1960s: "Mattel is energetic, deep-thinking, and far and away above the field in product development. I simply can't see its downfall."

Chapter 12

Hot Wheels and Hot Deals

The world of the young is the world of Mattel.

Early in 1968 a large ballroom in a New York City hotel was out-fitted with a stage and theater lighting, ready for the performers' arrival. Mattel's marketing department would put on a private show for toy dealers and wholesalers, for jobbers and retailers, then repeat the presentation at Toy Fair, which would open a few days later. Fifty percent of sales for toy companies came from toys that did not exist the year before, and every company faced the challenge of creating a pitch to make its toys stand out.

Mattel's shows were legendary. Certain members of the market-ing and sales departments became star performers. The ad agency Carson/Roberts helped write scripts and song lyrics. Professional lighting and costumes were designed. The highest-quality sound equipment was used. Production values rivaled Broadway theater. A young, ambitious professional, like Lou Miraula, could make his career on the Mattel stage or end it.

Miraula remembered his first stage show trip. He carried the sample bags, following Ruth, Elliot, and his boss, Cliff Jacobs, traveling first class to New York. "I was overwhelmed by this," he said. A big suite at the Tuscany Hotel had been reserved for a private show for Mattel's big national clients: Sears, Kresge, J. C. Penney, and W. T. Grant stores. Miraula had his first turn onstage, showing off the 1960 version of Barbie with her new wardrobe. "I parroted what I'd seen Cliff do. He was very entertaining. Ruth was in the room, and this presentation launched me. I was funny and got the buyers excited enough to say yes." Miraula was also the kind of young man Ruth adored, the handsome ones she called "her boys." Miraula was slim and dark, with chiseled good looks. Throughout the 1960s his star rose.

In 1968 he stood onstage before two hundred sales representatives. Dressed in a black turtleneck and black pants, he stayed as still as a mannequin as a spotlight came up in the darkened ballroom to illuminate the doll he held out in front of him in a moment of dramatic pause. Then the strains of the *Nutcracker Suite* began, and Miraula began to show what Dancerina, Mattel's new twenty-four-inch, battery-operated dancing doll could do.

The doll had blond hair, topped by a pink tiara that hid a knob to balance the doll and to push or pull, depending on what moves a child wanted her to make. She wore a matching tutu and tights. Her toes were permanently pointed, and she could turn in either direction and dance in place. With a showman's flair, Miraula demonstrated her charm. Boyd Browne, who acknowledged that Miraula was the master at these presentations, said, "You would never, ever, ever sit a doll down. You would talk to a doll and rub her head, pull her skirt down, kiss it on the cheek, and try to bring it to life. No other toy company was doing it like we were. They would bring a doll out by the neck and just sit it down." Ruth would have none of that.

When Miraula and Dancerina finished, the lights came up and the crowd gave him a standing ovation. Ruth rushed onto the stage and threw her arms around him. She loved the flamboyance of these shows and the effect they had on buyers. Every toy had a story ready for the stage. The Cowboy Ge-tar was the impetus for a show about the Wild West with hardworking cowboys sitting around a campfire and singing, accompanying themselves on their guitars. Ruth emphasized "romancing" every toy, even early ones like the jack-in-the-box. Mattel shows drove the orders that kept warehouse inventory from piling up. Ruth knew that toy companies with too much inventory went out of business.

By the end of the 1960s, Ruth was pushing her team harder than ever. She loved being the leader, much as she claimed to defer to Elliot. She took most responsibility for hiring management staff. She participated in meetings across departments, pushing, inquiring, goading, and motivating. Employees who loved her got tears in their eyes talking about her decades later. Those who hated her sputtered to find the worst invectives to describe her behavior. But no one was neutral about Ruth, and she was hardest on herself. "My standards are my toughest problems because for me they're higher than for anyone else. But I burn people out by my high standards. Monday morning the most incompetent [employees] of the moment will be gone."

Those who made it at Mattel thrived on the pressure. "The business was fast, exciting, romantic," remembered Rita Rao, who worked in market research. "They were wonderful days for all of us. There was lots of travel, and people were young, hormones were raging. There were lots of love affairs, which Ruth found amusing. She loved the gossip." Perhaps Ruth lived vicariously. All evidence points to her and Elliot being faithful and in love, but she was bawdy and outrageous enough to revel in other people's tangled sex lives. She also loved her coterie of male followers. "Ruth was just gorgeous. She'd come by with a group of handsome men all under forty, and they were just following her and jockeying to get close to her, and she'd be walking in front, leading them. She was big-breasted but tiny otherwise, and she always looked tip-top," remembered Pat Schauer. "She could be mothering to them, too, straightening their ties or picking a piece of lint off their shirt. But she ran the show." By the end of the sixties, running the show at Mattel was like riding a rocket. It had taken twenty years to get to one hundred million dollars in gross sales. It took just three more years, until 1969, to reach two hundred million.

Barbie accounted for a huge part of the company's success. In nine years the doll had brought in retail sales of more than half a billion dollars, which included sales of 103 million complete costume sets. Barbie now had a number of relatives and friends, including Christie, the "lustrous ingénue," as Mattel described the African American doll. Barbie had, among her innumerable accessories, a house with a 3-D fireplace and a bedroom fit for a doll focused on fashion.

It took a small army to turn out Barbie products. In Japan, ten thousand workers were employed to maintain inventory for Mattel's World of Barbie, with its thirteen million fans. Elliot described the Barbie phenomenon as if it were an addiction. "You get hooked on one and you have to buy the other. Buy the doll and then you buy the clothes. I know a lot of parents hate us for this, but it's going to be around a long time," he told the *New York Times* in 1968.

Ruth still roundly rejected criticism of Barbie as encouraging a sexist view of women or as harmful to young girls' view of themselves. Barbie, Ruth told a reporter, "is a very educational product: the children learn color coordination, fashion design, good grooming, hair styling, good manners, and people relationships—they interrelate through social situations." Ruth seemed to embody the lessons she described. "I had a nice figure," she said.

"I was well built, and I was proud of my breasts. I was proud of how I looked. I wore designer clothes, and they fit me tight and showed my body." Her wardrobe was stylish and in fashion, and her hair, makeup, and nails were as perfect as Barbie's. Unlike Ruth, of course, the new talking Barbie did not spout four-letter words or have an imperious side, and none of the doll's many pursuits included running the biggest toy company in the world.

Ruth's young executives had enormous responsibilities, often outside the expertise that had gotten them hired. "She did not care about past experience," Marvin Barab recalled. "She just put you where you'd be best. Management and foresight were what counted for her more than technical background, but she never hesitated to fire people who weren't making it." Sometimes Ruth's tactics were oblique. Stan Taylor was an advertising manager she wanted out. One day he came to work to find that an advertising director had been named. "I don't need any f-ing director over me," he protested. Shortly thereafter, Taylor went on vacation. He did not come back.

As Mattel grew, Ruth felt a responsibility to keep it growing, worried that her young tigers would leave if growth seemed to stall. "We had to believe that the business had to grow or we would die. We did not know how to slow down. Maybe we knew how but were unwilling to slow down." The costs of research, development, and tooling, however, were increasing. Layers of middle management had added large year-round personnel costs, just as the company's biggest moneymaker, Barbie, seemed to be waning in popularity. Ruth and Elliot agreed that toys would probably top out at about two hundred million dollars. The only way to keep growing was to diversify. It was a crucial decision that pulled the Handlers away from their core mission and the source of their success. Years later Ruth would say, "The thing that made Mattel great and permitted it to flourish as it did was its product, and I always trace Mattel through its product lines." But to keep the young tigers from growling, Ruth spun away from her company's center of gravity.

As Ruth began to focus on diversifying, Elliot kept his focus where he had received the most reward, on toys. "When you see your displays used in toy fairs all over the world and thousands of people producing for you, it's a little overwhelming," he told a reporter. He was still bursting with ideas, his imaginative genius undiminished, and Ruth never lost her zeal for selling what Elliot designed. Their love story had not changed either.

Elliot respected Ruth's natural business gifts, leaving her to her own devices, knowing she would respect his opinion if he felt he had to weigh in. "They were lovely together," Derek Gable remembered, and they did not need much beyond each other. They had few friends and did little socializing. "We are very simple people living a very simple personal life," Ruth said in interviews. "Our travel and entertaining is related to business; we're just not swingers. . . . A really good leader probably can't be a really good social mixer. Our favorite guests are our children and grandchildren." Ruth and Elliot had each other, their large Mosko and Handler clans, and Mattel, which was still a favored child. "They work too damn hard," a colleague told the *New York Times* in 1968, "and they put business before everything else. They have well over $50 million in stock, yet they don't seem to know how to enjoy it— they still worry over every penny."

Ruth drove to work in her El Dorado Cadillac and Elliot in his Rolls-Royce, but they still ate in the company dining room when they could, enjoying the kosher deli food and exchanging jokes. Ruth's intensity had not faded, and Elliot was still laconic, with a wry sense of humor. Asked by a reporter about a doll that recited fifteen full-length nursery rhymes and an equal number of long conversations, he said, "It recites when you punch her or kick her in the kidney, but then we found through voice-testing, the kids would kick her in the head if she went on for the full seven minutes she was designed for."

In 1967 Elliot had asked Jack Ryan to make improvements to a miniature two-inch-long die-cast car called Matchbox, which was made by Lesney Products, a British company. By that time, Ryan had amassed nearly one thousand patents in his name, including the joint movements for Barbie and sophisticated devices for talking toys. He was no longer on the Mattel payroll, but earned a half-million dollars a year on his royalties. With the toy gun market dying down, Mattel needed its next hit and Ryan was holding it.

Elliot and Ryan shared a love of cars. Ryan kept several customized Mercedes in his garage. Elliot had set Ryan to his task after noticing that his grandson Todd was playing with a non-Mattel toy car. Elliot and Ruth had given their children only toys from the company, but Todd, just three years old, loved the Matchbox cars. He'd say, "Papa car!" when Elliot walked into the room, and push the little toy around. That was all the incentive Elliot needed. Bringing one of the cars to the office, he said to Ryan, "Look at this. It's crazy. The wheels are molded right on the car. I want them to spin. See what you can do."

Three hours later Ryan stood in front of Elliot and put the retrofitted car on his desk. Elliot cleared a path across the desktop and watched expectantly as Ryan gave the car a hard push. It zipped across the surface as if a tiny accelerator had been pressed to the floor. "My God, those are hot wheels," Elliot said. He still spoke of the moment with childlike glee four decades later.

As the new little cars moved through the planning process, there was resistance. The marketing department was concerned that Hot Wheels were overpriced compared to Matchbox. Elliot thought they were wrong, insisting that sales would materialize despite the price. Even Ruth had her doubts, but she would not stand in Elliot's way. Then marketing refused to generate a sales forecast large enough to justify making the car. Josh Denham recalled Elliot's response: "Just raise the quota anyway." In a company built on razor-sharp forecasting, Elliot's command was out of the ordinary, but three million Hot Wheels went into production.

Two months later, the head of sales, Herb Holland, presented the toy to the J. C. Penney representative, one of Mattel's top accounts. As Elliot waited expectantly, the buyer said he liked it, without elaborating. "Well, how many will you buy?" Elliot pressed. "All three million and more if you have them," the J. C. Penney rep replied. According to Denham, Elliot cast a look at the marketing staff that let them know he thought they were idiots.

Sixteen customized cars scale-modeled with Mattel's usual level of detail were made to look like the hottest cars of the time, including Mercury Cougars, Pontiac Firebirds, and Volkswagens. Mattel promised that the cars would "out-race, out-stunt and out-distance," their die-cast competitors. To add to the play value, an elevated orange plastic track was designed, along with accessories like flags and a starting gate, so that cars could be raced using the power of gravity. "The secret of their speed," said an engineer, "is that we make the bearing diameters as small as possible—20/1,000ths of an inch." The little cars flew down their tracks and flew even faster off store shelves. Hot Wheels were captivating and another example of Mattel entering a market with a toy that was better engineered, designed, and marketed than the competition. Hot Wheels generated twenty-five million dollars for Mattel in the first year. The cars would generate eighty-eight million dollars in their best year. That first season, other buyers, like J. C. Penney, were afraid they would not have enough inventory, so they overordered. At the time, Hot Wheels looked like another dream toy for Mattel.

Worried over both the pace of growth and sustaining it, Ruth and Elliot agreed on a crucial new hire in September 1967. Ruth recognized that she lacked the formal training in finance that a company as large as Mattel required. Her skill for forecasting did not translate into accounting acumen. She also knew that Mattel had to keep its stock price high to afford to buy new companies. Bob Mitchell, Ruth's personnel manager, suggested a man at Litton Industries, the huge electronics company, who seemed perfect for the job.

Seymour Rosenberg was a LIDO, a Litton Industries dropout, as former executives of the company were called. Litton had recently experienced an unusually high turnover of top people. Rosenberg was part of a group of four who left in the fall of 1967. They took large stock options and a hunger for more challenge, opportunity, and independence than Litton offered. After Rosenberg arrived at Mattel, he told Josh Denham, "I was the brains behind the acquisition side of Litton, but I did not get the credit."

Litton was talked about on Wall Street as the "daddy of conglomerates," a company made rich through related but autonomous divisions and aggressive acquisitions. Divisions were meant to allow managers to be entrepreneurial. Central management was lean and focused on providing support services, and acting as counselor and critic. Litton grew into a $1.5 billion company with four large divisions and a continued focus on acquisition. Reasoning that diversifying through acquisitions was the only way to grow, Ruth and Elliot agreed on hiring Rosenberg, who presumably would bring with him what the *Wall Street Journal* called "Litton magic." They did not know that the magic was fading.

Rosenberg had left Litton at the right time. In the first quarter of 1968, the company would post its first decline in profits in fourteen years.

Rosenberg had a reputation as a financial genius who wrangled many of Litton's best-performing acquisitions, including Royal Typewriter. He was a confidant of Roy Ash, the company president. "Litton was the wonder company of Los Angeles," Ruth said. "Rosenberg was immediately regarded as a savior. He had all the financial and Wall Street experience." A brash, shrewd former patent attorney who had once worked for Howard Hughes, Rosenberg was so admired by Wall Street that Mattel's stock ticked up several points on news of his move.

A week or so after he arrived, Ruth went to Rosenberg's office to discuss some financial and accounting matters. She sat down and talked for about fifteen minutes, suggesting the people he should speak to about certain items. She did not know much about the personal side of this chubby elfin man with the Cheshire cat grin. She had heard that his wife was severely handicapped by polio. Word had also spread around the building that he liked flirting with the secretaries. "He used to crawl under our desks," said Pat Schauer, "and we all were just saying, 'I don't think so,' to his advances." As Ruth talked she noticed that Rosenberg was not taking notes. Suddenly he said to her, "Ruth, you won't do." Stunned, she said, "I beg your pardon, Seymour?" and he repeated, "You won't do. You're a woman, you're Jewish, and your style is all wrong. If you were to deal with the investment community you wouldn't create the right impression. To carry this company into the next stage of development you are simply the wrong person." Ruth remembered being "too stunned to respond." She got up and stumbled into her office, where she shut the door and cried. Elliot found her there, and she told him she wanted to fire Rosenberg, but he feared that such an abrupt move would hurt their stock price. Ruth agreed to let Rosenberg stay.

Ruth's story about the beginning of Rosenberg's tenure has hints of exaggeration, if not an entirely false note. To distance herself from the fraud charges that came later, she may have revised history to appear the helpless victim. In her autobiography, she concludes the story of her confrontation with Rosenberg by saying, "He *had* to stay and that conclusion flooded me with dismay . . . and a feeling of complete powerlessness. In one stroke, a man had gained power over me in my own company by putting me down. Thereafter I steered clear of him and left him to operate more or less on his own. As it turned out, I should have taken my chances and fired him." But her notes made after her criminal indictment for SEC fraud several years later seem closer to the truth. "We operated," she wrote, "with an armed truce."

If Ruth was powerless from 1967 forward, she could not be complicit in the fraud that took place. But up to that point, Ruth's reaction to male put-downs had been anything but tears and incapacity. Other than her private tears with Elliot over the initial reaction to Barbie at Toy Fair in 1959, neither she nor anyone who worked with her talks of Ruth being a person given to crying. Just the opposite. As her son, Ken, put it, "My mother was not very diplomatic always. She could be very tough."

Rosenberg also confronted Ruth near the height of her power. She had just taken the title of president, while giving Rosenberg and another executive the title she had abandoned: executive vice president. All evidence suggests she would have been more likely to fling a few expletives at Rosenberg and fire him on the spot or storm out than to stumble away.

Ruth had ammunition to fire back at Rosenberg. She had been the point person for the due diligence that took the company public. She had dealt successfully with the investment community for years on many levels. She was Jewish but so was Rosenberg, so why would that be a problem? And she reveled in having made it "her way," with her own style. Why would she collapse at the negative assessment of her style by a man she barely knew?

While it appears true that Ruth disliked Rosenberg, it seems an exaggeration that she was totally cowed by him or that she left him completely to his own devices. In other notes, Ruth wrote that she "gradually warmed up" to Rosenberg and that there was mutual respect. "He put me before financial people and told me what to say and seemed satisfied that I was doing well enough." There is no evidence that in the first years of Rosenberg's tenure she distanced herself from him, his ideas, or her role as president.

Rosenberg's influence at Mattel was obvious. After he came on board, Mattel began even more aggressive acquisitions and Ruth began to create divisions. Rosenberg had brought the Litton way, and it was taking hold.

In 1969 Ruth called a meeting of a six-member executive group and told them that she wanted to divisionalize the company. After several months of meetings a plan was developed that boiled Mattel operations down to four divisions. Each division ran like its own company, doing its own product planning, forecasting, marketing, and finances. Ruth now oversaw three toy divisions: Dolls, Wings and Wheels, and the catchall Toys. A fourth division, which Ruth had opposed, encompassed Standard Plastics, the New Jersey company that made Barbie carrying cases, and the general category of Games. Elliot insisted on this division, and he ran it with Art Spear. Ruth chose three of her most promising young tigers to head the other divisions, planning to go get the divisions operating in stages. "Divisions were meant to shift priorities so that everyone got a piece of the cake," Josh Denham, who became a division head, remembered. "This was going to be Ruth's thing."

As at Litton, there was a corporate umbrella of executives for finance, operations, and marketing, plus Ruth as president to service the divisions and provide oversight. The plan was supposed to phase in over three years. Ruth made it clear that initial plans for each division had to be run by her or one of the executive vice presidents, but there was resistance from the start. "Division managers were very possessive of the power I delegated to them," Ruth said. Infighting and jealousy infected the plan.

While the division plan had a shaky start, the company was still thriving. Hot Wheels was scorching the competition. The Wheels division head, Bernie Loomis, a large, effusive man bursting with marketing ideas, had pushed the bounds for the already popular toy.

In a company of hard chargers, Loomis stood out. "On a scale of one to ten in terms of aggressive marketing," remembered Josh Denham, "Bernie was an eighteen." He was also stubborn and argumentative. He argued with Ruth over product testing the first day he met her at Toy Fair in 1961. She hired him anyway, never shying away from people who challenged her, but as the company grew, so did the tensions between them. Like Ruth, Loomis was never satisfied. He pushed buyers relentlessly. He pushed Carson/Roberts to expand television advertising well beyond ads. Why not a whole show devoted to a toy? The Hot Wheels–themed television show was born in 1969 on ABC.

Mattel was testing the line the Federal Communications Commission had set regarding the amount of commercial matter in any given children's show. Another toy company complained about the idea of a show built around and named for a toy. Mattel was told to stop the program, but nothing could stop sales of Hot Wheels. The candy-colored toys became so popular that an entire plant was built to handle their production. If Hot Wheels had been its own company, it would have been the second largest toy company in the world next to Mattel.

Company profits were so great in 1969 that Mattel jumped into a charity program called Operation Bootstrap, set up to help minority-owned businesses by sharing expertise and making loans. Mattel financed Shindana Toy Company, an African American–owned business in South Central Los Angeles that made ethnically correct multicultural dolls.

Still operating on the "everything turns to gold" model, Ruth threw herself behind another Elliot brainstorm. In 1968, just as Hot Wheels was coming out, he had turned his attention to his Uke-A-Doodle roots, setting Ryan the task of creating a musical toy he called Optigan. As usual, Elliot was ahead of his time. His idea was to make a small piano-organ that could synthesize sounds by optically reading graphic images of waveforms off LP-size disks. Light beams shot through the transparent disks and were picked up on the other side by a photoelectric cell. Variance in the beams changed the voltage, which was amplified and passed through speakers as the sound of real instruments and a keyboard.

The name Optigan came from this optical organ idea. As the advertising proclaimed, "With the Optigan you actually play the real sounds of pianos, banjos, guitars, marimbas, drums and dozens more."

Elliot loved his new creation, which had the casing of a tabletop piano. As development went on, he decided it was not a toy at all, but a kind of instrument that adults could enjoy. A separate corporation was formed to market the novelty instrument. Elliot unveiled it at the company's annual meeting in May 1971. He tinkled the keys as shareholders waited, but there was silence. If Elliot had known the future, he would have seen the glitch as a sign, but then someone plugged Optigan into the wall and the show went on. No one thought it remarkable that once again Mattel was straying from its toy-centered roots.

Meanwhile, Rosenberg stepped up the pace of acquisitions,

using Mattel stock to pay for companies instead of cash. When he came on board, Mattel stock had just climbed out of a severe slump from two years before. Shares were back on a steady rise, which Rosenberg counted on. A higher stock price meant less stock was needed for acquisition deals.

In February 1969 Mattel bought three European toy companies for undisclosed amounts: a doll maker, Ratti e Vallenzasca, and a miniature die-cast car company, Mebetoys, both of Milan; and Ebiex in Brussels, a toy marketing company. In June Mattel bought Metaframe, a pet products company with stock valued at about twenty-seven million dollars. Recording a new high on Wall Street in January 1970, Mattel purchased Turco Manufacturing, a playground equipment manufacturer; Audio Magnetics Corporation, a blank cassette and reel-to-reel tape pioneer; H&H Plastics, a plastic molding company; and Monogram Models, a producer of plastic hobby kits.

In the early months of 1970, Ruth was expansive about her role as president. She toured factories around the world, hobbling on crutches from a minor accident but still thrilled at Mattel's worldwide reach. She admitted it was difficult to go from being "where the action is" to trying "not to stifle the creativity of others." She had sixteen vice presidents reporting to her. She told a reporter that it was becoming increasingly difficult to stay in contact with all of them. "For us, the change was traumatic," she said, referring to Mattel's growth, "but you can't have your cake and eat it too." She was becoming reconciled to her new role atop the toy company that was twice as large as its nearest competitor. She was also getting noticed. The Federal Reserve Bank of San Francisco asked her to sit on the board of the Los Angeles branch, making her the first woman to be given a seat.

Ruth began expanding Mattel in new directions. She announced new educational television programming for CBS, called *In the News*, consisting of mini-documentaries for school-age children, and a show on NBC called *Hot Dog*, which would explain the "who, what, when, where and why of things." But she was most proud of "the world of the young," as she called Mattel's conglomerate of acquired companies and related ventures. The latest entry was meant to challenge Disney's supremacy in children's movies. Ruth struck a deal with film producer Robert Radnitz, who made such highly acclaimed children's movies as *A Dog of Flanders*, *Island of the Blue Dolphins*, and *Misty*. Mattel would finance movies Radnitz produced and share in the profits. Its first success was the family drama *Sounder*.

Ruth also set in motion a deal to buy Ringling Bros. and Barnum & Bailey circus. She and Elliot had started a discussion about the merger at a dinner in the Houston Astrodome, where the legendary Roy Hofheinz held court.

Hofheinz was a major stockholder of the circus and owner of the Houston Astrodome Company and baseball team. He lived a large life, creating the Celestial Suite at the Astroworld Hotel, which rented for $2,500 per night. It had eight bedrooms, a mini nightclub, stocked bar and kitchen, and an eight-foot-by-eight-foot bed. He thought nothing of spending ten thousand dollars in overweight baggage charges when he traveled with his steamer trunks, footlockers, and assorted luggage. In Athens he settled his 250-pound frame into a pharaoh's chair and was carried to the Parthenon by four Greeks and two Houstonians. Most people called him Judge because as a young man he had sat on the Harris County, Texas, bench. He could have been called Mayor, too, for his time running the city of Houston before he ventured into business. Ever loyal and enthusiastic about his projects, he had coat buttons fashioned from gold-plated Ringling Bros. commemorative medals. As one reporter put it, Hofheinz was "a Texas capitalist and proud of it." Richard Blum, an investment banker at the time for Sutro Investment Partners, recalled Hofheinz as "the reincarnation of P. T. Barnum."

Ruth had never heard of Hofheinz when he called her during Toy Fair in February 1970, but her sales staff had. They encouraged her to fly to Houston to talk about an amusement park deal that he was proposing. Meeting her and Elliot with his usual flair, Hofheinz took them to the top of the Astrodome later that night. As they sat having cocktails, looking out at the empty stadium, the giant light board suddenly blazed with the greeting, "Welcome Ruth and Elliot Handler." They were suitably dazzled.

At dinner in the Astrodome restaurant, they were joined by Irvin Feld, who had bought Ringling Bros. circus just two years earlier, and Richard Blum, whose company also owned part of the circus. They were looking for ways to expand and modernize. Blum had the idea of introducing Feld to the Handlers for the purpose of getting Mattel to license Ringling-themed toys. He had no intention of talking about a merger deal, but Ruth hit on the idea right away.

Ruth and Elliot were not interested in Hofheinz's proposal for an amusement park in Houston, but bringing the circus into the Mattel family seemed perfect. They knew their grandchildren would love it, and from a business perspective, they always needed new ways to reach children, especially because some of their television programs were coming under fire. An activist organization called Action for Children's Television, founded by Peggy Charren in 1968, was growing stronger. Charren and the other mothers who founded the group demanded more quality educational television for children and petitioned the FCC to require it. Ruth had created new television shows partially in response to Charren, but she was also looking to mediums outside of television to protect her ability to sell Mattel's products. The circus seemed a perfect fit, the kind of magic that complemented Mattel's "world of the young."

Mattel was twenty-five years old and, as its own advertising proclaimed, more than a toy company. According to Ruth, Mattel filled "the educational and recreational needs of young people." The future promised even more fun and innovation than the past—or so Ruth and Elliot thought.

Chapter 13

The Cancer Within

Everything rolled downhill faster and faster, and there was no way I could stop it.

Starting around 1955, Ruth felt lumps in her breasts. She had a distinct memory of the first time she stood in the shower, lifting her arm to rub soap under it and over her breast, and suddenly feeling something unusual. She stood soaping and probing the lump for several minutes until she felt certain that a doctor should examine her. When she went to his office, he quickly detected what she had felt, but reassured Ruth that he did not think the lump was malignant. He told her he wanted to do a surgical biopsy, however, to be sure.

After that, every two or three years, doctors had been concerned enough about the lumps Ruth found to do surgical biopsies to rule out cancer. She had two on each breast and a number of less invasive needle biopsies. Her breasts were cystic, which meant that benign lumps developed often. All the procedures showed that she was cancer free, but every biopsy was a trial. "In those days they always made a big fuss over those biopsies. They would take you to the hospital. They would keep you there for a few days, and

I had scars on the sides of my breasts. They used the same scars over and over on each breast." Ruth found the procedures nerve-wracking, each time waking up from the anesthesia not knowing what she would be told.

After one of her biopsies, Al Frank, a New York representative for Mattel, was waiting in the hall outside Ruth's room. He had grown close to the Handlers over the years and was a warm, sweet man. As Ruth was awakening from the anesthetic, she heard a man crying and sobbing in the hall. She thought he must be wailing over her because the doctors had found cancer and taken her breast. Her breasts were bound so tightly with so many bandages that she had no way to know if her breast was there or not. She recognized Al Frank's voice talking to someone else. In moments, he was in her room, hugging Ruth and telling her that the biopsy was benign. Frank had been crying for joy.

It was at a family wedding in Denver in the 1960s that Ruth discovered a new, more worrisome lump. She was taking a shower before getting dressed for the ceremony and doing her usual soapy check of her breasts when she felt a lump larger than any she had discovered before. It seemed to come out of nowhere. Her cousin Dr. Joel Mosko was at the wedding, and she told him about it. He asked her to come to his office the next morning, and when he felt her breast he told her to see a doctor in Los Angeles immediately. Ruth called Dr. Paul Rekers, a Los Angeles surgeon, and said that she was coming home and wanted him to check her right into the hospital for a biopsy. He told her that it would be easier to come to his office, but she insisted that she did not want to wait. "That was typical of me," Ruth said. "That's how I did those things. If I was going to have to face the bad music, I did not want to have to screw around with it. I just wanted to get it done." Ruth planned to go to the hospital straight from the airport, and she expected the doctor to be waiting.

At the hospital that night, Dr. Rekers performed a needle aspiration of fluid from Ruth's breast, but because she was already in the hospital he decided to do a surgical biopsy as well. Ruth was scared, but once again the results were benign.

In 1970, however, Ruth felt something in her breast that was in a different place, a lump that for the first time had her doctor expressing concern. Leaving his office and walking toward her car in Beverly Hills, she burst out in tears. She was sobbing uncontrollably when a man passed her on the sidewalk. Looking at Ruth, he said, "Lady, it can't be all that bad." She turned away and thought, "You should only know."

Ruth set up another biopsy. The lump was not malignant, but since the doctor had opened her up he explored more deeply. Underneath the lump he discovered early signs of cancer. That morning, Ruth's breast was removed.

It was June 16, 1970, and nothing in Ruth's personal or business life would ever be the same. After years of living with the fear of cancer from numerous benign lumps, she had the disease and she was terrified. Would the cancer spread? Had the cancer already spread? She had lost her left breast. Would she find a malignant lump in her other breast, and what about the fibroids that doctors suspected in her uterus? Since the early 1960s she'd been diagnosed with mild diabetes, chronic tension, and diverticulitis. Would the cancer kill her or would something else?

Ruth could not help thinking about her sister Sarah, who had raised her. Sarah had died of ovarian cancer in 1950, after several years of extraordinary measures to save her. Ruth took charge of Sarah's care, not able to accept the initial postsurgery diagnosis that gave her sister six months to live. In her own words, she "embarked on a campaign" to find the best care in an era before chemotherapy.

During World War II, doctors had discovered that people exposed to mustard gas experienced a reduction in white blood cell count. Starting in the 1940s, doctors began experimenting with mustard gas in patients with cancers that had spread through the growth of white blood cells. Ruth found a doctor in Los Angeles using this experimental treatment. Sarah received the mustard gas through her veins, and though the treatment was painful, her tumors shrank enough to allow a second surgery to remove the cancer. She lived three more years, long enough for Ruth to treat her to a dream trip to Hawaii, where Sarah had always wanted to go. When Sarah returned, she needed another surgery, but this time she did not recover. Ruth, who had paced anxiously in the hospital hallway during Sarah's ordeal, never liked Sarah's husband, Louie, but she would never forgive him for "being out gallivanting" as Sarah lay dying.

As soon as she woke up from surgery, Ruth looked at her tightly taped chest and asked Elliot, "Will you still love me without this?" Her fears and insecurities overwhelmed her. She convalesced at the beach house in Malibu Colony that she had bought only two years before. The Malibu Beach Motion Picture Colony had been started in 1926 with cottages and leased beachfront marketed to Hollywood stars and executives. Four decades later, the colony was a gated, guarded, and exclusive beach retreat for the movie industry and business millionaires. Ruth bought the house of singer Frankie Laine on impulse after seeing how much her granddaughter loved the beach. The house, right on the beach, was a cherished retreat for Ruth and her family, but after the surgery it felt lonely and depressing.

Ruth's thoughts were dark. At times she just wanted to die. She remembered a story her mother had told her when she was a child about a friend's daughter who had lost a breast to cancer. Her mother whispered the terrible news in Ruth's ear. Perhaps

Ruth had seen the story about the previous month's conference of cancer researchers, all agreeing that any cure was years away. She was angry with the doctor who had scarred her, and ashamed. No one, not even her family, would talk about the ordeal, and there were no support groups at that time. For women in 1970, having a mastectomy was a secret, unspeakable brutality. Adding to Ruth's worries, Barbara came to the beach house to tell her mother that she was getting a divorce after eleven years of marriage.

Ruth returned to work five weeks after her surgery. She found it impossible to sit around doing nothing, but she was deeply shaken by the physical and emotional toll of the cancer. "I was unable to speak with authority," she wrote later. "I lost the courage of my convictions." Once proud of her body, she felt disfigured, unattractive, unwomanly. She was fifty-four years old. Deep new lines scored her face, which had grown fleshier. Bags showed under her eyes. Her clothes were chaste, buttoned to the neck and full enough to hide the inconsistent shape of her chest. She lost her broad, dazzling smile. Her shoulders slumped. She wore her gray hair in a flat, severe cut.

Ruth's modified radical mastectomy, in which her breast, some chest muscles, and lymph nodes in her armpits were removed, left permanent muscle and nerve damage. The pain would linger for the rest of her life.

Tensions at Mattel had grown more disruptive as the division heads competed to bring in the most revenue. They also struggled against top management. Yas Yoshida, the controller, had wanted the top finance job, and he resented Rosenberg for getting it. Ruth, relying on hard numbers, was fighting with Bernie Loomis in the Wheels division, believing that he wanted to overproduce a new gift set of the Sizzlers cars, a motorized version of Hot Wheels.

Darrell Peters had become the in-house master of sales data. He did extensive analysis of years of sales information and constructed a model that showed current demand, rather than future orders or past sales. As this model was refined, it became the single best predictor of the year-end quota for any toy. Mattel employees actually went to selected stores to count backroom inventory and items stocked on store shelves. Mattel could distinguish between those toys with early buys and those without, between new products and continuing items, between those with television advertising and those without. "It was a forecasting system and a W report [Weekly Sales and Shipping Report] as sophisticated as any in American industry for a comparably dynamic product line," remembered Joe Whittaker. Ruth believed in the Peters model, and at a planning meeting she fought openly with Loomis over his projected sales. Finally, he told Ruth to leave him alone.

Ruth felt out of control personally and at work. The corporate staff she had counted on to oversee the divisions was not working as she had planned. The death of her trusted executive, Herb Holland, which had come at the launch of divisionalization, had been a terrible blow. She tried to return to normal and put on a brave face, despite the continued pain from her surgery. Josh Denham, a division head who worked with her every day, remembers a social dinner where "she was doing her best to be the old Ruth, but perspiration was coming off her forehead and she looked like she was in pain." She felt even more vulnerable to the arrogant and bullying Rosenberg, who acted more and more like a former Litton superstar looking for a company to run.

Rosenberg was focusing less on acquisitions than on legal matters, finance, administration, corporate development, and long-range planning. He had overseen a hundred acquisitions at Litton but only eight at Mattel. His goal was to relieve the "stigma for seasonality," and use Mattel's people and facilities year-round.

Mattel's workforce, which shrank from thirty to forty thousand employees to as few as twenty thousand during the slow season, dragged on profits. Production workers could be laid off, but not executives and engineers drawing full-time salaries. Plus, by creating divisions, Mattel had driven up its year-round operating costs.

Rosenberg argued that the acquisitions were all profitable and that they would even out yearly revenue. He planned to move from 12 percent of the domestic toy market to 15 percent, and from 3 percent to 5 percent of the foreign market by the end of 1972. Rosenberg did not see the low growl of the emerging bear market as a problem.

After she returned to work, Ruth was more alone than ever. Elliot confined himself to research and design, having little interest in the business of Mattel. Ruth clashed personally with Art Spear, a rigid executive who had come to Mattel from Revlon in 1964 and been made executive vice president at the same time as Rosenberg. A lanky man with a long face and a high, balding forehead, he opposed Ruth's move to divisions and was growing more and more frustrated with the company's management. Sensing that she was "unable to grab back the reins effectively," Ruth began to feel as though she was on the outside looking in. No one in top management tried to make her feel differently.

Trouble began to emerge during the summer of 1970. One acquisition, Turco Manufacturing, was a poster child for the problems with the "world of the young" companies that had been added to Mattel. Many of these companies had been sold because, beneath their rosy projections, they were deeply troubled. With Turco, Elliot had been drawn to the idea of designing playground equipment, thinking of his grandchildren and what they enjoyed. But Turco's biggest and nearly only client was Sears. Turco management swore that the retail giant was loyal. But as soon as the sale went through, Sears abandoned the project and found another manufacturer. Buying a company with only one customer was foolish, as Ruth later admitted. "In fact," she wrote, "most of our acquisitions proved to be mistakes." She was right. Only Ringling Bros. and Monogram would consistently make money.

Meanwhile, projections for the Christmas season had grown exponentially. While Ruth hated to underproduce and miss out on possible sales, she knew that inventory losses were much more costly. If you shipped too many pieces to customers, they would make deep reductions in their orders the next year. "The product would be dead and you'd spend all the next year cleaning up inventory, both yours and your customers'," Ruth often explained. That was why everyone had been taught that the numbers counted above all. Executives came to meetings spouting sales figures that they had memorized for particular toys. Orders, forecasting, sales, reorders, production, timing of advertising—everything moved so fast in the toy business that only the most nimble and aggressive companies and executives survived. But in the months after her mastectomy, Ruth lost much of the spirit that she had used to lead her troops for so many years. After she returned from surgery she discovered that sales forecasts were running much higher than before she left. Even though she had told her division heads that forecasts were too high, they were competing and did not want to listen. Ruth felt that she could not get them under control, even as orders began to slow.

Mattel still produced Sizzlers on a fast track. The company projected big Christmas sales, but orders were slow. The first signal that Christmas might not be joyous for Mattel came in the fall. Like many companies, Mattel had built a factory just south of the border in Mexicali to take advantage of Mexico's lower wages. For the first time in a quarter century of production, a raging fire broke out that destroyed the plant and its entire inventory. Millions of dollars in Christmas orders went unfilled.

On the heels of the bleak news from Mexico, Hot Wheels sales began to slow. Topper Corporation introduced Johnny Lightning racers, a strong competitor. Hot Wheels buyers clamored for more variety and more styles, but that took time and money to produce. Designing and tooling could take months and months. There was a "giant backed-up wave" of cars, according to Josh Denham, that needed testing. Meanwhile, to keep his buyers happy, Loomis came up with a scheme to sell boxed sets of Hot Wheels. He promised buyers that the set would have a majority of new-style Hot Wheels and a few of the old ones, but the opposite was true. Between overordering in the first couple of years of Hot Wheels sales, and Loomis's pushing old cars in the boxed sets, buyers had too much inventory of old cars. They did not want or need to order more. Thirty million or more of unsold cars sat in Mattel warehouses, eventually sold at rock-bottom prices.

But the Wheels division was not the only problem. Optigan also was not being embraced by adult buyers. Its sound quality was poor and it was prone to break, resulting in high returns on the $300 novelty and a $6.5 million loss. Pat Schauer, who worked for the head of the project, thought the quasi-instrument needed more time to be perfected. Sears put in large orders but insisted that Mattel be responsible for repairs, which turned out to be the main problem. But Ruth had a different take that placed the blame not on her oversight or Elliot's design but on her manager. "Mattel had a big 'who did it?' complex," Josh Denham remembered, and it seemed to be in play more than ever.

Ruth felt that in the case of Optigan she was shielded from the truth. She had wondered about the size of the Sears orders and had asked whether they were firm. She had asked if they were cancelable and was told that they were not. She said that it would have been inappropriate, under the division structure, for her to check the orders herself. Optigan was a major project for Mattel, not just another toy. "It was like starting a whole new business," Ruth said, "and it went to hell. Obviously, our manager was incompetent. He had big fat dreams and delusions of grandeur that did not happen, and we got stuck with it and that was a total write-off."

As Barbie doll sales slowed in Europe, new problems arose at home. The Federal Trade Commission declared the television advertising for Hot Wheels and Dancerina "misleading." The commission claimed that the ads falsely portrayed the toys' appearance and performance. Hot Wheels cars were not self-propelled, and Dancerina could not stand up on her own, as the ads showed.

Despite the setbacks at the end of 1970, Mattel traded at thirty-four times the previous year's per-share earnings. Just before Christmas, the deal with Ringling Bros. was announced in the press. There were reservations on the circus board, especially from Richard Blum, who opposed the deal. As a young man he had briefly run a toy company. Taking the time to talk to some of his old contacts and some San Francisco toy retailers, he heard that Mattel was not doing as well as it seemed. "I made it clear I was against the deal," he remembered, but the circus's small, privately held board went forward. For Ruth, it was a bright spot. She told Josh Denham how thrilling it was to see all eyes in the audience turn to Irvin Feld when she sat with him in the big top, watching the show. "Now," Ruth said, "everyone will be focused on me."

During final negotiations, she and Elliot stayed at a hotel with a group of circus people in Venice, Florida. They were there to see firsthand how the business operated. One night she got into a poker game with eight or nine of the workers. The stakes were not high and Ruth did not want to take money off the circus hands, but she could not seem to lose. "I was playing the dumbest poker a person can play," she wrote later. "When the game was over, I'd won about eighty dollars." She saw her winnings as a good omen.

The deal stipulated that circus shareholders would receive

1.25 million shares of Mattel common stock in exchange for the 3.46 million outstanding shares of Ringling Bros. stock. The exchange was valued at just over forty-seven million dollars. Ruth saw Ringling as a "virtual money machine." Mattel, nearly twenty times the size of Irvin Feld's circus, had just reported more than seventeen million dollars' profit. Wall Street still held Mattel up as a glamour stock. Only certain top company executives knew that the good news was a mirage.

By January 1971, even as Mattel's stock hit an historic high of $52.25 per share, the Sizzlers line was in big trouble. Buyers had too much inventory. They were clamoring for Mattel to help them unload it. They did not want to buy into new lines of toys until they could be sure they would get relief. With orders down, inventory was backing up in Mattel warehouses, and revenue was not coming in to offset expenses.

Using an annualized accounting method, which was perfectly legitimate, Mattel became more aggressive about pushing expenses to later business quarters. Surely the revenue would be made up as it had been in the past. Surely Mattel buyers would send orders flooding in for the great new toys coming out in 1971. Profit targets were set, but unlike the hard-nosed number crunching of Mattel's earlier days, the targets were concocted based on what would keep Wall Street happy. Suddenly, "must-have" numbers appeared, and top management was pressured to figure out how to bring about the desired increase per share. The answer came in the form of bill and hold, a scheme for creating the appearance of continued company growth despite reality.

Bill and hold had been used before by Mattel as a legitimate business strategy. But that was not the case starting as early, at least, as 1971. Rosenberg was desperate to keep the stock price from falling because of the deal with Ringling Bros. He told Denham and Loomis that under the terms of the circus merger, if

Mattel's stock price fell too sharply, Irvin Feld, who remained as Ringling's CEO, would own the toy company.

Rosenberg's fears were justified. The merger agreement, signed January 5, 1971, warranted the truth and accuracy of Mattel's financial condition. Rosenberg knew that the result of lying would mean a lawsuit brought by Ringling. Specifically, Mattel promised that nothing it had submitted contained untrue or misleading statements. To keep up the facade memorialized in the Ringling merger papers, the bill-and-hold system went into effect. Charges for future sales were recorded immediately. False invoices and bills were prepared, and a second set of books was created. Customer signatures were forged. Routing and delivery instructions were incorrect. New product costs were deferred or amortized over unusually long periods, so that costs were understated. Legitimate orders were made fully cancelable. "Do not mail" invoices were created. Receivables mounted as customers became delinquent on their bills, yet the books showed some customers buying more toys. Between 50 and 80 percent of billed sales would be canceled by customers prior to shipping. Even the insurance claim for the Mexicali fire was inflated, with $10 million posted as a credit on the January 31, 1971, earnings statement. Six years later, only $4.4 million was actually paid. According to a later Special Counsel's report, Arthur Andersen, the company that conducted audits for Mattel, either turned a blind eye or was recklessly inept.

Denham and Loomis were uneasy as they saw the implications of the strategy. They went into Ruth's office and said, "We're going to ruin the company for the first six months of this year," explaining that there would not be any real sales. But Rosenberg saw them talking to Ruth and walked in. He told the two division heads to come to his office and he would "tell them what's going on." Ruth did not say anything.

In a company that had been charmed for so many years—a company that was the darling of Wall Street, that had given double-digit returns to its shareholders for the entire decade of the 1960s, it is not hard to imagine executives feeling sanguine. Bill and hold was risky and wrong, but when Mattel performed poorly in the past it had always bounced back. As long as the numbers were made up with strong sales in later quarters, maybe no one would find out about the fraud. But Denham explained that they had no time to reason it through. "The problems that came with bill and hold came so fast that we did not have time to think. We just thought we'd have big problems for five months or so." Instead, the economic recession deepened, and in the fall of 1971, a dockworkers' strike on the West Coast promised ruin for Mattel's second Christmas season in a row. There were years of problems ahead.

Rosenberg likely masterminded the initial scheme. The evidence is strong that Ruth knew about it. The federal court would later rule, over her vehement denials, that she knew all along. She insisted that she relied too much on trusted hands, that she was not up to par after her surgery, that 1971 did look like a "turnaround" year with exciting products coming on line and overhead reduced. In twenty-seven handwritten pages, Ruth later explained her version of events.

She said that she and Elliot were never aware of the magnitude of the bill-and-hold program or of the cancellation rights until much later. She thought her sales force was writing routine orders in the magnitude of two to four million dollars, which were noncancelable but would be held in Mattel's warehouse for later shipping instructions. She said, "I never, ever heard of phony invoices. We did not set 'must-have' numbers or profit 'targets.'" Ruth claimed that she constantly questioned sales targets and that she received assurances about them. Privately, she thought that if the sales were not achieved, it would still be acceptable to make ten or twenty cents less per share.

In retrospect, she acknowledged that it seemed impossible for her and Elliot not to have known what was going on. They were, however, very busy people, preoccupied with many other things. Ruth had a giant corporation to manage and was also spending increasing amounts of time on consumer issues that required her to be away from Mattel. She also believed that because she was recovering from a mastectomy, her staff was protecting her from problems at work. Rosenberg and Spear had reassured her after her mastectomy that she could depend on them to run and control things. Rosenberg had also pushed her out of reviewing accounting and financial numbers in detail. Ruth accepted this because she was told that Mattel was too big a business for her to be involved in every aspect of corporate affairs. She should let her people have their autonomy, she was told. She needed to delegate. Unfortunately, she said, she followed their advice.

Ruth's version of events grows more bitter as her notes go on, placing blame on the management team she had trusted: Art Spear, Seymour Rosenberg, Ray Wagner, Josh Denham, Bernie Loomis, Yas Yoshida, and Vic Rado. It quickly turns into a detailed explanation of company operations that is more revealing of Ruth's comprehensive grasp of company operations than of her innocence. She was president of Mattel and she sounds like it, but she stops short of admitting any knowledge of the fraudulent number crunching happening all around her. She still received weekly, sometimes daily, W reports. These would have shown that, for example, a hundred thousand units of a toy were sold, but only a dozen were in inventory ready to ship. It is unlikely that the woman who had caught the tiniest error in the past would miss the gross overstatements that bill and hold created. She admits to knowing about bill and hold, but only as a legitimate practice. She claimed to be shocked by the size of the overstatements, which totaled nearly eighteen million dollars.

The bill-and-hold scam did work for a while. Although Mattel's
share price fell to 19⅛ near the end of 1971, the fall was blamed on
a reported four-million-dollar loss and the ongoing dock strike.
Mattel remained a Wall Street darling, its stock kept artificially
high based on the belief that it would continue to grow. The full
extent of losses was still hidden and would remain that way for
another year.

The new layers of management were poorly organized. One
hand frequently was slapping the other with memos that con-
tradicted orders from different levels of the same department. In
marketing, an employee complained that it was "impossible to
get anything done on schedule . . . to get anything done, period."
Some executives burned out and left in a hurry. Others were hired
without the strict and taxing interview process of the past. Meanwhile, Ruth pushed for overly optimistic sales forecasts, saying
later that she based her exuberance on past experience. But later
revelations of hidden revenue targets suggest that her efforts were
also tied to the bill-and-hold scheme.

At the beginning of 1972, Ruth and Elliot were considering an
entirely new direction. No doubt, it was made more tempting by
the stress within Mattel. Rosenberg had told them in the summer
of 1971 that Kinney Systems, which specialized in leisure time,
real estate, and financial services, wanted to explore the idea of a
merger with Mattel. Kinney had spun off part of its conglomerate
after buying Warner Brothers and, in September 1971, changed
its name to Warner Communications. Ruth could see the logic
of joining with Kinney/Warner, which after its merger had more
money and earnings than Mattel but was trading lower. Steve
Ross, the aggressive deal maker who was running Kinney, wanted
to merge under the Mattel name, believing it would greatly raise
the value of the new entity's stock.

In May 1972 a meeting was set at Ruth's Malibu beach house

for the investment advisers, lawyers, and company executives, including Ruth, Elliot, and Seymour Rosenberg, who were planning to close the deal. Perhaps the roller coaster created by Wall Street increased Ruth's desire to reduce the pressures in her working life. She liked and trusted Felix Rohatyn, who had negotiated the deal for Kinney. She and Elliot would continue as minority board members, and Ruth had agreed to run the toy division after the merger.

As she sat with the group reviewing the final documents, Ruth was startled to see that Rohatyn, rather than being one of Kinney's majority board members, was listed as a minority member. She liked Rohatyn, but she did not intend to have Kinney pick her representatives to the board. Making her feelings clear, Ruth examined the rest of the document with growing unease. Kinney was proposing that its eighty-year-old founder be made president of the conglomerate, but Ruth expected Steve Ross to act as president. It did not make sense to her to place this old man at the operational head of the company, unless something else was intended.

Ruth suspected that Rosenberg had cut a deal behind her back to be made president once the merger was done, knowing she would veto such a plan if she could.

Barely controlling her anger, Ruth told the group that she would agree to serve as head of the toy division, but she would resign as soon as the president did. Elliot spoke up, asking how the elderly man, who had no active role, could be made president at all. The Kinney representatives erupted, insisting that Ruth was needed to run the toy division, but their distress only confirmed to Ruth what she suspected. "This whole thing is a farce," she barked. Turning to Rosenberg, she accused him of disloyalty and orchestrating a takeover behind her back. He was the first person out the door. Later, executive vice president Art Spear would say that the merger failed over a "problem of politics and egos."

. . . .

That spring, Rosenberg must have been desperate. A new operating committee had been formed to run Mattel, which included him, Elliot, Ruth, and three executive vice presidents. Were they going to talk about the failure of the bill-and-hold strategy? Were they going to try to find a way to make up for the false postings? If so, they never did. Rosenberg must have thought the Kinney merger could be his salvation, and he had almost gotten it. But Ruth upended the deal and any hopes he had of taking charge of the company and figuring out a way to cover the fraud that had been going on for more than a year.

On Monday, after the aborted merger meeting, as Pat Schauer remembers, Ruth stormed into the office and ordered that the locks on Rosenberg's office door be changed. She left instructions that he be told to leave when he showed up. But after she went into her office, Elliot came in and quietly told her, "Now, Ruth, you can't do that." They both feared the reaction on Wall Street if Rosenberg were precipitously thrown out. Angry but resigned, Ruth decided Elliot was right. She was livid for days after the incident but quietly negotiated a deal with Rosenberg. He agreed to retire in August, replaced by Robert Ehrlich, who was told to redo reporting systems and keep Ruth informed.

Rosenberg, the forty-nine-year-old financial whiz kid would leave with a package that included sixty thousand dollars a year for twenty years and a promise to act as a consultant for Mattel. He agreed to surrender forty thousand shares of rapidly declining stock, sold another eighty thousand worth nearly two million dollars, and remained a board member. It seemed that he had gotten out just in time.

At the end of March 1972, Mattel announced that for the first time in its history it had operated at a loss in the previous fiscal year. Elliot, as chairman, struggled to appear cheery about the future as he explained away a staggering $29.5 million deficit, compared to more than $17 million in profit the previous fiscal year. Large write-offs for restructuring of the European toy operation were blamed, as was the dock strike, surcharges, currency devaluation, and nonrecurring losses from inventory and retooling write-offs.

Ruth and Elliot continued to act as if all was well or even better than ever. They announced a new fifty-million-dollar Circus World theme park in Florida, part of the deal they had made with Feld. At the May annual meeting, Elliot proclaimed, "We have many reasons to believe we are making a turnaround and are moving toward an innovative and profitable year in the traditional Mattel fashion." But history was far from repeating itself, and Wall Street did not find his words persuasive.

In June, 450,000 shares were dumped by Mattel's biggest institutional investor, who had lost faith in the company's management. The stock dove from $20 to $16 in one day. Paper losses were mounting. Ruth often vented about people she did not like, and she had a style of finding someone to blame when things went wrong. In frustration, Ruth fired the man she felt most responsible for the losses, next to Rosenberg, Bernie Loomis.

Hoping to help the Handlers deal with the mess, the division heads and Art Spear arranged a dinner with Peter Drucker, the man who invented modern management. They met at the Los Angeles airport restaurant. While the instigators went off to the bar, Drucker and the Handlers talked for more than two hours. After Ruth and Elliot left, the others rushed back to the table to ask Drucker what he thought. "There are very, very few entrepreneurs that start big companies," Drucker told them, "and can survive through the next phase."

In that long summer of 1972, millions were being lost in discontinued operations and special charges. In August shares slumped to their lowest price of the year after Mattel announced that sales for the first half of 1972 would be even worse than for the previous year.

In October, the first of what would be a cascade of lawsuits was filed by a shareholder. Lawrence Seftel alleged that Elliot, Ruth, Rosenberg, and five others had sold $118,000 worth of their own Mattel stock, based on inside information, before the August announcement that caused the share price to sink by 10 to 15 percent. In Ruth's case, she seemed to have sold the stock to help Barbara buy a bigger house, but there was still the appearance of insider trading. The attacks came from all sides, and they were about to grow more fierce and far more dangerous.

Chapter 14

The Plot Unravels

We started getting hit with catastrophe.

In early January 1973, Ruth and Elliot were on a cruise ship in the Caribbean. They had made a last-minute decision to join her brother Max and his wife, Lillian, flying to New York and staying at the Plaza Hotel before embarking on the SS *France* on December 21. They sailed to Port-au-Prince, Haiti, on Christmas Eve and on to Cristobal in the Panama Canal Zone on Christmas Day. From there they went to Curaçao, then Barbados, and docked for New Year's Eve in Martinique. When they arrived in St. Thomas on January 2, Ruth phoned her secretary to check in. Something in the woman's tone made her uneasy. The cruise was not scheduled to end for three more days, when Ruth and Elliot would fly to Sarasota, Florida. Ruth made an abrupt change. Leaving the ship in St. Thomas, she and Elliot made arrangements to get back to Los Angeles as quickly as possible.

When they got back they discovered Ruth's intuition was sound. About fifteen bankers were assembled in the boardroom along with Art Spear and some other executives when Ruth and Elliot made their unexpected appearance. "They were all very surprised and embarrassed to see us," Ruth said. "Surreptitious meetings with the bankers had been going on for some time. There was a terrible plot going on."

Ruth was right. A crucial lunch meeting had already taken place at Mattel headquarters. Executive vice president Art Spear had asked Bob Ehrlich, who had taken Rosenberg's place, and another Mattel executive to meet with a key group of bankers. The group included Dick Bingham, a partner at Kuhn, Loeb, the eminent investment bank. With two hundred million dollars in short-term financing outstanding, the banks that lent Mattel money were worried. Once the plates were cleared, the first order of business was a management shake-up focused on getting Ruth out of the president's chair.

The meeting was open and casual, but Spear wasted no time in getting to his main point. He and Ehrlich made clear that they considered Ruth the heart of the company's problems. They did not believe that she understood the financial implications of her actions or that she had a strong enough commitment to controlling Mattel's subsidiaries. Spear hoped to get her to agree to step down as president, but his relations with her were tense. He was closer with Elliot, but explained that Elliot could not be counted on. He would act as husband before chairman. Spear proposed that the bankers support efforts to pressure Ruth out of the president's job.

Bingham and the others agreed; they wanted to do whatever it would take to protect their investment. They would not agree to support Spear in a company takeover, but new management was certainly in order. They also pushed for an outside board, reasoning that no one would want to join a board with the Handlers as the majority shareholders. After the meeting, Spear started looking for ways to pressure Ruth to step aside. Within weeks, the crisis he needed broke into the financial news.

. . . .

Elliot and Ruth were at the Toy Show in February 1973, overseeing Mattel's new toy line and talking to customers. They received
a call from Art Spear saying that he was coming in from Los
Angeles and had to see them at their hotel the next morning. At
the meeting Art, Ruth's nephew Ron Loeb, and Ray Ferris told
Ruth and Elliot that Mattel had run into a serious problem. A
few weeks earlier, on February 5, 1973, Elliot had announced that
the company would make a good profit for the fiscal year. His
statement predicted a "definite turnaround" for Mattel. Earnings
problems were blamed on Optigan, but Elliot predicted that the
company report would show "satisfactory earnings from continued operations."

Spear told Ruth and Elliot that, contrary to the February 5
statement, the last quarter was going to show a substantial loss.
A new statement had to be immediately released to the press. On
February 23, Mattel issued another press release saying, " . . . the
company now expects to incur a substantial operating loss for the
fiscal year ending February 3, 1973, rather than a profit as previously anticipated." The release should have read "spectacular
loss." It was thirty-two million dollars.

Ruth remembered the conflicting reports as coming months,
rather than weeks, apart, but she had a clear memory of the fallout.
"All hell broke loose. That was like a bad dream; the nightmare
came much later. That was the beginning. We were out of control and did not really know how badly, because when we finally
did announce our loss it was quite obvious that we still hadn't
accounted for all of the things that had to be written off. [But] we
did not know this until much later, unfortunately."

In full "who did it?" mode, Ruth blamed her financial and
public relations staff for the reporting fiasco. She said that she

and Elliot had relied on Mattel's financial people for the numbers, and allowed the public relations staff to write the statement that was released to the press with Elliot's signature. She argued that she was not a "financial pro," but having remained as president, there was only one place for the blame to stop. Later she said she had been out of control of the company, at least from the time she returned from her surgery, but few people accepted that excuse. Ruth had built her power with staff much like her. She quickly dispatched those who could not keep up, and she had always stayed abreast of every company operation.

The truth behind phony sales and false revenue was starting to leak out. Ruth was desperate for allies after Mattel's Bank of America representative told her and Elliot that their creditors wanted Spear as president. She called Josh Denham into her office. He had always been apolitical, a slightly built, well-spoken peacemaker, and he worked for Spear. She asked him to help, but he told her there was nothing he could do, the problems were too deep.

Ruth confronted the bankers, arguing that Spear did not know enough about marketing or the toy business to take over, but they had made up their minds. They threatened to shut off Mattel's credit if she did not go along. On March 27, 1973, Spear was named president of Mattel. Ruth became a cochairman with Elliot. Three days later *Fortune* would list Ruth, alongside *Washington Post* owner Katharine Graham and Olive Ann Beech of Beech Aircraft, as one of the ten highest-paid women executives in the country. Unlike the others, however, Ruth now held a largely empty portfolio of duties, although she insisted publicly that the move was long planned.

Full control of Mattel passed to Art Spear and other executives. Ruth came to work every day and sat in her office with little to do.

She knew that everyone was avoiding her, sometimes in ways that were obvious and distressing. On one occasion, she was walking down the front hall past all of the executive offices. She was going in the direction of Jay Jones's office just as he started to walk out his office door. Seeing Ruth, he turned around and went back into his office, closing the door behind him. Ruth saw his panicked look. He was hiding from her.

In another humiliating incident, Ruth asked Ray Wagner to come to her office. She wanted to talk to him about a marketing plan that had landed on her desk, which she believed had flaws. He kept avoiding her. Finally, he came to her office. As they went over the plan, Wagner bit his fingernails, something Ruth knew he did when he was nervous. He was also shifting in his chair as if he could not sit still. When Ruth was half through going over the plan he told her that he had to leave for another appointment. He got up and left without waiting for her reply. "I was so hurt," Ruth said. "He would never have done anything like that. He was a nice man." When she thought about the incident years later, she said it still "hurts terribly."

Spear made quick work of a bloated conglomerate. By June he had done away with 125 marginal toy lines. One new toy line was doing well. Big Jim, a male nonmilitary action figure with flexing biceps, met with good reviews, and Barbie's home furnishings, in the burnt orange and robin's egg blue of the 1970s, sold briskly. Mistakes in foreign sales, like releasing Barbie clothes that did not reflect European tastes, were being corrected. "The previous management was preoccupied with achieving a big jump in growth," Spear told the *Wall Street Journal*, "and did not pay attention to capital structure. We plan a moderate growth, and we have put in tighter financial controls, which will result in assured profits." He was trying to reassure shareholders that the corporate ship had been steadied, but they were not mollified easily. After two fiscal years of losses totaling sixty-two million dollars, Mattel's stock plunged like a plane that had lost its engines. From a high of $52.25 just eighteen months before, shares were trading at $5.

Mattel had become the butt of insider humor. The *Wall Street Journal* printed a joke going around the financial community: "Have you heard about Mattel's new talking doll? Wind it up and it forecasts a 100% increase in sales and profits. Then it falls flat on its face." Five new class-action shareholder suits had been filed, including one by Ringling Bros., which Roy Hofheinz joined. Circus shareholders charged that at the time of the merger Mattel overstated earnings, understated losses, and misrepresented finances on the proxy statement used for the deal. Shareholder actions caught the interest of the SEC, ratcheting up the scrutiny of the previous years' financial machinations.

For Ruth, each day at the office turned into an exercise in pretense. Executives at all levels avoided her. No one threw her out of meetings, but when she spoke no one listened either. People she considered loyal friends, like division head Ray Wagner, were completely unavailable. "I went through a period," Ruth said, "when I thought there was not a person in the world who wanted me or wanted anything from me, which was an absolute opposite from what it had been in my life for the prior thirty years." She hated the feeling of not being wanted, of being rejected. She felt like a leper, and that people were not sincere in showing their respect for her. "It was a very demeaning, humiliating experience," Ruth recalled. She told her lawyers that she wanted out of the company, that she hated being there, but they wanted her to stay. They felt she would weaken her legal position by leaving. They were not considering her emotional state. Every day she came to Mattel increased her sense of isolation and embarrassment.

Ruth found some relief with her family. Ken and his wife, Suzie, had added three grandchildren to Barbara's two, and the Malibu house became a haven for Ruth and Elliot to enjoy their grandchildren. Increasingly, however, Ruth left Los Angeles altogether.

In January 1973, President Richard Nixon created an Advisory Committee on the Economic Role of Women and made Ruth one of sixteen inaugural members. "I remember her as a gutsy lady," said Jacqueline Brandwynne, who also served on the committee. "She was a firecracker with bundles of energy and enthusiasm. We were both strong consumer and women's advocates." Besides attending meetings of the committee, Ruth began giving speeches. "The Challenges of Consumerism" and "Mandatory vs. Voluntary Regulation" for the Better Business Bureau. "Safety in the Marketplace" for the Business and Professional Women's Clubs and manufacturers' associations. She talked about what she knew: "Anything you do starts with identifying the consumer's need and ends up with a product satisfying that need." She traveled around California, to Wisconsin, to Hawaii, to Washington, D.C., and to Fort Worth, Texas. With Elliot, she traveled around the world to some of Mattel's plants and subsidiaries, but she always returned to an office cold with inactivity and a workplace turned increasingly hostile.

In the summer of 1974, the SEC acted on the complaint that had been filed against Mattel. The company had been cooperating over the past year of investigation. Ruth had agreed that Art Spear should go to Washington, D.C., to work out the problems with the agency.

She still believed Spear was an ally. Later she became convinced that he connived against her with the SEC. "Art was the worm in the woodpile," she said. To her, he was much worse than Rosenberg because he betrayed her trust. When Spear went to Washington he negotiated a deal that changed Mattel's board so that he was in charge of finding new board members, whose names would be submitted to the SEC for approval. Ruth said Spear chose his cronies for the board. She and Elliot were forced to acquiesce because of the pending lawsuits and threat of federal criminal action. Spear also agreed to the SEC's appointment of a special counsel, Seth Hufstedler. Although there is no evidence to support her contention, Ruth suspected that Spear helped choose Hufstedler, paving the way for them to become, in her words, "bosom buddies."

Ruth believed Spear saw his chance to take over the company on the back of her and Elliot's problems. He was establishing contacts with the government and the banks. She said she found documents that indicated that Spear felt that if he got Ruth to leave, Elliot would follow. In August, Mattel agreed that it had filed false and misleading financial reports. The Federal District Court ordered the appointment of unaffiliated directors and the creation of new committees to look deeper into the financial mess. The court gave the directors and committees several years' worth of power, but it only took a month for the next blow to fall. Mattel announced that "information had been discovered," about possible financial irregularities. The new committees were doing their work.

In October, just after Arthur Andersen resigned as Mattel's auditor, the SEC made an unprecedented power play. More violations had been uncovered, and the agency asked to be given effective control over the corporation. Bypassing shareholders, who had the traditional role of picking directors, the SEC set criteria for appointing a new majority group of directors to the board. Agreeing, the court forced Mattel to pick directors unaffiliated with it or any company that had dealings with Mattel. Special Counsel Seth Hufstedler was charged with investigating the company's financial dealings. He was given four months to interview employees and look at Mattel's records for the crucial years of 1971 and 1972.

Mattel shareholders had stopped receiving dividends eighteen months earlier. As the SEC closed in with the new order, Mattel asked for a halt on trading its shares on the New York Stock Exchange. New directors were announced before Christmas, even as two new lawsuits were filed. In one of its first acts, the board abolished Ruth's and Elliot's operational titles, leaving them only their diminished role on Mattel's board. "The new board really shunned her and Elliot," Tom Kalinske remembered. "They weren't welcome."

Elliot found solace in his painting, getting a studio near their penthouse and going to Malibu to paint on weekends. Without an outlet, Ruth was consumed with bitterness and anger. She did not know what to do with herself. She hated the endless meetings with attorneys. She missed working. "Under the circumstances," she told a reporter later, "some people would have seen a psychiatrist, other people would have blown their brains out, somebody else would have escaped to a desert island. I tried a little of each." Too often, Ruth drove her red Rolls-Royce to Gardena, the gambling town on Los Angeles's outskirts. She was known for her foul-mouthed outbursts at the tables and general disregard for cash won or lost. On a trip to Las Vegas shortly after she and Elliot left Mattel, Ruth was playing craps and losing. Elliot told her to stop and then went to get the car. By the time he got back she had won back the fifty thousand dollars she had lost. "How do you cope?" she said. "You cry, get sick, feel terrible." She tried teaching at the University of Southern California and UCLA, but she resented working for free. She felt that the universities did not think she was worth anything since they did not put a dollar value on her teaching. She started gambling every day, toying with the idea of becoming a professional gambler. Meanwhile, she and Elliot were required to give two million shares of stock to Mattel to settle class action suits. "There were days," Ruth said, "when I could have done away with myself."

Hufstedler, the special counsel, was finding a more complicated web than the SEC had imagined. He needed a year to finish his work. Ruth was one of the last people he interviewed. He questioned her closely, occasionally recommending that she consult with counsel before answering, but she did not. What she did not deny she did not remember. "I don't recall," she told the special counsel. "I'm now having trouble separating recent recollections from past memory."

Ruth said she knew nothing about tooling or obsolescence calculations. She had only realized the magnitude of bill and hold after a "computer blow-up." When she called Yoshida into her office to ask why her morning report had only "negative numbers," he told her he was reversing out the bill-and-hold orders. She was shocked to learn the amount was eighteen to twenty million dollars, and ordered him to correct it. "I was an absolute nut on receiving accurate numbers so that I could review our quotas," Ruth told Hufstedler. But the bill-and-hold numbers were put back into the computer and then taken out again. Had she talked to Yoshida about that? She did not think so. And she had not talked to any of the division heads. If shenanigans were going on with the numbers, it was news to Ruth.

Hufstedler zeroed in on the connection between the circus deal and earnings pressure. "Did Seymour Rosenberg discuss with you any possible effect of a downturn in sales on the circus acquisition?" Hufstedler asked several times in various ways. Ruth's answers never varied. She did not connect sales with the circus deal at all.

She believed earnings at that time were fine. Rosenberg was secretive. Rosenberg was the financial mastermind, not her. Rosenberg was always pushing for higher targets; she hated that pressure. Rosenberg was the villain, with Bernie Loomis, the Wheels division head, in a supporting role.

Years later Hufstedler remembered Ruth with some sympathy as "a tough lady," but she had no kind words for him. She did not think he believed anything she told him. She was insulted when he told her that she was lying. She was certain that he was good friends with her attorney, Francis M. Wheat from the law firm of Gibson, Dunn & Crutcher. Wheat had worked for the SEC, which was the reason that he was recommended to the Handlers. He was one of the most respected attorneys in Los Angeles and a major power in his law firm, but Ruth was told that he had gone on mountain-climbing expeditions with Hufstedler. She said, "I don't think Wheat believed I was innocent of many of the things I was accused of because his buddy Hufstedler had it all figured out that I was the guilty one. So I had a lawyer who did not believe in my innocence." As Ruth's legal problems increased, she saw conspiracies all around her.

The month before Hufstedler announced his findings, Ruth and Elliot resigned from Mattel's board, severing their remaining connection with the company. They announced that they were giving two and a half million shares of their stock to settle shareholders' lawsuits. It was half of what they owned of their company, but in the end, thirty-four million dollars would be paid by Mattel for the civil actions. Ruth still hoped, however, to find a way to gain control, or at least wrest it from the man she felt had plotted against her—Art Spear.

On December 16, 1975, Ruth met with Bob Ehrlich, the man who had taken Rosenberg's place. Ehrlich said that he told the special counsel that Rosenberg and Loomis were the plotters of the fraud, but he was also certain that Spear knew about it. He told her that he had gone to Hufstedler after the report came out and told him that Spear had been involved and that much of the report was wrong. Supposedly, Hufstedler said he agreed, but it was too late to change the report.

Ruth concluded that Hufstedler had not tried hard enough to find out the truth about Spear. In her notes from the meeting she wrote, "All [Spear] had to do was raise the issue to us and he could have stopped the whole thing." Ehrlich offered to cut a deal with Ruth to take over Mattel by buying the Handler shares. He laid out his plan, assuring her that he would choose board members loyal to the Handlers. But she was not ready to sell out, even if she and Elliot were on the outside looking in.

Finally Ruth realized that Mattel was out of her control. The pain of separation was acute. She had come to the lowest point of her life. "It was heartbreaking. By the time we left I was devastated. I couldn't believe what was happening. I was actually traumatized and kept saying, 'this can't be happening.'" Elliot struggled as well, though he had an easier time accepting a quieter life. "It's a heartbreaking thing to lose your baby; what you built over the years, and to lose stock. But the important thing was we lost our baby." Ruth was about to take the first steps toward a different kind of salvation, one that only she could have conceived. But her long, painful fall from power was not over. She was about to be sent toward a terrifying abyss.

Chapter 15

Nearly Me

I couldn't just screech to a halt after racing my whole life.

Ruth worked the presentation of her new product down to a studied and predictable performance during 1977. She knew when the uncomfortable looks would come, the nervous laughter, the shocked and embarrassed stares. She had first brought the show to Neiman Marcus, then Bonwit Teller and I. Magnin. She insisted that everyone take part: the company president, managers, sales staff, even stock boys, electricians, and warehouse workers. After all, they had mothers and sisters and wives, too. If she was not satisfied that a store could market her product exactly as she wanted, she would not sell to them.

The show started with Ruth talking about her mastectomy. She was matter-of-fact. That was important. She was remaking the marketing of prosthetic inserts, demystifying and taking the horror out of the process, all to give women like herself their dignity back. She would tell the story of driving her Rolls-Royce to the department store in Beverly Hills shortly after her cancer surgery. Elliot had urged her to do it, telling her to face up to the change in her body.

Ruth had asked the sales clerks about a prosthetic. They had huddled, whispering and grimacing, and to Ruth's mind, drawing straws for who would fit her. Finally, the "loser" showed her into a dressing room and closed the curtain. When the clerk came back, she dangled a surgical brassiere with built-in pockets over the top of the curtain rod, clearly unwilling to see Ruth undressed. Next came the ill-formed lumpy globs that were the inserts. Ruth struggled to get them into the pockets. The sizes had no relation to bra sizes. She tried a six—too big. A five looked less awful. She bought one for home and one for the beach house, and left feeling miserable. After that, Ruth explained to her audience, she gave away her form-fitting couture clothes and found anything shapeless and dull-colored that would cover the odd, malproportioned contours of her chest.

Then she would throw her shoulders back a bit more, emphasizing her well-defined and balanced bustline and bright-colored tapered blouse. "I call it Nearly Me because it's not me, but it's a great improvement over what was available," she would say. She would challenge the store staff to tell her which breast was fake. Sometimes, she would invite one of the men to step up to her. Taking their hands, she would put them on her breasts, telling them to feel free to squeeze, and demanding they guess which was the prosthetic. The crowd tittered. There were red faces, but Ruth made her point. Usually they guessed wrong. In the grand finale, Ruth would pull open her blouse or fitted suit so that her whole buxom bra could be seen. After buttoning up, she would reach inside and pull out the Nearly Me breast and pass it around.

Once again, Ruth revolutionized not only a product but its marketing. Men designed the old prosthetics, she would explain scornfully. They did not realize that breasts have lefts and rights, just like feet. They were so embarrassed by their product that they called the inserts "pads" or "forms." She insisted on calling hers "breasts." Coining a new term, she called the women who came to her for help "mastectomees," because "like amputees, we feel we have been amputated." She wanted to remove the shame from the disfiguring surgery.

Ruth remembered her unexpected fits of crying after her own surgery. One night at a cocktail party she started talking to a stranger about her cancer and mastectomy. She remembered, "The tears stopped and the hostility began to disappear." She wanted to give other women that kind of relief by creating a place where they could be open about their feelings, their needs, and their struggle. She helped women with their pain in the way most natural to her—designing a product to sell and market. She pulled the marketing of breast prosthetics out of the shadows along with the women who needed them.

After Ruth's first awful visit to the department store in 1970, she tried other shops. "I bought everything I could find as prosthesis, and they were all globs," she explained. "Your ego goes to hell then, and walking into a store to an untrained person who doesn't understand your situation is torture. I decided the prosthesis fitting was worse than the surgery." Then she heard about Peyton Massey, a world-famous arts sculptor in Santa Monica who specialized in making custom prosthetic noses, hands, legs, and breasts.

Massey wrapped wet plaster-covered gauze bandages around Ruth to make an impression of her chest, designing a custom prosthetic that she found more comfortable and attractive than the egg-shaped lumps she was using. She bought two for $350 each. The new breast was contoured and stood up against Ruth's chest wall, but there were problems. The breast material had a funny smell, and if Ruth had to take off her blouse, the edges showed outside her bra. And there was another error reminiscent of problems with the early Barbie dolls molded in Japan.

In retrospect, Ruth found the story humorous, and often repeated it. Massey's first prosthesis for her had large, distended nipples. Massey had placed the gauze for shaping the breast on Ruth as she stood in a cold room, which made her nipples become erect. Although some women have distended nipples much of the time, Ruth's were normally flat. Massey formed the prosthetics based on his molds, and Ruth kept trying to find clothes that would hide the unnatural nipples.

Just before she left Mattel in 1975, Ruth went on an aggressive weight-loss program as an attempt to pull herself out of her depression. She lost inches off her size, and when she went back to Massey for a new prosthesis she told him just how she wanted it. The new insert was more comfortable and natural looking. Ruth realized what needed to be done to make a prosthetic that worked for women, as opposed to the artificial breasts then on the market.

One day after Ruth was no longer with Mattel, she drove about halfway to Gardena to gamble, but according to her, "my car turned itself around and went back to Massey's place." She walked in, unsure of what she wanted to say until she stood in front of Massey, and then blurted out, "Peyton, I'm going into the breast business." She told him she wanted to make customized breasts that could be sold over the counter. She wanted stores to fit women to their size. She was not sure how many sizes would be needed, but she wanted to have them all available in stores to be tried on. She wanted to have separate right and left breasts, similar to the custom breasts Massey made for her, but able to be manufactured. Massey thought the idea was impractical, but Ruth was undeterred. She talked him into helping her, telling him that she would figure out how to manufacture them if he would do the sculpting.

Ruth had found her salvation. As the meetings with lawyers

over the myriad Mattel-related lawsuits ground on, and the threat of federal criminal charges loomed, she went full speed again into a new business. She had spent her life marketing and designing products. She had often lectured on defining a need and targeting consumers, on never going into business as me-too, but to solve a problem in a new way. You had to know *why* you were in business, Ruth lectured. "Every product has to have a reason to be." She announced that making prostheses was what she wanted to do for the rest of her life.

She had a loving husband and a close family, and she wanted to "spend my retirement years doing something that needed doing, and something that had to be done by a woman who had had a mastectomy." Good intentions were part of the explanation, but she also needed an outlet for the entrepreneurial energy that had always driven her. She also needed something more. Tom Kalinske, who considers her a mentor, recalled, "No one was better at spotting trends, but she also had to get redemption, had to prove she was not a bad person."

Painting Ruth as a bad person, however, or at least a malfeasant corporate officer was just what Special Counsel Hufstedler's report had done. The exhaustive five-hundred-page tome fell like a boulder into Ruth's new world. She was working on her breast idea with a team of engineers, chemists, designers, material experts, and model makers, some of whom were Mattel retirees. Her attorneys showed her the special counsel's report in mid-November, soon after it was filed. His implications were unmistakable and scrupulously documented.

Hufstedler found that Mattel had sent to the SEC, and had publicly released, false and misleading financial information. The fraud arose from a desire to show a pattern of "ordered growth with regularly increasing sales and earnings." Mattel's accounting firm, Arthur Andersen & Co., should have discovered the fraud in the ordinary course of its work, but if it did, there was no evidence that it tried to stop it.

Hufstedler gave a nod to the creativity and innovation that brought Mattel success through 1970. "The successes in turn generated a belief among management," he wrote, "that the company's growth would continue indefinitely." But Mattel management showed an "inability to adjust its beliefs to changing realities," which led to the decline in sales and profit that triggered the fraud.

Hufstedler reconstructed a nearly day-by-day calendar of corporate meetings and actions over three years. He explained how the switch to the legitimate practice of annualized accounting, started after Mattel went public, set the stage for later abuse. He laid out the plan for sales incentive programs that turned sour, and the disastrous move to diversify that began after Mattel passed the hundred-million-dollar sales mark in 1965. That year Ruth had set a new corporate objective: "to increase earnings per share in a manner which will foster further growth and enhance our stockholder investment." She was looking to increase sales volume by 10 percent per year, and earnings by 25 percent. To get there, Hufstedler wrote, Ruth had brought in Rosenberg. Rosenberg jumped on his mandate to improve Mattel's image with the financial community and fulfill the objectives Ruth had set, quickly succeeding in creating more interest in Mattel stock. Meanwhile, the acquisition program went forward.

Hufstedler pinpointed the problems with diversification. "Mattel as a toy manufacturer," he wrote, "had little expertise in the fields represented by the acquired entities. As a result, these acquired companies had to be run in large part by the previous management, with little or no active supervision by Mattel." In the case of Ringling Bros., the contract stated that Mattel would not interfere, and Feld continued to run the show.

When it came to organization, Hufstedler was blunt. Organizational charts were a fiction, and "Mattel was operated in much the same manner as when it was a small company." He noted that even Mattel officials had admitted that divisionalization was a mistake. He laid the blame for the $55 million loss in fiscal year 1972 on false hopes. The company had failed to "restrain its optimism of earlier years," and "certain company officials wanted to keep up the growth rate of the past." He was pointing his finger at Ruth, Elliot, Rosenberg, accountant Yas Yoshida, and the division heads. In a minor bright spot for Ruth, he saw no evidence of significant insider trading, except by Rosenberg.

The report, accompanied by an audit by Price Waterhouse, detailed the method used for the fraud: bill-and-hold "sales" of about fourteen million dollars that were never shipped or paid for, understating the amount of excess inventory by about seven million dollars, deferring several millions of dollars in tooling costs, and overlooking a billing error that added nearly five million dollars to the 1972 first quarter report.

Ruth tried to keep her mind on her new business. When she was asked about the special counsel's report, she offered a stock answer, "I worry about it, but there's nothing I can do. Whatever will be, will be." But she had a good idea of what would be. Hufstedler's report was being used to prepare a federal criminal case against her and others at Mattel.

In between endless meetings with lawyers in which Ruth took copious notes, she moved forward with producing Nearly Me. She also named her new company Ruthton, an awkward combination of "Ruth" and "Peyton." While she did not think it was a great company name, it did relieve one of her long-held resentments. Ruth explained that it was she who "really started Mattel" with Matt Matson, but when a name was chosen that combined Elliot's and Matt's first names, Ruth was left out. The same had been true for Elzac, which combined Elliot's and Zachary Zemby's names. "I was extremely active in the business," Ruth said, "but somehow Elzac came out." She admitted, "Ruthton really is a shitty name, but I couldn't figure out a name that worked. Really what I was declaring in the name was that this was something that I was going to do my way."

Ruthton started in a storage room behind Massey's office and laboratory. The space was "dirty and junky," according to Ruth, but Elliot and some friends cleaned it out and painted it. Ruth got an old tin desk and bought tools from Sears. She would park her Rolls-Royce in the alley, which had the only entrance to the storeroom, and go into work, often laughing at the incongruity.

Ruth told her team that she wanted the "world's first breakthrough design," a prosthesis that resembled a real human breast, not just a blob to plop in a bra cup. She could always spot a woman with a prosthesis, as its weight made one shoulder lower than the other. Her breast would have its own chest wall, so it would sit more naturally on the body. The core of sculptured foam was surrounded by sealed compartments of silicone fluid, not gel, because it was more "living feeling." The foam was similar to that used for Mattel's Tender Love dolls. The breast was encased in a nonstick polyurethane outer skin. It was relatively light and odor free. Ruth made forty lefts and forty rights, tapered at the top and sides and sized, like bras, from 32 to 42 and from A to DD cups. They cost a reasonable $98 to $130, depending on size, and could be worn against the body, with a cover that was included or with a pocketed bra. Hating the expensive and ugly surgical bras that were pushed on mastectomees, Ruth tested dozens of bras already on the market and then recommended which over-the-counter brand fit best with Nearly Me.

Once the breasts were constructed, Ruth needed a corps of women to test them. She went to the office of a leading Beverly

Hills breast specialist for an examination, hoping to get names of other women who would try Nearly Me breasts. After her exam she showed the doctor her prosthetic. He refused to give her names of any of his patients, no doubt out of ethical concerns, and his nurse suggested another doctor.

Ruth took a sample breast up to that doctor's office. He and his nurse were sympathetic and excited about the product. Ruth explained that she did not intend to sell the prosthetics to the women, but needed them to try on the inserts. The doctor agreed to give Ruth names of his mastectomy patients. Ruth, resentful that the other doctor had refused to help her, transferred her care.

By April 1976 Ruth began selling the breasts from a store attached to a 5,000-square-foot factory in West Los Angeles. She was not sure how to market the breast. She thought about opening her own stores, wanting to be sure that the fitting was done right. She worked on brochures, advertising Nearly Me with the slogan, "The best man-made breasts are made by a woman." In the past, she had used her gender subtly. With Ruthton, and the tragedy that spurred it, she saw her gender as a marketing tool, but Ruth had discovered something more.

The previous summer she had spoken at the inaugural event for the new Women at Mattel group. Despite her mounting problems and the rumors that raced through the company, the women embraced her. In a note that Ruth saved, one woman wrote, "You inspired us. You help us to recognize our weaknesses without self-imposed guilt, but most of all to maximize our strengths. You set the example for us to find our own unique dimension." On a collage of pictures from the event, which show Ruth laughing and relaxed, she wrote, "Women were finally starting to organize at Mattel." In one of her files from the period labeled, "Notes on Women," she kept a letter from Gloria Steinem promoting *Ms.* and a feminist essay by Cynthia Fuchs Epstein. Both pieces were frank discussions of sexism, workplace discrimination, and the need for women's activism. Ruth, who had never sought or sustained close friendships with women, was beginning to understand the power of sisterhood.

By that summer she had joined a Los Angeles group called Women in Business. The group met once a month and had occasional outings. Ruth signed up for a trip to Tecate, Mexico, that fall to stay at Rancho La Puerta, a rustic resort and spa on three thousand acres with a gorgeous mountain view and emphasis on wellness and healthy food. About twenty women drove down, sleeping two to three in each of the simple casitas dotting the property.

A few women from Mattel were in the group. Rita Rao remembered that they went out to the big Jacuzzi after dinner. "There was a lot of drinking and Ruth got ripped." The women took off their clothes and sank into the water, but Ruth held back. These women were young. None had been disfigured like her. "She had never shown her scar to anyone but Elliot," Rao explained. But that night, with the other women urging her to join them, Ruth finally pulled off her jeans and sweater and climbed in. No one seemed to notice. "We were yelling and being so rowdy," Rao said. "Eventually, management came and threw us out, and we went to someone's room and Ruth just kept telling us stories." Pat Schauer, another Mattel employee, remembered, "Ruth could hold her audience pretty well. She was always the center of attention. It soon became Ruth's hot tub."

Something happened for Ruth in that evening of camaraderie with those fun-loving, bright, ambitious women. Years later Ruth would say, recalling the evening in the Jacuzzi, "I find that I enjoy women better than I enjoy men. My world has changed. I think I may have felt victimized by men." Her transformation may have started at Tecate, but it did not end there. The little girl who had not liked other little girls, the woman who enjoyed her power among men and their attention, was discovering what she had missed. Women would restore her confidence and her hope, and make her their hero. "I was trying to rebuild my self-esteem," Ruth said. "I seemed to find friends with strangers and, strangely, with women. I had never made friends with women, and suddenly I found women were becoming my friends. I never sought them out. I found a whole new breed of women seeking me out. Young women, career women, professional women sought me out as a role model, and they sought me out as someone who could help them understand how they could achieve."

Ruth enjoyed her new role. She felt that these women were being honest with her, and she was honest with them. Although she was older than they and had done more in the business world, her loneliness pushed her to ignore their differences. She let them pull her into their circle, and they helped end her isolation.

When Ruth returned from Tecate and went to her factory in Los Angeles, she sought out Alex Laird. Laird was moving up in management at Mattel when Ruth brought her in as a marketing specialist at Ruthton. Ruth was building a woman-run company, and like all of Ruth's hires for the new company, Alex had had a mastectomy. That morning Ruth apologized to Alex for not paying more attention to her when she was trying to move up at Mattel. The trip had made her realize that she could not hold Ruthton back anymore. She was ready to market Nearly Me, not in her own stores but in high-end retail department stores. She wanted to start with Neiman Marcus in Dallas.

Even as she was building her new business, Ruth's legal problems required her attention. She was accused of criminal activities and felt as though she was constantly being called to her lawyers' office. Her legal obligations came more in conflict with her business in January 1977, when she started traveling all over the United States, promoting the Nearly Me prosthetic. Her first promotion, as she had hoped, was at Neiman Marcus in Dallas. Her second was at Woolf Brothers in Kansas City, after which she traveled to Neiman Marcus stores in other cities. A crew of women traveled with her, helping to train sales ladies as well as fitting customers. Ruth felt the marketing was working better than she had expected. She was full of plans for growing the business and creating new product lines, but when she came home, she would have another lawyers' meeting. "The meetings," Ruth said, "put me down to the ground. It was just an awful experience. I couldn't wait to get out of town and go back to get into the fitting rooms and fit women with breasts."

Nearly two million women had lost one or both breasts by 1977. Ruth had done her research. She knew that eighty-three thousand women had breast cancer in 1975 and the incidence was likely to grow by forty thousand in a decade. "The market is not expanding but exploding. Breast cancer strikes one out of every fourteen women in the United States," Ruth said in an interview. "There's no way we can cover the United States, but we're expanding as rapidly as possible."

Ruth knew that surgery could destroy these women's self-images. She also knew that "personalized service and understanding are the way to a customer's heart and pocketbook." She built a team of women like herself: positive, no-nonsense women who had also had the surgery. Many of them were her original customers. "I am possessive and I have put in too much blood and sweat to entrust anything about Nearly Me to the uncaring," she told a reporter. She encouraged husbands to come to the fittings. "They go through their own kind of hell when their wives have mastectomies," she said. "They're brought up in a breast-conscious society, and they need to have this brought out of the closet as much as women." She was speaking from her own experience, knowing the toll her illness had taken on Elliot.

They were still in love, but she felt more distance from him as she built a business alone. Elliot was a member of the Ruthton board and managed all their personal affairs, but it was much lonelier founding a business without him. "I can't share intimate experiences with Elliot, can't share in a deep sense," Ruth said wistfully. Elliot seemed to understand. "She loved to put a breast on someone," he remembered, "and see them smile, and it made her happy and opened up her life . . . it brought her back to life. I just did not want to go back into business. Ruthton did not make much money, but she loved traveling and she loved it."

Ruth traveled four out of every six weeks. "My calendar looks like a racetrack. I've never worked so hard in my life nor enjoyed it so much." She went to Bonwit Teller, Bloomingdale's, and Marshall Field. She sold in home health stores for women who found the upscale stores too intimidating. Some of the stores were reluctant at first, but soon Bonwit's was creating a special store within the store, just for Nearly Me. Store management announced that they were rejecting the idea that women who had mastectomies were bad people. "She's lost a part of her body," their spokesman explained, "she hasn't committed a crime." Bloomingdale's opened a Nearly Me boutique.

Ruth found that being in the fitting room with strangers that she would never see again and whose names she would not remember gave her great emotional satisfaction. "To take a woman who comes in, and I will work on her and very often she will be quite hostile or confused or uptight or all so unsure of herself. I take that woman, take her through a fitting, have a happy experience where at the end she's laughing and joking and sticking her chest out and showing off what she's wearing. Half the place is enjoying it with her, and she walks out and she gives me that look and a hug and a kiss. I never see her again [but] that's my high." Even though the traveling took Ruth away from Elliot, she was enjoying her hands-on work too much to stop.

Ruth was planning for a 25,000-square-foot factory in the latter part of 1977. The department store employee training and fittings and attendant public relations had been wildly successful. On television shows she was funny and loose and joyful. She still strode around like a dynamo, her white hair cut in a close cap, brown eyes full of sparkle, and skin that belied her age and any ravage from her illness. She still found time to keep her nails and makeup perfect. She would drop her famous one-liners, flashing a broad ruby-red smile and arch her left eyebrow. "I'm surrounded by boobs. Just call me the booby hatch, or the booby hatcher," Ruth told one interviewer. She was often asked about the Barbie doll, and she came up with a standard response: "I've come full cycle from the first doll with a real breast to answering a real woman's need for a breast." Interviewed by Jane Pauley on the *Today* show, Ruth said she wanted to make it so "women could stick their tits out." On another television show, she discovered that she did not have a sample prosthesis with her, so she pulled one out of her bra and handed it to the shocked host. The ploy worked so well that she began using it to "liven things up," as she put it. "We were getting lots of publicity," Ruth said, "and I was turning on again to life. It was a wonderful, wonderful experience to stand there toe to toe with women and fit them with this prosthesis, which I had designed and made. I was really thrilled. It became my salvation." In April *People* magazine ran a story on Nearly Me with a picture of Ruth, her blouse pulled wide open and a broad smile on her face. She was her best advertisement.

To the women she fitted, Ruth was their salvation. She received letters, heartrending and heartfelt. From Detroit, a woman wrote, "I had to walk the road of acceptance alone . . . being raised in an orphanage and foster homes, I had to face this nightmare alone. The pain, the fear, the ugliness of the scar . . . being a secretary, I couldn't return to work. . . . I thank God for the inner strength and guidance and I thank you for allowing me to look 'Nearly Me.'" From Honolulu, another woman penned her gratitude, "After my radical surgery twenty years ago I was *never* without pain. Even at night my right side and upper arm ached. I was fitted and walked out of the shop. When I went to bed I lay there in peace with no pain for the first time in twenty years." A woman in Czechoslovakia carefully inscribed a letter, "I wear it and call it my comforter because during the most critical period it helped me to overcome my complexes and regain my self-confidence. I treat it with great care because I shan't be able to purchase a new Nearly Me here."

There was one letter Ruth made sure to keep in her file. She had driven to Rancho Mirage, California, to fit former first lady Betty Ford. She wrote to thank Ruth both for fitting her and for sending an alternate insert for her to try.

NBC correspondent Betty Rollin helped bring to light the courage of women like Ruth, Ford, and Marvella Bayh, Senator Birch Bayh's wife, who had revealed their surgery. Rollin wrote the book *First, You Cry* in 1976 about her own breast cancer and mastectomy. "Part of that coming out," Rollin said, "is that women want to make the best adjustment possible. It's the beginning of recovery when you want to do things about it, when you want to look as well as you can. It's happened to so many of us that we have to deal with it in a straightforward way."

Ruth had her own take on putting her life back together. "When and if life isn't beautiful to some degree you've got to take stock of yourself and figure out what you are doing to destroy

its beauty. You can't really accept life until you accept yourself."
She had found the way to accept herself as a cancer survivor, but
another role awaited her that would again make her feel horrified
and demeaned.

On January 10, 1978, Ruth met with her new criminal attorney,
Stan Mortenson, in preparation for the ordeal of the following
day. She was going to appear before the federal grand jury, and he
told her that an indictment would likely follow. He was right. Just
after her meeting with Betty Ford, on February 17, 1978, Ruth
Handler was indicted on ten counts of mail fraud, making false
statements to the SEC, and making false statements both in her
Registration Statement and to federally insured banks. She faced
a fifty-seven-thousand-dollar fine, the maximum allowed by law,
and forty-one years in federal prison.

Chapter 16

The Wages of Fraud

I learned a long time ago that when something starts to go
bad, get the hell out of it, don't hang in, because in most cases
if it ain't going right, it ain't going to go right.

In the late afternoon of Tuesday, September 5, 1978, Judge Robert
Takasugi's courtroom in the Federal District Courthouse in Los
Angeles was packed with reporters. Word was out that Ruth Handler would make a plea to the raft of felony charges against her.
Ruth was big news in Los Angeles, where Mattel had been a major
employer and generous charitable contributor for more than two
decades. Her fall from power as one of the few top corporate
women in America had national interest as well.

She had the dubious distinction of being part of the most high-
profile corporate scandal of the 1970s. Junk bond dealer Michael
Milken had yet to be investigated by the SEC. The scandals of
Enron, Tyco, and WorldCom were more than a decade away.
Martha Stewart was just beginning to build her empire, years away
from the felony charges that would send her to federal prison for
five months. The white-haired grandmother who had given little

girls their beloved Barbie dolls was an irresistible magnet for the reporters who lined the courtroom.

Assistant U.S. Attorney John Vandevelde, parked at the prosecution table, looked annoyed. There had been meetings in U.S. Attorney Andrea Sheridan Ordin's office, where Ruth's lawyers, Herbert "Jack" Miller and Stan Mortenson, argued for a plea deal. Miller, a legal legend, would sit quietly listening, but when he pulled himself up to the table he was a commanding presence. Ordin was less than a year into her job as head of the office, and Vandevelde was a young assistant, but they would not budge from the government's position. They wanted at least one guilty plea out of the ten counts. They felt the public deserved that much. The final decision, however, rested with the judge, and after meetings in his chamber Vandevelde knew that Takasugi would be more lenient.

Ruth had been lucky to get Takasugi assigned to her case. There were eighteen federal judges on the bench in Los Angeles. According to one experienced prosecutor, only two or three of them would have been likely to agree to her no-contest plea.

Ruth arrived with an entourage of family, including Elliot, her children, and her grandchildren. She needed their support. She was desperately trying to end the legal case so she could get back to the work she loved at Ruthton.

The day of her indictment back in January had been horror enough, but what followed had terrified her. Ruth had endured the court hearing and followed instructions to go to the basement of the courthouse to be processed. She stood with Elliot and her two attorneys in a stark anteroom but could see two holding cells, one for men and one for women, behind a locked door. Within a few minutes, a police officer led Ruth alone through the door. She thought she was going to sign papers, but instead she was fingerprinted and a card was placed around her neck before mug shots were taken. "Cold horror crept down my spine. This is what they do when you're going to jail," she thought. A woman officer ordered Ruth to follow her, saying that she had to get rid of her jewelry, adding, "They'll kill for them." Shoving Ruth into a windowless room, she had her take off her watch, wedding ring, earrings, gold chain, and belt, and then led her toward the women's cell. As the guard put the key in the lock, Ruth ran toward Elliot, screaming his name. Her lawyers stepped in, explaining to the jail attendant that there was a mistake and Ruth was not supposed to be incarcerated. Only then did Ruth, still shaking with fear, complete the paperwork that put her in the federal criminal justice system.

The charges filed in January by the government relied on special counsel Seth Hufstedler's report, but focused on examples of fraud and false statements that had misled Wall Street and influenced borrowing from banks. Ruth, Rosenberg, Yoshida, and two others were charged. Forty-five "overt acts" of fraud over a five-year period were listed, including bill-and-hold orders, annualization of financial statements to falsely defer expenses and manipulation of excess inventories, tooling costs, and royalty expenses. Jack Ryan, who held many Mattel patents and supported his grand lifestyle on his royalties, had allegedly been cheated. As with the other charges, Ruth claimed to know nothing about Ryan's royalties. Perhaps, she speculated, he had asked for the reduction because of his own divorce proceedings.

The charges gave the auditing firm Arthur Andersen a reprieve, with the indictment finding that it, too, had been given false information by Mattel. Unlike Hufstedler's conclusion, the indictment charged that Ruth traded in Mattel stock, based on her insider knowledge, to enrich herself. In 1972 she sold 8,300 shares for $191,000. She was infuriated by the charge, but she was devastated by another allegation. She and Elliot always prided themselves on taking care of the "Mattel family." In November 1970, the indictment charged, Ruth and Rosenberg discussed eliminating approximately $2.6 million of Mattel's contribution to the employee profit-sharing plan to improve earnings.

Ruth immediately issued a press release pronouncing her innocence and setting up one of her defenses. She claimed the government had delayed too long by waiting eight years to bring charges. She said she had "turned the other cheek," and allowed false accusations to be made against her because she wanted to do what was best for Mattel. She had resigned from the company for the same reason, hoping she could help speed Mattel's financial recovery. But she was changing her tactics. "I cannot ignore these accusations any longer," Ruth said. "It is now my turn to put the lie to those who prefer to blame me for Mattel's problems. I am not guilty of any criminal conduct, and I intend to exert every ounce of strength I have to prove my innocence to the Court and to the public generally." For Ruth, the only bright spot was that Elliot did not get charged. He was helped by a lie detector test offered by his attorneys that affirmed his innocence. Getting a confidential polygraph with a certified polygrapher was a common tactic for defendants trying to ward off an indictment. None was produced for Ruth. Considering the time Elliot spent in R & D and the lie-detector results, the government declined to prosecute him. "I was very glad to get [Elliot] out. There was not an ounce of resentment or jealousy or anything else you might think about," Ruth said. "I felt very lonely, but that had nothing to do with any bad feelings toward Elliot. I don't know whether I was more lonely alone than with Elliot. You can be lonely with someone. Even when the two of us were in this thing together at the beginning, I still felt very lonely."

. . . .

For a year Stan Mortenson told Ruth that he was certain the government was going forward. The delay played to her advantage, he assured her. He advised her to try to weather the publicity and focus on her business. There were ways to delay the case, perhaps derail it. There were statute-of-limitations arguments. The government's case was tenuous. If they gave immunity, their witnesses could be challenged. The trial date was June 13, but motions would be flying and there would be months of wrangling. Mortenson also guessed that the government would offer Yoshida a deal. He was right.

On February 28, 1978, former Mattel vice president of finance Yas Yoshida pleaded guilty to one count of filing false annual reports with the SEC, including one that overstated the company's sales by ten million dollars. He had cut a deal that left him facing a possible two years in prison and ten thousand dollars in fines, but with assurances from prosecutors that his cooperation would be brought to the judge's attention at sentencing. To ensure that he followed through, his sentencing was set to occur after Ruth's trial. Yoshida's testimony against Ruth would make the government's case. It was laid out in the transcript of his appearance before the grand jury the previous summer.

Yoshida implicated all of the other defendants without equivocation. Did Ruth routinely scrutinize all the sales reports? Yes. Did she generally conduct the daily business of the company? Yes. Rosenberg had set targets that had to be met regardless of sales. Had Yoshida told Ruth what he had done to achieve those targets? Yes, he told her that he had deferred over two million dollars that in the past he would have recognized. Did he discuss eliminating the contribution to the pension plan with Ruth? Yes. Did he outline for Ruth those items that had been falsified in the reports and records, and did she order that the false bill-and-hold documents be purged? Yes and yes.

Yoshida testified for hours, detailing each year and each event that involved the fraudulent scheme to boost Mattel's sales and profits. His testimony was precise and damning. He had worked for Mattel since 1950. He would be a difficult, if not impossible witness to impeach.

While Ruth's lawyers maneuvered to delay the trial or avoid it, she tried to get on with her life and her new business. It was a tense and bitter summer. One day she would meet with her attorneys at her Century City apartment. The next day she would fly off to fit more grateful women at a Ruthton event. Her activities with the business, however, could not overcome her despair. Every article Ruth read in the *Los Angeles Times,* the *Wall Street Journal*, or the *New York Times* seemed to proclaim her guilt. She was embarrassed to see neighbors on the elevator in her apartment building. She avoided the Hillcrest Country Club, where she and Elliot had been regulars. She sold her Rolls-Royce, not wanting to stand out in any way. Elliot was "in a state of shock," too, as Ruth wrote in her autobiography. "He tried in every way to help me get back on track, and he was concerned and supportive during my terrible flashes of despair. But the fact is, I felt very much alone—facing the specter of a prison sentence. . . ."

Ruth's lawyers challenged the use of Hufstedler's report for the government's charges, claiming it was gathered in violation of the defendant's constitutional rights. They argued that the government had improperly delayed getting the indictments and that a five-year statute of limitations barred prosecution of any acts before 1973. In all, they filed eight motions trying to dismiss the indictments. On August 4 Judge Takasugi rejected them all. "Motions were all stacked up and we marched down, and the judge denied them all. We were elated," Vandevelde remembered.

Three weeks later Seymour Rosenberg pleaded no contest to the charges against him. Like Ruth, he faced more than forty years in jail. At a meeting with the judge, the Justice Department attorneys protested Rosenberg's request for a plea deal and the guarantee of probation rather than jail time. Rosenberg implored the judge to consider his wife's poor health. Takasugi, the first Japanese American appointed to the federal bench, had been serving less than two years. As a twelve-year-old living in Tacoma, Washington, he had been interned with his family during World War II. He was known for being fair and for protecting minority rights. Then–U.S. Attorney Andrea Ordin remembers that he was known as a more compassionate and sympathetic judge than some others from his time in Superior Court. Rosenberg's sentencing was set for December, but the judge made clear that he would not have to worry about being sent away from his ailing wife.

Ruth's trial was set to begin October 3. Her lawyers, telling her it could last three months, accelerated their demands for meetings. She sat with them in total misery. She wrote extensive notes, desperate to prove her innocence and obsessed with restoring her reputation, yet she wanted the ordeal to end.

One day Ruth found the pressure unbearable. Her lawyers were insisting that she appear in court on a date when she had scheduled an out-of-town promotion for Ruthton. Her promotions were set two or three months in advance, and she did not want to cancel. Her lawyer explained that she was under court order and had to appear. In frustration she told him that she would not do it and asked if there was something that could be done to end the continual pressure her legal problems were creating. He said she could plead no contest, explaining that the plea was the equivalent of admitting guilt but that she probably would not be put in jail. But she was not guilty, she protested. She told him she wanted to plead no contest and also say that she was innocent.

Her idea flew in the face of accepted practice, but her lawyers promised to do some research to see if she could have her way. Assistant U.S. Attorney John Vandevelde had already made a statement to the press after Rosenberg's plea that the Justice Department "did not think it [was] in the best interest of the public to accept" no-contest pleas. No doubt, Justice would be equally vociferous in fighting Ruth's attempt to follow Rosenberg, especially if she wanted to thwart the common understanding of the plea as an admission of guilt. Judge Takasugi had made it clear to Rosenberg that his plea was equivalent to an admission of guilt, although it could not be used against him in other proceedings.

Within days, hanging his theory on an obscure legal maneuver called an Alford plea, after a Supreme Court decision from 1970, Ruth's lawyer told her she could plead no contest but still assert her innocence. As she sat at the defense table, feeling like the whole world was watching, she held tight to her prepared statement and her fierce desire to claim her innocence.

Judge Takasugi, a short, stout, and serious jurist, announced that an "agreement" had been reached. He decided to allow Ruth to plead no contest. In exchange, she would not be imprisoned. She must realize, however, the judge made clear, that her action was the equivalent of a guilty plea. Did she understand that she was making a guilty plea, he asked? "I believe that I am innocent of any criminal wrongdoing," Ruth answered, "but I decided, with my attorney's concurrence, to plead nolo." The judge seemed satisfied, but the prosecutors were not. Takasugi ordered that a judgment of conviction be entered on all ten charges and set a date for sentencing in December. Then Vandevelde rose to protest. He said the government was not taking part in the agreement. As with Rosenberg's case, the Justice Department lawyers felt the public was entitled to a full airing of the charges and evidence.

When the hearing ended, the judge told reporters that there

was a "tacit agreement" with the prosecutors that Ruth would not have to go to jail, but U.S. Attorney Andrea Ordin did not agree. "We believe the public interest requires a final, public, and unambiguous resolution," she told the *Los Angeles Times*. Ruth's claim of innocence despite her plea "calls into question the integrity of the system," Ordin argued. She had not yet seen the statement that Ruth was handing out as she left the courthouse.

"It is my understanding that I am not admitting that I am guilty of any of the charges leveled against me," the statement read. "In fact, I steadfastly deny that I am guilty of any criminal wrongdoing. And I feel that were I to stand trial, I would be able to demonstrate the falsity of these accusations." Ruth had, however, "lost my zeal to fight." Her new company had totally consumed her life. "In light of this new venture, which I do not wish to jeopardize by personal commitment to a lengthy trial." In her only nod to the court's authority, Ruth concluded, "I recognize, of course, that even though I continue to assert my innocence, that for purposes of this particular proceeding, the court will consider my plea as the equivalent of guilty. And I am prepared to accept the consequences that flow from that fact."

The prosecutors struggled to contain their anger. Ordin gave an interview to the *Herald Examiner*. Two days after the hearing, the paper ran a story with the irresistible headline "Did Mattel Official's Plea Toy with Justice?" Ordin was quoted saying that a no-contest plea deprived the public of the facts. Ominously, she said that she would never agree to a "no jail" commitment without "acknowledgement of guilt." Ruth's lawyers wrote to Ordin, protesting her public statements and laying out their justification for Ruth's actions, but the prosecutor was up in arms. "We intend to point out to the court at the time of sentencing . . . our views of the relative culpability of the defendants." Ordin made clear that whether a defendant had "acknowledged their wrongdoing and accepted responsibility for it" would be a key factor in the Justice Department's recommendation regarding prison.

Ruth had a momentary victory, but the cost was dangerously high. The Justice Department attorneys were poised to recommend jail time. All she could hope for was the continued mercy of the judge. But Ruth's lawyers learned that Judge Takasugi was also angry about Ruth's written statement of innocence. He had full discretion to put aside his "tacit agreement" about jail time, and rising pressure from prosecutors could be enough to change his mind. Ordin concluded her letter to Ruth's attorneys with the dark promise that she would have a sentencing memorandum to the court before the hearing. Ruth could not understand Ordin's hostility. "This U.S. attorney, Andrea Ordin, she was a bitch," Ruth said. "I'll take all the men rather than one bitchy woman. She felt something was wrong with her career by reason of me. I don't know why she went after me. She said there was a flaw in the system, and she went on a rampage."

Ironically, like Ruth, Andrea Ordin was a woman pioneer. In 1918 the first woman was appointed U.S. Attorney. In 1977 President Jimmy Carter appointed the second. Ordin was the third. She was also the first Latina to get the job. She had never even met Ruth during the course of the litigation, but as head of the office, she became the focus of Ruth's resentment.

Three months later at her sentencing hearing, Ruth sat waiting for Judge Takasugi to enter his courtroom. This time she had no statement prepared. She only hoped and prayed that he had not changed his mind about putting her in jail. She accepted that she would be sentenced to community service. She was prepared for that. She had even tried to influence what her service might be.

Cathryn Klapp, Ruth's probation officer, had prepared a presentencing report. If the judge followed through with probation, he would likely rely on Klapp's recommendation. Ruth had carried a proposal into her first meeting with Klapp in October. For her public service, Ruth suggested, she would be prepared to give free breasts to women who needed them and could not pay for them. She was willing to give away hundreds of thousands of dollars' worth of the inserts. She loved her idea and argued with passion that it would be a major community service. Klapp was skeptical. Wasn't Ruth just trying to get good publicity for Nearly Me? How could the court be sure she would not spend most of her time running the for-profit side of the business and delegating the giveaway? Despite heartfelt letters from Elliot and friends attesting to Ruth's sincerity and goodwill, the probation officer seemed unmoved.

In Ruth's mind, Klapp was another "bitch" with a chip on her shoulder about Ruth's lifestyle. On a visit to the Handlers' penthouse to discuss appropriate service for Ruth, Klapp looked at the artwork on display—Monet, Renoir, Pissarro, Picasso. The apartment was like a small art museum, its walls covered with millions of dollars' worth of paintings. "You people have no right owning art like this," Klapp burst out after a few minutes of looking around. "It belongs in a museum. I hope you'll at least put them in your will for some museum." All Ruth could think was "Who is she, telling me what I can and can't own?"

The courtroom quieted as Judge Takasugi took the bench. He looked grave. After arranging some papers, he spoke directly to Ruth and Rosenberg, who was being sentenced at the same time. Your crimes, he told them, "are exploitive, parasitic, and disgraceful to anything in society." He ordered that they pay the maximum fine, fifty-seven thousand dollars, and that it be used as reparation on a program of occupational rehabilitation for federal offenders. Then he ordered them placed on five years' probation with a sentence of five hundred hours of community service each year.

Turning to Ruth, the judge said that her service must be with a charitable organization picked in consultation with the probation officer. Personal participation was required. A monetary contribution or efforts "utilized by reason of defendant's wealth" were not acceptable. Finally, he struck the last blow. Any participation, he told Ruth, "promoting defendant's business enterprises shall be carefully examined, screened, and avoided. The court, however, does not discourage Mrs. Ruth Handler's donation of her company's prostheses to indigent mastectomees." Judge Takasugi used the word Ruth had coined, but not in the way she had hoped. He gave her the longest public service sentence ever handed out, and not a minute of it could be spent working at Ruthton.

Chapter 17

Forced Service

I decided to give in gracefully.

Ruth was sixty-two years old, a wife, mother, and grandmother; a business founder and entrepreneur; a mastectomee and a felon. During the years she ran Mattel she had been named Outstanding Business Woman of the year by the National Association of Accountants; received the Brotherhood Award from the National Conference of Christians and Jews; been named Woman of the Year by the Western States Advertising Agencies Association; and been honored by the City of Hope, the Jewish Community Foundation, the American Cancer Society, and many smaller charities and organizations. She had been a presidential appointee, and served on the National Business Council for Consumer Affairs and the Advisory Committee on the Economic Role of Women. She had taught in the School of Management at UCLA, made innumerable speeches, and received thousands of fan letters for inventing Barbie as well as Nearly Me.

As Ruth considered where to turn for her court-ordered community service, however, she felt despair. She could not face going to people who knew her before she was labeled a criminal. Through her charitable work, Ruth knew many leaders in the philanthropic circles of LA, but she did not think she could bear the embarrassment and humiliation.

She tried to find public service efforts where she did not know anyone. Some of the work she found pleasant, but she could not reconcile herself to following orders and being monitored. "I had to have my hours signed off by each charity, each time. It was humiliating to go to somebody and describe what I've done and have them sign off."

Ruth finally took a job at her temple, which she had helped found. A woman member assigned Ruth gofer tasks alphabetizing and filing. The woman kept careful track of Ruth's hours on time cards. "We had donated hundreds of thousands of dollars," Ruth said, "and here I am being told by this person how to do the filing, and she was talking down to me like I was a ten-year-old. Humiliating." Ruth quit in short order. She haggled with her probation officer, insisting that travel time be counted toward her service. She complained that Ruthton took so much time, she had no time or energy for the service. She wanted to do meaningful work. "Don't knock your brains out," her probation officer told her. "Just get something close to your house. You walk home and do it slow and easy and just get your hours. Don't try to prove anything. You won't get any brownie points." Ruth tried to follow his advice.

She found the parole system chaotic and frustrating. Just when she felt she had an understanding with her first parole officer about what activities counted as public service, he moved to another office. She started over, again having to argue about the eligibility of work she did, but this man left as well. Ruth found the changes traumatic. "I was fit to be tied," she said. "I was ready to commit suicide. It was awful . . . another one, after I had gotten these other two so well trained."

To her, Steve Wishny, the young man who took over her case had a "pie-in-the-sky face." She thought of him as a dreamer and do-gooder full of idealism. He told her he had been watching her case. He had decided that the parole office had not been using her correctly. When he said that, Ruth burst into tears. "For Christ's sake," she said, "I don't want to be used correctly." Wishny was undeterred. He told Ruth that she was not the type for emptying bedpans or other menial work. He had bigger plans for her talents.

Wishny was working on a program to get white-collar probationers to help blue-collar probationers with job training and life planning. He connected Ruth with three men, also on probation: an accountant, a former plastics company owner, and a public relations executive. Together they began discussing a program. Steve explained that the idea stemmed from a recent case in which meatpacking executives were convicted of bribing Department of Agriculture inspectors. The job training program they established, placing young ex-offenders in the meat industry, was a great success.

Ruth grabbed on to the idea. She wanted to start planning; however, she found her fellow probationers were happy to hold discussions but reluctant to act. They frustrated her with months of talk about the problem but refusal to plan what they would do about it. They would not have gotten past the first interview at Mattel, Ruth thought in disgust. "I really thought the whole thing was a farce," she said. Although she liked the idea, she gave up on making it happen. Instead, she turned her efforts to cutting short her probation. Her lawyer filed an application to end her obligatory service. She threw her energy into the scheme, angering the probation department. Wishny, who had been warm in his relations with Ruth, was furious when he received the application. His tirade caught her by surprise. "He tore into me something terrible," Ruth said. "It was just awful."

Besides the filing of an application to shorten her probation,

Ruth's doctor Elsie Giorgi sent a three-and-a-half-page letter to Stan Mortenson, her lawyer, in March 1979. Giorgi must have felt a close kinship to Ruth. She was the tenth child of Italian immigrants, and she worked in the office of a trucking company for twelve years to earn money for medical school. She was the moving force behind establishing a hospital in Watts where the ratio of doctors was 1 to 2,900 residents and the infant mortality rate was double the national rate. Like Ruth, she was a fighter, especially when it came to her patients.

Ruth, Giorgi said, was severely depressed and anxious. She suffered from low self-esteem. Ruth's physical symptoms included high blood pressure, cold sweats, fatigue, and burning chest pains. All of her symptoms started after her sentencing, and the only place she felt any satisfaction or solace was at Ruthton. After a three-and-a-half-hour session with her patient, the doctor concluded that Ruth's sentence was taking a detrimental physical and emotional toll. Giorgi feared a complete breakdown. She asked Mortenson to tell the court that Ruth's work with Ruthton was service enough. The breast prosthetics company was losing money. Ruth did it only because of the good it did for women. Why should she be forced to do additional meaningless work? She assured Mortenson that Ruth had not asked her to write the letter, and offered to speak to the judge directly if that would help.

Giorgi was right about Ruth's distress. She felt as though everyone was pulling at her—her probation officer, the women in her company, even Elliot. He was concerned about her health. He did not understand why she could not relax a bit, take some things off her overfull plate. He thought selling Ruthton would be a good idea, but Ruth could not even contemplate that. "Elliot's saying 'dump it, just take the whole loss and write it off on our taxes,'" Ruth said. "He wasn't on the same wavelength as I after all these years if he can say that so easily."

Giorgi's letter and Ruth's entreaties were not enough. Wishny depended on Ruth for his project. "Do you know how special you are?" he said to Ruth. "There's no one in the whole world quite like you. You're the kind of person who can fall in a pile of shit and come out with a bed of roses." He offered to try to change her sentence, holding out the possibility that she might reduce her time based on the quality of her work rather than its quantity. Finally, Ruth gave in, with the caveat that she be allowed to work directly with Steve and his boss. She still hated the humiliation of having him sign off on her time card every day. Creating her own document, she insisted he sign off on her version of a time card. "I had done that deliberately," she said, "to humiliate him the same way I have been humiliated." He told her more than once that no one had ever asked him to sign a paper. "Now you know what it's like," Ruth shot back.

She began to warm to her role with Wishny. He did need her. When he asked for a recommendation for someone to head the citizens' board of Foundation for People, the organization they were forming, she suggested Ed Sanders, a civic-minded lawyer who served on many prominent boards and would soon head to Washington, D.C., to work in President Carter's administration. She arranged a lunch with Sanders and Wishny at the Hillcrest Country Club.

Sanders loved the idea of Foundation for People, but more important for Ruth, he gave her the affirmation she craved. "You know why this thing's bound to succeed?" he said to Ruth. "Because you're doing it. Do you know why I want in? Because you're doing it." Looking back, Sanders recalled Ruth as "an outstanding woman, smart as hell. I knew it was a tough time for her, and I was willing to help her in any way." She had been trying to get out, but Sanders's words helped to reconcile her to her sentence. She was amazed to hear that even the judge believed in her. Wishny told her that he had asked Judge Takasugi to allow Ruth to serve on the organization's board. He had agreed. "He feels you can move mountains," Wishny told her.

The board met at the Price Waterhouse offices in Century City, near Ruth's apartment. She was named president. They voted to work together with a program called Boys Republic, to help troubled young men aged eighteen to twenty-one find work, stability, and direction. The Foundation for People renovated a building near the University of Southern California campus, a broken-down hotel that they turned into a residence with space for tutoring and a library.

Ruth felt proud of every phase of the program. She struggled to find meaning in the terrible events that had consumed the decade of the 1970s—her cancer, her fall from power, her criminal indictment, plea, and sentencing. In her autobiography she wrote, "In some ways, [the Foundation for People] also presented me with a reason for the ghastly sequence of events that had cost Elliot and me the control of a company we founded and loved, that had cost us millions of dollars, that had affected my health and my relationships, and that had drastically changed my life. At least now I could . . . see that my own misfortune had helped me turn around some lives for the better."

Now with a program and purpose, Ruth became more comfortable using her contacts. One night, she and Elliot went to the Saloon restaurant. As they walked in, a man sitting at one of the tables began to wave at them and call Elliot's name. Alex Green had met Elliot when they both paid five dollars for a ride from Denver to California in 1936, when Elliot had first come to join Ruth. They had not kept in close touch, but Ruth knew that Green was running a shoe business.

She asked Green how his business was doing. He told her he

had five hundred employees and was the only shoe manufacturer in the United States, because the industry had moved overseas. Ruth told him that he might be just what she was looking for. She called him the next week, asking for a time to bring a team from the probation department to his factory. Green said he would love to have them.

Ruth was delighted when Wishny brought his boss, Dr. Jack Cox, on the factory tour. She realized how important the project was to the department. "In my wildest dreams," she said, "I never thought [Cox] would want to go visit a shoe factory."

Green's factory was a model of production and efficiency. Like factories in Asia, his workers were packed into narrow aisles so tightly that they had little room to move. His small factory was turning out three thousand pairs of shoes a day.

Green delighted in showing Ruth and the probation staff his entire operation, praising her entrepreneurial acumen as he went. She felt as though he idolized her. "It was a thrill in itself," Ruth said, "that he felt that way about me because I hadn't known I had any friends." Ruth was also proud of what Green had accomplished. He was two years older than Elliot, and like the Handlers, he had started from nothing.

Green brought his shop foreman over to talk to the group. The foreman ran an operation that had little room for downtime or error. He did not like the idea of a program that might slow down production. Ruth saw that she would have to persuade him to help or working with Green was doomed. "I set about turning him around," she said. "Eventually, he got the point through his head that he has a responsibility to himself and his wife, if he doesn't want some kid to knock him over the head and rob him or kill him, to cure some of the social ills that exist."

The foreman came up with the perfect idea. He told Ruth

and the others that there was a shortage of shoe repairmen. The makers of shoe repair equipment, he told them, would happily supply trainers and training equipment. The course took about eight weeks. There would be plenty of work, he assured them. Shoe repair was a dying art.

Ruth ran with the idea. As Wishny had predicted, her years of management experience were invaluable to the project. Ever curious, she enjoyed learning about and improving the lives of people she otherwise never would have known. She still hoped, however, to complete her service quickly. She found the shoe repair idea "terribly rewarding and very exciting," but also, she said, "it made me all the more valuable to the probation department when I'm trying to get out of it." She was right. Wishny and Cox saw how hard she worked to make the program a success.

In May 1982 they recommended to Robert Latta, the chief probation officer, that Ruth be allowed to finish her service early. Latta wrote to Judge Takasugi. Ruth had made "diligent efforts" in the Foundation for People program he said, recommending that her probation be terminated. On June 8, the judge signed the order that cut eighteen months off Ruth's sentence and released her from probation. She was free of lawyers and lawsuits and courtrooms and judges. She was free to devote all her time to Ruthton. She was free to do nothing at all. She was free.

Chapter 18

Ken and a Time of Plague

I think the best people, the ones who have
reached the highest plateaus as human beings, are those
who have known a great deal of adversity and have
dealt with it and then moved ahead.

Sometime in late 1991 or 1992, Ken and his wife, Suzie, went to Ruth and Elliot's beach house in Malibu, bringing along Dr. Pamela Harris. Ruth's son had come on a heartrending mission. Harris had offered to help.

Harris, a diminutive woman with sharp, intelligent blue eyes, was trained as a hematologist and oncologist. Her medical intuition put her at the cutting edge of unraveling the secret of a national scourge.

In 1978, before she met Ken, Harris was working around the clock. Her day job was at Memorial Sloan-Kettering Cancer Center in New York, and in the evenings she volunteered at a methadone clinic in Harlem. Gay men were coming in during the day with a mysterious and terrible illness. In the evening, she saw a similar disease in the drug addicts she was treating. At the time, doctors called it "gay lymph node syndrome" or just "the wasting disease," for the toll it took on bodies over time. By the mid-eighties, Harris was on a quest. She had done a fellowship in Washington, D.C., and had seen a certain kind of anemia that went with the disease. Traveling to Miami, she observed the same symptoms that she had seen in New York in Haitian detainees. Around the same time, Dr. Anthony Gallo announced that he had found the virus responsible for the disease—HIV. Soon a new disease name would enter the national lexicon: acquired immunodeficiency syndrome, or AIDS.

Harris moved home to Washington, D.C., and opened an oncology and AIDS practice in a condominium office she owned in the multicultural Adams Morgan section of the city. One day in 1990 Ken Handler walked into her office.

Ken had a sick look, but he was tall and stood straight and was fairly robust. He was still married to Suzie, but he believed he had contracted the disease from an intimate encounter with a young man. He had been desperate to heal himself, taking monthly trips to Ecuador, where he had found a man with a "cure" that used native plants. Ken was financing research on natural remedies in the South American country. He came to Harris for help with his symptoms and for her opinion as a researcher. She became his primary doctor and his friend.

Harris helped Ken break the devastating truth to Suzie. "She is the most loving human being," Harris remembered, and Suzie stood by her husband even after learning his secret. "Their life was very rich. Suzie was a great Italian cook. When you saw Ken play the piano it was like watching something fantastic." Harris remembered a time when she visited Ken's house with her boyfriend and they had both been moved to tears by his piano playing. Ken had a Renaissance sensibility, and had grown up with the money to follow his artistic passions. He made three movies, staged plays, wrote and played music, and took endless photographs. In 1987, at the 4th Street Photo Gallery in New York City, he put on an exhibit of haunting photographs of gay men beset by AIDS. He called it *A Time of Plague: New York City Under Siege.*

Ken often voiced his resentment of the doll that bore his name. He hated the materialism promoted by Barbie and Ken dolls and the negative effect the toys had on children's images of themselves. In a plaintive and sometimes incoherent letter to his parents in 1970, he argued that the dolls were, "cow-towing [*sic*] to those who can't accept the issue of their own sexuality." His parents knew nothing about his secret, but they had to be told. Ken did not have much longer to live.

After settling in at the beach house, Ken said he was going to take a walk. He had already agreed with Suzie and Harris that he would leave so that they could tell his parents the sad news. Sitting in the glass-fronted room that faced the ocean, the two women explained as gently as possible about Ken's condition. Tears filled Elliot's eyes. "So that explains why he's going to Ecuador all the time," Elliot said. He got up, walked over to Ken's bar mitzvah picture, and stared at it as if "it was the most important thing in the world," according to Harris. Ruth sat, repeating, "Oh my God." And then she said simply and forcefully, "OK, we have to deal with this." Harris went outside to find Ken on the beach, and within minutes Ruth had caught up with them. "We're going to deal with this," she assured her son. Harris was moved by Ruth's reaction. "At that point in time," Harris said, "I couldn't believe how awful some parents were to their kids. But Ruth and Elliot were very loving."

Ruth may have thought that she had suffered enough grief and tragedy for a lifetime. She was not, however, a person who engaged in self-pity. She threw herself into finding some way to help Ken, in the same way she had pulled herself together after her mastectomy and the way she had assailed her legal battles. She fought down her fear, she marshaled her resources, and she pushed ahead.

. . . .

Ruth had spent the previous decade reordering her life after probation. She wanted to keep her focus on her new business, although at times she still struggled to quell resentments over Mattel. She also had to confront continuing, serious health issues. Before she learned about Ken's diagnosis, she had been completely immersed in Ruthton's growing product lines, as well as taking feelers about selling the company.

In 1982, as if flaunting her newly won freedom from probation, Ruth was the swimsuit model in advertising for Nearly Me's Wear Your Own Bra swimsuits in the 1980s. In the ads she smiles at the camera in different poses for the Malibu Swimwear collection. A handsome white-haired woman with doe eyes and a shapely body, not thin but solid, she wears the maillot with a "sunburst neckline" and another with the V neckline available in teal, lilac, raspberry, and turquoise blue. The tagline reads: "Because looking good is only the beginning." Lengthy brochures showed the materials and various products, along with fitting instructions and questions and answers for women to shop at home. There were various "silicone gel equalizers" for women to choose from, depending on size and comfort. Ruth also created ubiquitous spreadsheets for factory workers' salaries, for office workers' salaries, for promotions and tours, and for manufacturing, sales, and marketing. Once again, she was in control. She was also in demand.

Fern Field was a television producer and director for such hit shows as *Maude* and *A Different Approach*. After seeing a magazine story about Ruth's life, she called Ruth about turning her story into a television movie. Ruth wanted editorial approval and the project never came off, but Ruth agreed to hours of taped interviews with Field, starting in 1981 and spanning more than a decade. Ruth spoke frankly, often passionately. The two women, both groundbreakers, became close friends, going out as couples and traveling to Israel together.

Organizations sent a steady stream of requests to speak about being a woman in business, despite Ruth's legal problems. She was still the mother of Barbie, the founder of a company that grew from a garage to a toy industry behemoth, a woman who had succeeded while surrounded by men. Whatever her transgressions, other women wanted to know what it had been like and what advice she could offer. Who was this woman whose life had taken such dramatic turns? Ruth accepted a limited number of requests for such talks. She kept her focus on Ruthton, on the women who needed her, the women who, like her, were suffering.

Despite the pace she kept, Ruth's health was poor. As a result of her first surgery, she had near constant nerve pain and occasional muscle spasms on the left side of her chest where her breast had been removed. She felt extreme burning when she swallowed food and suffered a variety of gastrointestinal problems, combined with fatigue and shortness of breath. Her right hip started to hurt, and doctors were inconclusive about whether she was diabetic.

For the nerve pain in her chest, the doctors tried putting a neurostimulator under her skin, but it did not help. She found some relief in biofeedback relaxation techniques. For her shortness of breath, the doctor recommended brisk walking to build up her cardiovascular capability, though he must not have realized that Ruth was already a brisk walker. She went to UCLA for an evaluation in late 1982. The doctors recommended various techniques, including acupuncture, trigger-point injections, and self-hypnosis. The staff psychologist found Ruth to be "quite depressed."

The wound of her ouster from Mattel and public humiliation was as painful at times as her physical maladies. Mattel had recovered, but she had not. By 1980 Mattel was again a prosperous company. Art Spear steered it back into the black within a year of pushing Ruth out, although in 1986 he would leave Mattel after a restructuring caused by massive losses incurred on his watch. Ringling Bros. and Monogram Models turned out to be money-making acquisitions. "Mattel had a life of its own. There were such good people and processes in place, when they left it hardly made a ripple in the business," recalled Sandy Danon. Ruth and Elliot had sold their about $18.5 million of stock, about 12 percent of Mattel, after leaving the company, but shares were spread out across their family and given as stock options to many employees they considered friends. They could not help feeling invested in Mattel's success, no matter their feelings about how they had been treated.

Ruth decided that sexism was responsible for her unfair treatment by Mattel executives and government lawyers. "A great deal of what went on," she said, "was colored by the fact that I was a woman." She felt that her attackers were trying to build their reputations, and she provided a good target. She was famous and controversial because of her gender. "To bring down a woman," she said, "a famous woman who had had the nerve to get up there, just think of the reputations that could be made on bringing her down."

Still protesting her innocence, Ruth developed a philosophical response that made sense of her ordeal. She would tell various television, newspaper, and radio interviewers, "I'm not sure I would have grown much had I not lived through such grief. I think there's nothing like adversity to make one grow." She contrasted her old and new selves as she spoke of a world not of haves and have-nots, but of the carefree and the careworn. "I think people who have not known adversity, who are lucky enough to have a self-image that enables them to be successful and powerful and move forward with total confidence . . . are not as complete underneath as those of us who have experienced some real suffering."

She had learned. She had grown. She had found meaning in her misfortune. By the end of the 1980s Ruth no longer blamed the debacle at Mattel on her breast cancer. Instead she chose to see it as part of a larger plan. She saw a mysterious universe where individuals have to choose to find meaning. What happened to her at Mattel had to happen, she reasoned, for her to create Nearly Me. She suffered, but that was the price of doing so much good in the world and finding her own peace. "Making money doesn't necessarily mean one is moving ahead," she said in an interview. "Making peace with yourself is what I'm talking about. I think sometimes, at least for me anyway, it is much harder to grow as a human being than it is to make lots of money."

In February 1987 Ruth and Elliot were at a breakfast at New York's 200 Fifth Avenue Club to receive the *Doll Reader* magazine Lifetime Achievement Award. To the audience's delight, Ken and Suzie and their children attended, despite Ken's misgivings about the dolls. He was still his mother's adoring son. Ruth had received other industry honors, but the most prestigious did not come until 1989. That year she and Elliot were inducted into the Toy Industry Hall of Fame. Ruth's reemergence as a respected leader in the industry and among her peers had been gradual but steady. Her hardest reconciliation was with those people she had left behind at Mattel.

The Mattel employees Ruth had hired and worked with were in many ways her family. Before 401(k) plans, she and Elliot had pioneered a profit-sharing plan that had made many employees rich. Yet Ruth was certain that everyone from the company was "mad at her," as Derek Gable remembered. Gable, who had worked in R & D, tried to stay in touch. "We loved them," he said. In the late 1980s, some of the longtime Mattel employees like Gable organized the Mattel Alumni Association, a group for networking and philanthropic work. They started a two-year class in business called Life Skills, which empowered inner-city young people to run companies and allowed them to keep half the profits. "I called Ruth up," Gable said, "and told her we wanted her to be involved. She was guarded and reluctant. She was nervous, not bubbly or connected like she used to be." Ruth agreed to come to a meeting at a local Denny's restaurant. The Mattel employees greeted her warmly. She told them that she thought everyone was disappointed in her and did not like her or Elliot anymore. They assured her she was wrong, that her leaving had been a big loss for them. "By the end of the meeting, you could see the spark come back into her eyes," Gable said.

The boost Ruth got from awards and recognition, from the growth of Ruthton, and from her rediscovered friends in the Mattel Alumni Association helped her face a problem that was wearing down her body and mind.

In 1986 her right breast started feeling lumpy again. She had a surgical biopsy, and her surgeon assured her that the result was fine. A few days later, however, he called to say that he had found a precancerous condition after conducting more tests on the specimen. Ruth asked him what the result meant, and he told her that they would keep the breast under observation. Nothing needed to be done immediately.

For several years after that biopsy, Ruth went to her doctor for regular mammograms and checkups. She got the same cautious advice that her breast was fine but needed to be watched. "One day," she said, "I got disgusted with 'just watching it.' I was tired of talking to that doctor and those people. I was going to go to someone new and get it over with."

After years of fitting women for breast prostheses, Ruth was familiar with the various types of breast surgeries. She could recognize a particular surgeon's work by looking at a woman's scars. She called a surgeon whose work she admired and made an appointment.

Ruth walked into the doctor's office, and when he asked what he could do for her, she told him she wanted to remove her right breast. He looked at her and laughed, saying that it was the first time anyone had said that to him. She invited him to look at her records, X-rays, and lab reports. After he did, he told her that he agreed with her. It would be a good idea to remove her other breast.

Ruth gave the surgeon instructions. She told him that she did not want big clumps of flesh in the back of the underarm like she had seen on many women. When she came out of surgery, however, she found a clump of flesh not behind but in front of her underarm. The doctor claimed it was there before and she had not seen it. She was not sure he was right, but she was relieved that the operation was over.

After the surgery, Ruth's doctor told her that the precancerous condition had not spread or moved, but she did not regret her decision. She tried to believe that she had put her years of fear and the endless doctors visits and treatment for cancer behind her.

Trying to find outlets for her energy, Ruth took up bridge and spent more time with her grandchildren. Barbara's son, Todd Segal, sent her an invitation to his Whispering Maples Bed and Breakfast in rural Massachusetts to attend a workshop on macrobiotic holiday cooking. "Hope you can come, only 3,000 miles from LA!" he wrote. He had written her about his interest in macrobiotics, concerned about her health. Todd's sister, Cheryl, still in Los Angeles, was particularly close to her grandmother. Ruth had saved a letter from an official at Pepperdine University letting Ruth know that Cheryl had been accepted in 1983. Writing to Cheryl eleven years later, Ruth said how proud she was of her granddaughter, who had also gone to law school. "Keep your self-confidence high and keep plugging," Ruth wrote.

Even as she attended meetings with new doctors to learn about possible help for Ken, Ruth tried to keep the family together and on track. Ruth received an invitation to go with the United Jewish Appeal on the organization's President's Mission to Budapest and Israel. She wrote Ken, Suzie, and their daughter Samantha, who already had a trip to Israel planned, encouraging them to join her. She was, as always, hopeful, but Ken's condition was deteriorating.

Thanks to Pamela Harris, they had access to the latest information and the work of the top researchers in the field. Once again, Ruth took extensive notes at every meeting. "Virus is so complex . . . immune response of human system should be pumped up . . . skin lesions get better with expensive drug. . . ." Ken was experiencing dementia. High doses of the drug AZT seemed to help, but he refused to take it, preferring his natural remedies. By spring 1994 he was critically ill. His daughter Stacey was planning to be married that summer.

The end came in June. Ruth and Elliot were there to help, and everyone took turns at Ken's bedside. Dr. Harris was alone with him at the moment he died. She came downstairs where Ken's family sat talking quietly. "It's over," Harris told them, knowing that there was some relief after the suffering Ken had endured. Only a moment went by before Ruth popped up out of her chair and announced, "I'm going to make some corned beef sandwiches." Suzie went to the kitchen to help. They all sat around a table laden with chopped liver and corned beef sandwiches, fussing over Harris, telling her she had to eat.

Ken's daughter Stacey's wedding was scheduled for the next

day. Although in Jewish tradition a funeral is supposed to be held as soon as possible, it was acceptable to wait a day for the wedding to take place. Elliot led Stacey down the aisle. As Ruth told her, life had to go on.

Ruth was finishing the manuscript for her autobiography. She rewrote the sections about Ken, saying only that he "remained happily married to Suzie, his childhood sweetheart for thirty years . . . until his untimely death." She omitted his cause of death, but she told of his many trips to the Amazon. She recounted his theory that the plants in that region were more powerful because they were closer to the equator, where the sun was more intense. She acknowledged his work to find a cure for HIV and AIDS, among other diseases. If she did not give a full account, she also did not lie. There were family members to protect, after all. But perhaps Ruth understood that, like her, Ken had suffered from a disease that carried fear and shame with it. Like women who lost breasts to cancer in 1970, his disease was closeted. Ruth helped change the need for women to hide their mastectomies, but she could do little about the public revulsion toward AIDS sufferers.

The subtle cloaking of Ken's story, however, was never corrected. Various versions of his cause of death circulated—that he died of a disease he picked up in his exotic travels, that he died of encephalitis or of a brain tumor, as was reported in Ruth's obituary in the *New York Times* and *Los Angeles Times* eight years after his death. Meanwhile, the Ken doll had become a gay icon with Mattel's production of Earring Magic Ken in 1993. The doll was a response to children's requests for a hipper Ken, but the lilac mesh shirt, diamond earring, and black lace-up dance oxfords he wore had more than a child-centered appeal. For the gay community, still closeted and discriminated against, there was affirmation in the idea that the Ken doll could be straight or gay.

In a letter to Dr. Harris written weeks after Ken died, Ruth offered her heartfelt gratitude in a way that had often been difficult for her to express. "Pam, you were the only one Kenny trusted and you understood him so well. In the end you came when you knew we all needed you . . . the work you do and the heart you give to your patients is so wonderful. I've never known anybody like you . . . keep on trying, maybe one day it will get easier. Thank you, thank you, thank you. Love, Ruth."

Three years earlier Ruth had sold Ruthton to Spenco Medical Corporation, then a division of Kimberly-Clark. She wanted to devote as much time as needed to Ken's health. Now he was gone, and his absence left a terrible, aching void.

Chapter 19

Her Way

Barbie always represented the fact that a woman has choices.

In spring 1994 Bernie Kivowitz, who had been an East Coast sales representative for Mattel back in 1967, saw Ruth at a celebration for Barbie's thirty-fifth anniversary. Ruth had been brought back into the Mattel fold after twenty years of exile. She was asked to make appearances around the country, including a signing on Barbie's "birthday," March 9, at FAO Schwarz. The store had an entire section devoted to the doll, called Barbie on Fifth Avenue. Ruth told a reporter, "So many people stood in line for hours for my autograph that I did not have the heart to go to lunch, even to go to the bathroom. Realizing that I made a product that meant so much to people . . . was an amazing experience." For many women, Nearly Me had made Ruth a saint, but Barbie had made her a star.

Kivowitz made plans to meet her later in the summer at a Toys "R" Us flagship store in New York, where she would be signing her newly published autobiography, *Dream Doll*. He called her the night before the event and learned that Ken had died just weeks before. When he asked how she could go through with the signing, Ruth said, "You have no choice but to go on."

More than a thousand people lined up in a driving rain for Ruth to sign their books or their Barbie dolls, still in their original boxes, or any piece of memorabilia where they wanted to have a remembrance of the woman they thought of as Barbie's mother. "Ruth sat there all day," Kivowitz remembered. "Sometimes she teared up, but she talked to everyone and signed until the line was gone." She was seventy-eight years old and still struggling with a myriad health problems.

Dream Doll was less about telling her life story than justifying it. There were still scores to be settled, although those who wronged her are referenced rather than named. The book has the cautious quality of someone conscious of the problem of lawsuits but determined to tell her side. Ruth had help from Jacqueline Shannon, her collaborator. "I was a very enthusiastic Barbie player, and that was very important to Ruth," Shannon said. "But Ruth was an activist with the book."

Ruth retold the story of her ouster from Mattel, her criminal indictment, her plea, all the while protesting her innocence. The book has many villains, some demons, and little evidence of the self-reflection and recognition of responsibility that occasionally found its way into Ruth's taped interviews. "Eventually," she writes, "the man who had been put in place by the banks to replace Elliot and me was eased out of the business very quietly with no bad publicity even as the company nearly collapsed." She was talking about Art Spear, who escaped indictment and, to Ruth's mind, the public humiliation that he deserved and she endured. Asked about whether she had let go of her resentments over her ouster, Josh Denham, one of the unindicted former division heads who was close with Ruth, said, "She never put it behind her—ever." A better answer is that she managed to put her shame and anger behind her gradually, but never completely.

In *Dream Doll*, Ruth praises the new management of Mattel

brought in after Spear, while noting that the company depended on her legacy. She was right. Barbie, her clothes and accessories, and Hot Wheels, were the company's biggest sellers at the time the book came out. Barbie went through nearly eighty careers, including the army Barbie, a medic with the rank of sergeant serving in Desert Storm, which was made in 1992. President Barbie made her debut the same year. Barbie dolls could be bought in more than 150 countries. Mattel flaunted the staggering statistic that three Barbie dolls were sold somewhere in the world every second. By 1998 the doll accounted for $1.9 billion in sales for Mattel.

The company even had a CEO who some people said looked like the doll. Jill Barad, thirty-five years younger than Ruth, had the narrow face, dazzling smile, and model-perfect body of a Barbie come to life. She enjoyed posing with the dozens of Barbies she kept in her office, but like the other woman who ran Mattel, she was driven and competitive. She was also known as a marketing genius. When she was put in charge of the Barbie line in 1983, she reasoned that Barbie sales were flagging because of criticism that the doll was sexist. She started a campaign to market Barbie as a professional role model, coming up with the tag line "We Girls Can Do Anything."

Resurrecting Ruth as a company spokesperson fit Barad's theme and served as a counter to the argument that Barbie objectified women. "I brought Ruth back to Mattel after years of exclusion, and it was a great moment for the company," Barad recalled. Ruth spoke with a creator's authority, telling audiences that Barbie was made so girls could be free to imagine themselves as anything they wanted to be. Barad was the first Mattel executive to recognize the importance of Ruth's legacy.

The United Jewish Appeal had a group called Women of Distinction, and Ruth was invited to join. Barad was a member and attended Ruth's first meeting with the group in New York City.

Ruth loved the idea of getting to know accomplished Jewish women from all over the United States. She saw them as true achievers. Many of them were well-known.

About thirty or forty women sat in the opulent Fifth Avenue apartment of philanthropist Mona Riklis. They started the meeting by standing up and introducing themselves. When it was Barad's turn she said, "I'm Jill Barad. I'm president of Mattel, and I have my job only because such a woman as Ruth Handler existed before me and created the company that I now work in." Ruth, sitting in the back of the room, was touched, and the two women became friends.

After that meeting, UJA made Ruth their first Women of Distinction honoree, an award she coveted, and Jill Barad made the presentation. As more groups chose to honor Ruth, she would often ask Barad to introduce her. Ruth was still a demanding perfectionist, and Barad laughs as she remembers, "She'd yell at me for getting some fact about her wrong." At the time she met Ruth, Barad was president of girl dolls, while a man was the president of boy dolls. Ruth told her, "You can't do that. You need to have the title for yourself." By 1997 Barad had taken more than the title of president. She became chairman and chief executive of Mattel. Giving Ruth credit for her rise, Barad said, "She had great respect for me and she was a mentor."

Ruth's faith in Mattel began to return. After having sold all her shares, she began to buy back in. "A year or two after we left Mattel we sold all of our stock. Everything. But starting [in 1992] I personally started to buy a little stock, and I have a few thousand shares along with a portfolio of other shares. I treat it as I would any other stock, as an investment." Buying the stock at all contradicts Ruth's claims of dispassion. She never emotionally let go of the company she had founded. As Barad brought her back into the company as a kind of emeritus marketing star, she felt comfortable being enmeshed again, however tangentially, in the company's fortunes.

Barad was building the Barbie line overseas and invited Ruth to join her on a trip to Germany, where Barbie was popular. There were grand plans for a series of events for the doll's twenty-fifth anniversary in that country. The Berlin wall, dividing Communist-controlled East Berlin from West Berlin, had come down in 1989. A picture in the *New York Times* of a little girl climbing over the cement and twisted metal carrying a Barbie doll captured the poignancy of the moment of freedom for those in the East. "We had a warm feeling for the people there," Barad remembered.

Ruth and Barad attended a huge event in East Berlin for the reopening of a museum that had been shuttered since the end of World War II. Barad brought Ruth up onstage, and the audience gave her a standing ovation. "She was wearing this gorgeous dress and heels," Barad remembered, "and she just jumped in the air and clicked her heels, you know the way people turn their legs to the side and tap their heels, and she was about eighty years old!" Ruth had not lost her exuberance for life, for an audience, or for telling stories. Her energy on the Germany trip left Barad exhausted.

Ruth personified her own ideal for Barbie, a woman who defied convention and culture to realize her dreams. She referred to her legal transgressions as "when I resigned from the company" or "when I was forced to resign from the company," without reference to her plea and time in probation. Whether people judged her innocent or guilty, she had atoned in her own way and she did not dwell on the past.

Barad ordered up even more glamour and glitz for Barbie's fortieth birthday in 1999 than she had for the thirty-fifth. At a black-tie event at the Waldorf-Astoria hotel in New York, movie stars entered the anniversary gala on a pink carpet. With Dick Clark as master of ceremonies, the popular singer Brandy performed. There was a time-travel fashion show of Barbie clothes with Barbie-faced models strutting down the runway. Annie Leibovitz unveiled her Barbie doll artwork, and Mattel introduced the Ambassadors of Dreams. They were described as "women of achievement" who helped teach girls that they could be anything they wanted to be. There was Muriel Siebert, the first woman to buy a seat on the New York Stock Exchange; Emmy-winning talk show host Rosie O'Donnell; the president of *People* magazine, Ann Moore; the great track star Jackie Joyner-Kersee; and entertainment executive Geraldine Laybourne. For Ruth, who sat in a place of honor as the original Ambassador of Dreams, there must have been huge relief in this grand recognition. She had never understood or agreed with the criticism of Barbie as somehow damaging to girls' image of themselves. When Brandy sang the song from the new Barbie ad campaign, Ruth must have felt vindicated. It was called, "Be Anything."

One thing Barbie was not, unlike Ruth, was a wife and mother. While Mattel marketed a number of wedding-themed Barbie and Ken outfits and accessories, Barbie's marital state was always inconclusive. For Ruth, her marriage was the one immutable and transcendent fact of her life. In 1998 she and Elliot marked their sixtieth wedding anniversary with a celebration attended by family and friends. "And we went together five years before we were married," Ruth reminded everyone. Derek Gable, who stayed close to the couple after they left Mattel, remembered, "They did not get old. They were very connected with the real world. Ruth talked about new ventures where she was adviser, consultant, or lecturing." Elliot continued to paint, delighted with and ever trusting of his wife's course. "She could do anything," he liked to say.

The conventional view holds that couples who work together create problems in their marriage. For Ruth the opposite applied. In her mind, the key to her marriage's longevity rested on the

Handlers' collaboration in the workplace. When asked the secret to their marriage she said, "It has to do with respect. Sure, we had love, but more important, I don't think we could ever have survived the life we had without mutual respect. He respected me and my talents enough to let me do my thing, and I respected his talents enough to not only let him do his thing, but to take what he did and run with it and be enthusiastic about it and try to make something of it. Without that there is no way we could have lived the life we lived."

With Ken gone, Ruth grew closer to Barbara. She, Elliot, and Barbara had traveled to the Far East just before Ken's death. The perspective of time had given Ruth a greater appreciation of the toll her work life had taken on the children. She understood that it must have been difficult growing up as the Handler children. "We tried very hard to give them enough time and enough attention," she said, "but we were very preoccupied with the business, we were consumed by the business." She and Elliot loved the children and felt loved in return, but she knew the children were confused by having famous parents who traveled and were unlike other parents. She also knew that naming the dolls after them had added to their confusion and anger. After years of strained relations, however, she and Barbara found friendship. "Both of us decided," Barbara said, "that we weren't going to get at each other anymore."

For her extended family, Ruth became the matriarch. Her nephew Ron Loeb, who became a lawyer, remembered, "When Sarah died, I think Ruth really took her place in the family structure. Everyone seemed to go to Ruth after that. Ruth was always a very concerned person, deeply concerned with all her relatives and their children and people outside of the family. She was interested in the children's development, and she was always interested

252 Barbie and Ruth

in my career and my grades, and from time to time helped me financially. Ruth was never short on advice, even if sometimes that advice was not always welcome, but she was ever willing to lend an ear when there was a problem to discuss."

Half a century earlier, after the deaths of Jacob and Ida, Ruth's brother Joe had reminded her that the family had to support one another as their mother and father would have wanted. At the beginning of a new century, Joe was gone, as were all Ruth's siblings except Aaron, but Joe's words still resonated. "Everybody in the family admired Ruth," Aaron said. "She was the best-hearted person. She'd help any of us; no one was jealous. She'd break her neck to help you."

Ruth liked to joke that she had "lived my life from breast to breast," but no humor could be found in the toll that cancer and a lifetime of illness took on her body. In 2001 she kept a daily log of her health for her doctor at the pain clinic at Cedars-Sinai Medical Center. On November 20, her rating, with ten being the most pain, was seven or more. She woke up at three in the morning, again at four, again at five, tried to read, tried to sleep again. She managed to bathe and dress and get in an hour of work from nine until ten before receiving an injection to stop the pain. Afterward she was dizzy with shooting pain, forcing her to lie down. She managed to drive three miles for an hour of bridge, her pain logged at a seven, but she grew dizzy and drove home to lie down. She watched television, the pain radiating from the side of her head to the top, the level rising. She tried to sleep but managed only two hours for the night. In the margin at the end of the log she wrote, "The shot made my pain much worse. For hours I was dizzy and sometimes slightly nauseous. Please, no more shots!"

Always at her side, Elliot wanted Ruth at home and not in the hospital, but in January 2002, she was lying down in the bedroom when blood seeped out onto the sheets. Elliot rushed her to the hospital. After operating on her colon, her doctors could not agree on the cause of the bleeding. She came home, but her problems persisted as a bacterial infection invaded her stomach and recurred despite medication. By April she was again hospitalized. Elliot kept a vigil at her bedside. Barbara came every day. On April 27, as Elliot went to kiss her good night, Ruth did not respond but stared off into the distance. He knew she was gone. "Perhaps the fight's the thing," Ruth had said, and she had fought as hard as anyone could right up to the end.

A traditional Jewish prayer reads, "So long as we live, they too shall live, for they are now a part of us." For Ruth, this held true not only for those who knew and loved her, but for a much broader part of humanity. She created Barbie in all her molded-plastic outsize glory, in reality simply a doll, but for Ruth, and those who understood her vision, a statement about women and life and a belief in limitless possibilities.

It had taken a long time and much heartache for Ruth to imagine her life as her own. Once she did, she found what she had been seeking since little Ruthie Mosko rushed toward her future: dignity, approval, and acceptance. In her last decade, she liked to sum up her life for adoring audiences by describing a simple yet powerful chronology:

"I feel like I have lived three lives. In my first life we did it our way. In my second life, we did it their way, and in my third life, I did it my way."

Author's Note

I first read about Ruth Handler in *Enterprising Women: 250 Years of American Business*, by Virginia G. Drachman. I had no idea that the Barbie doll was conceived by a woman or, even more astonishing given the sexism of the era, that Mattel, Inc., was founded and built by a woman. When I discovered that there was no previous biography of Ruth, I realized that once again, to paraphrase Arthur Schlesinger, history's greatest casualties are women's stories.

Ruth could have been my mother, a child born in the 1910s to Polish Jewish immigrants who spoke little English and labored for their claim to the life America offered. In this way, Ruth's story is not only one of corporate success, hubris, and redemption, but of the American dream. In one generation the Handlers went from poverty, fear, and repression to unimaginable wealth, comfort, and security. In my family as well, and in many of those I grew up with in Skokie, Illinois, immigrants saw their children become doctors, lawyers, and successful entrepreneurs.

Ruth's spectacular ascent as a capitalist coupled with her disregard for legal and ethical boundaries is also part of America's recurring story. The popular novels of Horatio Alger in the nineteenth century told only the bright side of stories with darker facets. History is full of Ruth Handlers, magnificent entrepreneurs who disregarded or felt above the rules. They continue to make news, although an untold number will never be caught or suffer the retribution that Ruth endured. There is nothing to her credit in being among the scoundrels of American business, but there is much to admire about her redemption. Without it, I would not have chosen to write her story.

Three women recognized the importance of Ruth Handler's story and preserved critical primary source material, which I used for this book. Fern Field, a television producer, approached Ruth in the 1980s about making a movie of her life. To prepare for that project, Field conducted hours of interviews with Ruth over a period of a decade, and generously provided me the transcripts. Unless otherwise noted, all of the quotations attributed to Ruth are drawn from these documents.

In 1999 Barbara Haber, then curator of books at the Arthur and Elizabeth Schlesinger Library on the History of Women in America at the Radcliffe Institute for Advanced Study at Harvard University, began discussions with Ruth about bequeathing her papers to the library. Jane Knowles, Radcliffe College archivist, worked to acquire and archive the thirty-five boxes, first available in 2004. These materials provided an invaluable window into Ruth's personal and business life. I am particularly grateful to Elliot Handler for giving me permission to access the boxes of otherwise restricted family correspondence. Thankfully, Ruth saved everything, from early invoices, bills, check stubs, receipts, and bank statements to family correspondence, fan letters, appointment calendars, and her own copious notes, which were extensive during the years she was investigated and indicted by the federal government. The Schlesinger collection also contains photographs and a number of videos of Ruth speaking at various events, which helped me discern her style, speech, and manner later in her life.

Former Mattel employees, besides providing invaluable insight through interviews, also gave me a number of useful documents. Sandy Danon provided forecasting documentation modeled on Ruth's W reports. Joe Whittaker provided a copy of his marvelous and illuminating Mattel Alumni Association speech from 1991. Tom Kalinske gave me videos of Ruth and early Mattel toy commercials, as well as valuable documentation.

In addition, the materials listed in the bibliography were used for reference, background, and citation.

Bibliography

Books

Allison, Jay, and Dan Gediman, eds. *This I Believe: The Personal Philosophies of Remarkable Men and Women.* New York: Holt, 2007.

Amerman, John W. *The Story of Mattel, Inc: Fifty Years of Innovation.* New York: Newcomen Society of the U.S., 1995.

Bailey, Beth, and David Farber, consultants. *The Fifties Chronicle.* Lincolnwood, IL: Publications International, 2006.

BillyBoy. *Barbie: Her Life and Times.* New York: Three Rivers Press, 1992.

Byrne, Chris. *Toys: Celebrating 100 Years of the Power of Play.* New York: Toy Industry Association, 2003.

Crawford, Roy J., and James L. Throne. *Rotational Molding Technology.* Norwich, NY: William Andrew Publishing, 2002.

Dichter, Ernest. *Getting Motivated by Ernest Dichter: The Secret Behind Individual Motivations by the Man Who Was Not Afraid to Ask "Why?"* New York: Pergamon, 1979.

——. *The Strategy of Desire.* Garden City, NY: Doubleday, 1960.

Drachman, Virginia G. *Enterprising Women: 250 Years of American Business.* Chapel Hill: University of North Carolina Press, 2002.

Gallagher, Carol. *Going to the Top: A Road Map for Success from America's Leading Women Executives*. With Susan K. Golant. New York: Penguin, 2001.

Handler, Ruth. *Dream Doll: The Ruth Handler Story*. With Jacqueline Shannon. Stamford, CT: Longmeadow Press, 1994.

Handler, Stacey. *The Body Burden: Living in the Shadow of Barbie*. Cape Canaveral, FL: Blue Note Publications, 2000.

Kalinske, Thomas, Ryan Gunnigle, and Neil Friedman. *The Business of Toys and Games: Top Executives on Launching New Products, Developing a Recognizable Brand, and Competing for Shelf Space*. Boston: Aspatore Books, 2006.

Kreuzer, Franz, Gerd Prechtl, and Christoph Steiner. *A Tiger in the Tank: Ernest Dichter, an Austrian Advertising Guru*. Riverside, CA: Ariadne Press, 2007.

Lord, M. G. *Forever Barbie: The Unauthorized Biography of a Real Doll*. New York: Walker & Co., 2004.

Melody, William H. *Children's Television: The Economics of Exploitation*. New Haven, CT: Yale University Press, 1973.

Miller, G. Wayne. *Toy Wars: The Epic Struggle Between G.I. Joe, Barbie, and the Companies that Make Them*. New York: Times Books, 1998.

Packard, Vance. *The Hidden Persuaders*. New York: David McKay, 1957.

Pecora, Norma Odom. *The Business of Children's Entertainment*. New York: Guilford Press, 1998.

Place, Irene, and Sylvia Plummer. *Women in Management*. Skokie, IL: VGM Career Horizons, 1980.

Pope, Daniel. *The Making of Modern Advertising*. New York: Basic Books, 1983.

Rand, Erica. *Barbie's Queer Accessories*. Durham, NC: Duke University Press, 1995.

Sarasohn-Kahn, Jane. *Contemporary Barbie Dolls: 1980 and*

Beyond. Dubuque, IA: Antique Trader Books, 1997.

Schneider, Cy. *Children's Television: The Art, the Business, and How It Works.* Chicago: NTC Business Books, 1987.

Shiach, Morag. *Feminism and Cultural Studies.* New York: Oxford University Press, 1999.

Stern, Sydney Ladensohn, and Ted Schoenhaus. *Toyland: The High-Stakes Game of the Toy Industry.* Chicago: Contemporary Books, 1990.

Sutton-Smith, Brian. *Toys as Culture.* New York: Gardner Press, 1986.

Uchill, Ida Libert. *Pioneers, Peddlers, and Tsadikim: The Story of Jews in Colorado.* 3rd ed. Boulder: University Press of Colorado, 2000.

Woolery, George W. *Children's Television: The First Thirty-five Years, 1946–1981.* 2 vols. Metuchen, NJ: Scarecrow Press, 1983–1985.

Movies

Shlain, Tiffany. *The Tribe.* DVD. www.tiffanyshlain.com/The_Tribe.html. 2005.

Stern, Susan. *Barbie Nation: An Unauthorized Tour.* DVD. San Francisco: El Rio Productions, 2004.

Newspaper and Magazine Articles

Auerbach, George. "American, Foreign Toy Makers Display Wares Here This Week." *New York Times,* March 8, 1959.

Burton, Susan. "About a Doll." *New York Times Magazine,* December 29, 2002.

Bush, Thomas W. "Mattel Again Toying with Profit Uptrend." *New York Times,* May 5, 1965.

Carberry, James. "How Mattel, Inc. Went from Thriving

Concern to Not-So-Thriving One." *Wall Street Journal*, June 20, 1973.

———. "Mattel Holder Suit Says Top Officers Used Inside Data in Trading; Firm Sues Insurers." *Wall Street Journal*, March 13, 1973.

Cook, Anthony. "Life After White-Collar Crime." *Savvy*, May 1980.

Davidson, Joanne. "Handler Overcame 'Nightmares.'" *Denver Post*, February 5, 1996.

Delugach, Al. "Ruth Handler Changes Plea; Won't Be Jailed." *Los Angeles Times*, September 6, 1978.

Dorfman, Dan. "Heard on the Street." *Wall Street Journal*, March 4, 1968.

Groves, David. "A Doll's Life: Barbie's Inventor Has Seen Her Grow from Hunch to Hit Ageless—and Controversial—Symbol of Womanhood." *Los Angeles Times*, December 15, 1994.

Hammer, Alexander R. "Mattel Plans Sale of Ringling Bros." *New York Times*, December 19, 1973.

Harris, Roy J., Jr. "Judge Upholds Use of Special Counsel Data in Mattel Case." *Wall Street Journal*, August 4, 1978.

Heinzel, Ron S. "Mattel Spreads Happiness in Form of Toys, Record Profits." *New York Times*, May 29, 1969.

Hill, Gladwin. "Toy Missile No Flight of Fancy." *New York Times*, February 7, 1959.

Holles, Everett R. "American-Made—in Mexico; Satellites of U.S. Plants Employ Low-Cost Labor." *New York Times*, January 31, 1971.

Holsendolph, Ernest. "Ex-Executives as Consultants; Many Get Fees from Their Old Companies." *New York Times*, March 31, 1974.

Jennings, C. Robert. "In the Toy Business the Christmas Rush Is On." *New York Times*, May 19, 1968.

Johnston, David Cay. "Arthur Spear, Who Led Mattel Through Fiscal Crises, Dies at 75." *New York Times*, January 4, 1996.

Lindsey, Robert. "Mattel Settles 5 Class Lawsuits." *New York Times*, November 4, 1975.

———. "A Million-Dollar Business from a Mastectomy." *New York Times*, June 19, 1977.

Loercher, Diana. "From Rag Dolls to . . ." *Christian Science Monitor*, March 21, 1972.

Loper, Mary Lou. "Man-Wife Team Partners in Firm." *Los Angeles Times*, September 29, 1959.

Los Angeles Times, Display Ad 129, November 26, 1959.

Los Angeles Times, Display Ad 77, October 29, 1959.

Los Angeles Times, Marriage Announcement 18, May 17, 1959.

Lukas, Paul. "How a Stylish Doll Became a Head-Turning Classic and Put a Pair of Fledgling Entrepreneurs in Play." *CNNMoney.com*, April 1, 2003. http://money.cnn.com/magazines/fsb/fsb_archive/2003/04/01/341015/index.htm.

Martin, Judith. "Interview with a Superstar." *Washington Post*, April 7, 1974.

Meyer, Wendy Haskell. "Traveling Abroad 'Imperial V.I.P. Class.'" *New York Times*, July 18, 1971.

Milton, Brock. "Case of the Teen-Age Doll." *New York Times*, April 21, 1963.

Morris, Kathleen. "The Rise of Jill Barad." *Business Week*, May 25, 1998.

New York Times, "Business Is Brisk as Toy Fair Opens," March 10, 1959.

New York Times, "For Christmas, Dolls That Grow and Dolls That Don't," November 22, 1975.

New York Times, "4 Ex-Officers of Mattel Among 5 Indicted on Conspiracy Charges," February 17, 1978.

New York Times, "New President Named by Toy Manufacturer," June 10, 1967.

New York Times, "16 Named by Nixon to Panel on Women," June 7, 1973.

New York Times, "Toy Factory Started in a Garage Parlayed into $4,000,000 Business," July 22, 1951.

Nuccio, Sal R. "Toy Makers Plan Off-Season Drive." *New York Times*, October 15, 1961.

O'Connell, Patricia. "To Ruth Handler, a 21-Barbie Salute; So What That Her Creation Was Anatomically Impossible?" *Business Week*, May 1, 2002.

Penn, Stanley. "Securities Analyst Rues Rosy Reports He Wrote for Investors in Mattel Stock." *Wall Street Journal*, November 5, 1975.

Quinn, William G. "Ruth Handler: Intrepid Entrepreneur." *Dynamic Years*, March 1985.

Ramsey, Sonya. "Women Inventors; Women's Inventions Improve Our Lives." *USA Today*, March 22, 1989.

Rosenblatt, Robert A. "Leaders Heckled; Game Gets Rough for Mattel as Stockholders Yell Foul." *Los Angeles Times*, May 30, 1974.

———. "The Mattel Debacle: How It Took Shape." *Los Angeles Times*, November 9, 1975.

Salt Lake Tribune, "A Talk with the Woman Who Created Barbie," December 6, 1994.

Sansweet, Stephen J. "Mattel Ex-Aides Tried Cover-Up, Report Asserts." *Wall Street Journal*, November 4, 1975.

———. "Study of Mattel's Past Financial Affairs Begun by U.S.; Lengthy Report Involved." *Wall Street Journal*, November 11, 1975.

Sederberg, Arelo. "Ruth Handler Happily Toys with Big Business." *Washington Post*, January 3, 1968.

Simross, Lynn. "10 Honored as Times Women of the Year." *Los Angeles Times*, March 11, 1975.

Sloane, Leonard. "Toy Industry Sees Sales Surge in '64." *New York Times*, March 11, 1964.

Smith, David C. "Feel for Kids' Tastes, Massive TV Use Help Mattel Lead Toy Field." *Wall Street Journal*, November 24, 1964.

Talbot, Margaret. "Little Hotties." *New Yorker*, December 4, 2006.

Taylor, Frank J. "Million-Dollar Music Box." *Saturday Evening Post*, December 6, 1952.

Time, "All's Swell at Mattel," October 26, 1962.

Wall Street Journal, "Changes in Stockholdings," September 19, 1968.

Wall Street Journal, "Commerce and Industry," June 6, 1967.

Wall Street Journal, "Ex-Official of Mattel Pleads Guilty to Filing False Reports to SEC," February 28, 1978.

Wall Street Journal, "Ex-Officials of Mattel Placed on Probation for Five Years, Fined," December 11, 1978.

Wall Street Journal, "Federal Judge Accepts Plea of No Contest of Ex-Mattel Officer," August 28, 1978.

Wall Street Journal, "Mattel and Remco, Big Toy Makers, Indicate Pre-Christmas Sales Trailed Expectations," December 28, 1964.

Wall Street Journal, "Mattel Appoints Panel to Review Operations," July 28, 1972.

Wall Street Journal, "Mattel Expects Fiscal '66 Net Above Prior Year," August 27, 1965.

Wall Street Journal, "Mattel Founder Pleads No Contest to Charges of Falsifying Reports," September 6, 1978.

Wall Street Journal, "Mattel, Inc. Says Net and Sales Increased in Year Ended Jan. 31," March 9, 1967.

Wall Street Journal, "Mattel Names Spear President and Omits Its Quarterly Dividend," March 21, 1973.

Wall Street Journal, "Mattel Posts Profit for Fourth Quarter, Fiscal 1974 Net Loss," April 3, 1974.

Wall Street Journal, "Stockholder Meeting Briefs," May 20, 1970.

Wall Street Journal, "Three Former Mattel Aides Seek to Block Use of Data Collected on Alleged Fraud," January 10, 1977.

Washington Post, "Five Mattel Executives Indicted in Stock Fraud," February 18, 1978.

Washington Post, "Mattel Sued for Ringling Acquisition," March 3, 1974.

Weinstein, Mark. "Creator of Barbie Thriving, Surviving." *York (PA) Daily Record*, September 27, 1996.

Woo, Elaine. "Ruth Handler Was Creator of Barbie Doll." *Los Angeles Times*, April 28, 2002.

Yockel, Michael. "Living Doll," *City Paper Online*, December 25, 2002. www.citypaper.com/special/story.asp?id=3367.

Interviews
The following people were interviewed for this book:

FORMER MATTEL EMPLOYEES
Marvin Barab
Jill Barad
Boyd Browne
Sandy Danon
Josh Denham
Derek Gable
Fred Held
Cedric Iwasaki
Tom Kalinske

Bernie Kivowitz
Lou Miraula
Rita Rao
Pat Schauer
Frank Sesto
Lou Silberman
Joe Whittaker

HANDLER FAMILY MEMBERS
Elliot Handler
Ron Loeb
Aaron Mosko
Barbara Handler Segal

OTHER INTERVIEWEES
Richard Blum
Jacqueline Brandwynne
Fern Field
Gordon Fitzgerald, toy industry professional
Alix Getty, interviewer
Pamela Harris
Seth Hufstedler
Isaac Larian, CEO, MGA Entertainment
Catherine Leicester
Andrea Ordin
Ed Sanders
Larraine D. Segil, acquaintance of Ruth
Jacqueline Shannon
Barbara Smith, secretary
John Vandevelde
Zachary Zemby

Acknowledgments

The proposal for this book languished in a drawer until Larry Shames, novelist, friend, adviser, suggested I send it to Stephanie Tade, who became my wise, wonderful agent. She immediately understood why this book had to be written. Genoveva Llosa, at Collins, bought the manuscript and helped set my course along with my second editor, Toni Sciarra. But it fell to Ben Loehnen to read, edit, reread, reedit, and guide this book to publication. He did so with all the diligence, attention to detail, and wise counsel that authors lament not finding in editors today, and I am a better writer for it. Thanks also to Matt Inman, Hollis Heimbouch, Teresa Brady, Angie Lee, Janina Mak, Richard Ljoenes, all at Collins. Tom Green, at DesignWorks Group, designed the perfect cover.

The staff at the Schlesinger Library was unfailingly patient and good-humored as I labored through Ruth's papers. The collection, and those who assemble and protect it, renders an invaluable service to women's history. Particular thanks to Jane Knowles for her archival work and Sarah Hutcheon for helping with many questions.

Thanks to my sister, Dee Francken, for her first read; my brother-in-law, John Francken, for genealogical advice; my

sister-in-law, Marguerite Records, and Sheila King for reading and research help; Birgit Muller for assistance in Germany;
the Washington Biography Group and James McGrath Morris;
Peggy Engel for her early and enthusiastic input; Mary Boland
for her perceptive read; and friends Lisa Dobbs, Fern Field,
Sandy Foote, Ilana Bar-Din Giannini, Robin Gradison, Cindy
Hallberlin, Marylu Jordan, Kitty Kelley, Susan Land, Anne
Maher, Peggy McCormick, Judy Rosener, and Pamela Toutant
for their support.

As always, the love and faith of Tony, Ariel, and Sam makes
everything else possible.

Index

Paul, Harry, 87, 90, 130
Pauley, Jane, 210
Peerless Plastics, 75
People (magazine), 210, 250
Pepperdine University, 241–42
Peters, Darrell, 170
Phillips, Leonard, 29–30
piano toys, 82–83, 85, 94, 160
picture frames, 58–59, 61, 77
Plexiglas, 46, 47, 49, 50–51, 63
polyvinyl chloride, 12
Price Waterhouse, 203, 230
prosthetic breasts. *See* Nearly Me

Radnitz, Robert, 162
Rado, Vic, 178
Rao, Rita, 149, 206
Reed, Donna, 17
Rekers, Paul, 166
Riklis, Mona, 248
Ringling Bros. and Barnum and
    Bailey circus, 162–64, 172,
    174–77, 190, 194, 202; as Mattel
    money-maker, 238
Rohatyn, Felix, 180
Rohm and Haas, 46, 50, 51
Rollin, Betty, 211
Roosevelt, Franklin D., 27, 35
Rosenberg, Seymour, 155–58,
    160–61, 169, 170–71, 175–79,
    183, 191; influence at Mattel
    of, 158; Mattel fraud case and,
    195–96, 203, 215, 217, 219,
    220, 223–24; Mattel severance
    package for, 181; reason for
    hiring, 202; Ruth's reactions
    to, 156–58, 180, 181, 194, 195
Ross, Steven, 179, 180
Roy Rogers Show, The (TV pro-
    gram), 94
Ruthton, 203–5, 207–12, 214, 218,
219, 221, 224, 226, 228, 232,
236; Ruth's focus on, 237, 240;
sale of, 244
Ryan, Jack, 3, 10–11, 13, 17, 117,
    120, 135–41, 160; Barbie's en-
    gineering and, 132, 138, 145,
    153; Hotwheels and, 153–55;
    patents held by, 153, 215

Sanders, Ed, 229
Schauer, Pat, 114, 150, 156, 173,
    181, 206
Schneider, Cy, 99, 107, 108
Sears, Roebuck, 4–5, 18, 47, 68,
    82–83, 93, 102, 148, 171–72,
    173
Securities and Exchange Commis-
    sion, 157, 190, 191–96, 201–3,
    212, 213–24
See 'n Say toys, 141
Seftel, Lawrence, 183
Segal, Allen M. (Ruth's son-in-
    law), 109
Segal, Cheryl (Ruth's granddaugh-
    ter), 131, 241–42
Segal, Todd (Ruth's grandson),
    241
Semon, Waldo, 12
Senekoff, Ben, 68
Sesto, Frank, 125, 129, 141
Sew Magic (toy), 139
sexism, 117–18, 122–23, 247
sex toy, 9–10
Shannon, Jacqueline, 246
Shindana Toy Company, 160
Shockett Lighting Fixture Com-
    pany, 33, 35
Siebert, Muriel, 250
Sizzlers (cars), 169, 172, 175
Skipper (doll), 132, 143
Sounder (film), 162

Spear, Art, 158, 171, 178, 180, 182; fraud case and, 191–92, 195, 196; Mattel management shakeup/restructuring and, 185–90, 246, 247; Mattel's financial recovery and, 237–38
Spenco Medical Corporation, 244
Standard Plastics, 158
Steinberg, Paul, 53
Steinem, Gloria, 205
Sugarman, Art, 75
Swedlin, Abe, 117

Takasugi, Robert, vii, ix, 213, 214, 218–24, 230, 232
talking toys, 129, 140–41, 152–53
television. *See* advertising; children's television
Temple Isaiah, 76, 130, 226
Tender Love dolls, 204
Tillie the Toiler, 7
Time magazine, 99, 100, 141
Today (TV program), 210
Topper Corporation, 173
Toy Association, 117
Toy Building (N.Y.C.), 67–68
Toy Fair, 1–5, 73, 74, 75, 82, 87, 147; Barbie and, 5, 17, 18, 104, 108–9, 110; Burp Gun and, 94, 97; history of, 3
Toy Industry Hall of Fame, 239
Toy Line Projection (TLP), 128
Turco Manufacturing, 161, 171–72
Tutti and Todd (dolls), 132

Uke-A-Doodle, 72–78, 82, 88, 160
Union Station (Los Angeles), 39
United Jewish Appeal, 131, 242, 247
United Jewish Welfare Fund, 130
University of California, Los Angeles, 114, 130, 193, 225, 237

University of Denver, 28, 35
Urban League award, 86

Vandevelde, John, vii, 214, 218, 220
V-RROOM! bicycle, 144

Wagner, Ray, 178, 189, 190
Warner Brothers, vii, 179
Weber, Franz Carl, 9
Weissbrodt, Max, 10
westerns, 94
Westmore, Bud, 13
Wheat, Francis M., 195
White, Leo, 74, 75, 87–88
Whittaker, Joe, 121, 128, 146, 170
Wishny, Steve, 227, 229–32
Women at Mattel group, 205
Women in Business, 206
Women of Distinction, 247–48
Women of the Year award, 145, 225
World War II, 46, 53–54, 58, 64–66, 219

Yoshida, Yasuo, 96–97, 169, 178, 194, 203, 215; Mattel fraud testimony of, 217–18
Young, Jerry, 50
Young, Loretta, 86

Zacho's (gift shop), 49
Zemby, Zachary, 52, 53, 204
Zukerman, Sam, 76, 78